THE

HAPPY
IN A HURRY
COOKBOOK

ALSO BY STEVE AND KATHY DOOCY

The Mr. & Mrs. Happy Handbook

The Happy Cookbook

ALSO BY STEVE DOOCY

Tales from the Dad Side

THE
HAPPY
IN A HURRY
COOKBOOK

100-PLUS FAST AND EASY NEW RECIPES
THAT TASTE LIKE HOME

STEVE AND KATHY
DOOCY

WILLIAM MORROW

An Imprint of HarperCollins*Publishers*

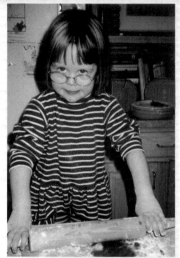

To the Original Doocy Test Kitchen, Peter, Mary, and Sally:
Without your ideas, suggestions, and dramatic food reviews,
this cookbook could have been finished in a fraction of the
time . . . but it would not have been as much fun for our family.

CONTENTS

INTRODUCTION

WELCOME TO *HAPPY IN A HURRY*

We know there's a happiness that comes with foods that remind us of something good. Meals or menus or restaurant smells can suddenly activate something in the Official Nostalgia Department of our brains and instantly take us back to a happy time in our lives. It's like a personal time capsule that you can open every time you turn on the stove.

There's a certain magic to certain foods made a certain way. That was the idea behind *The Happy Cookbook*, and that general theme continues in this one . . . but there's a new twist.

Kathy and I were at a book signing for *The*

Warming up her cooking hands.

Happy Cookbook at the Barnes & Noble in Palm Beach Gardens, Florida, and met a woman who told us about the foods from her childhood that still have special meaning to her. We assumed that was why she bought six copies of our cookbook. As Kathy was autographing one, she said to the woman, "Hope you enjoy making the recipes!"

The woman paused and said, "Kathy, I don't cook . . ."

"Then why are you buying half a dozen cookbooks?"

"My sister got one and told me I'd love the stories—and I read some in line waiting for you, and they're hilarious! So I'm buying a copy for me and for some of my friends."

Pleased with the sale, but a bit puzzled, I had a follow-up: "Out of curiosity, why don't you cook?"

And then she said something that we would hear so many times during that book tour: "Look, I am a terrific chef . . . I would love to cook . . . but I just don't have time."

People all across America told us the same thing: They'd love to cook more, but there just weren't enough hours in the day. That is the unspoken truth of home cooking in the 2020s; chances are you won't make your next meal from scratch—because you're busy with life.

And that's where the idea for this cookbook came from. These are still the recipes that make people happy, and as a bonus, you can whip up

It's not Christmas until the gingerbread is made.

This won't last long . . .

most of them in less than an hour. Think of it as your Happy Hour. You were going to have a glass of wine anyway . . . am I right?

"We should call this cookbook *Happy in a Hurry*," my brilliant wife, Kathy, announced, and so we did.

The 100-plus recipes in this book are all about making people happy—and about prep that's faster and easier, so you can be happy in a hurry. Just know there is an exception to that general rule, and that's our holiday recipes chapter. Christmas, Easter, and Thanksgiving are days dedicated to family, food, and fun. And since so much emphasis is on food, those recipes are a little more elaborate and encourage you and your family to come together to make them, and make your own new happy holiday memories.

By the way, before the lady in Florida who bought six books left, my curiosity got the best of me and I asked her, "Does your house even have a kitchen?"

"Yes, and it's beautiful—we just had it redone last year, all Sub-Zero appliances!"

"Well, maybe one day you'll have an idle afternoon and our cookbook will inspire you to turn on your new oven."

An odd look crossed her face. She said, "Oh, I can't do that . . . I keep my shoes in the oven."

One hundred percent true story.

And with that we welcome you to *The Happy in a Hurry Cookbook*, for fast, easy, happy recipes that taste like home.

Steve and Kathy Doocy

HAPPY IN A HURRY HACKS

Because of simple physics, getting a meal on the table requires a certain amount of cooking time at a certain temperature. Elon Musk could be secretly working on a nanoparticle kitchen that can prepare a perfect prime rib in six seconds, and that will be great—someday. But until then, one of the smartest ways to save time is to not waste time. These hurry hacks are commonsense tips from a lifetime of reading recipes and those little cookbooks in the checkout aisle at the grocery, as well as observing loved ones in the kitchen and pros on TV shows turn stuff in cans and cartons into something delicious for the family to enjoy.

BEFORE YOU TURN ON THE STOVE

How many times have you wandered into the kitchen, opened a cupboard, and wondered what you could open or mix with something else to make dinner? We've all done it, but that only works well on *Chopped*. In real life you need a plan. As the legendary Yogi Berra once observed, "If you don't know where you're going, you'll end up someplace else."

First, **review your recipe.** You don't want to start an hour before dinner and discover that the recipe instructs you to marinate something overnight, or longer.

Let time do the work. If a recipe requires marinating, do it in the morning. It saves time later, and the flavor is better.

Cook in volume. Leftovers are one of the greatest inventions ever. Plan to cook enough once to allow you to eat twice or thrice, which means less time in the kitchen and more time watching cat videos on YouTube.

Delegate. If you have young adults in your household, one night a week have them create a meal. It might be tacos or a mac and cheese concoction, but at least you're off the hook, and they learn how to cook.

Let "previous you" do the work. Holiday meals are often exactly the same, year after year, so for Thanksgiving Kathy uses a holiday shopping list she made ten years ago (it's two pages long), and she keeps it paper-clipped to the recipes. On Monday of Thanksgiving week, she can pull it out to start gathering the supplies before the anxious kids arrive home wondering if there are some White Claws hidden in the fridge behind that seventeen-pound turkey.

Lean on prepared foods. It's okay to farm out parts of a meal, small or large. We get a precooked ham at Easter because we know the Easter Bunny has her hands full. And because Kathy is wearing an apron, people assume she's made everything on the buffet table.

GROCERY STORE GAME PLAN

The typical grocery store has half a million different items, so you cannot go to the store without a list. Don't argue—you just can't. If you walk in and wing it, you'll get winged-it dinner (and will likely forget something, which means you have to run back to the store—not a time-saver). Here are some of our favorite grocery navigation tips!

• Most people make a grocery list in random order as items occur to them, but that's frustrating because when you're actually shopping you're likely to end up backtracking (the store isn't going to re-order itself to match your list). Better to write the list according to the layout of the store you'll be visiting. Our produce department is first, followed by the bakery, canned goods and baking supplies, meats, dairy, and bread. Picture the store and write the list to follow your footsteps. I love shopping in the exact order of the store's layout because I never get to the cash register and realize I forgot the slivered almonds.

• If crushed for time, order groceries online for delivery; every major chain has a pick-up and delivery service. When Kathy had surgery, and during the pandemic, we used this service, and the groceries were the exact same items we would have spent an hour finding for ourselves. Thank you, stock team!

THE LIFE-SAVING MAGIC OF TIME-SAVING INGREDIENTS

• If we need a couple of cups of cooked chicken for a recipe and don't have leftovers, we'll either buy a small amount of the precooked grilled chicken from the deli or get a whole rotisserie chicken. At our store it's cheaper than uncooked chicken, we don't have to spend time cooking it, and we get both white and dark meats.

• Grandma made great bread doughs and pie crusts, but she also had all day. You probably don't, so just buy the store-bought crusts, doughs, and phyllo pastry. They're terrific time-savers, and they'll taste the same as homemade to 99 percent of the people you're feeding.

• Chopping takes time, so we'll often buy pre-cut vegetables in the produce department. They're especially handy if you don't have a spiralizer to make zoodled zucchini. Frozen works too.

• Waste not, want not. If your recipe only requires ¼ cup chopped celery, ½ cup diced beets, or 10 olives, don't buy whole packages that may never get used. Instead, buy exactly what you need at the salad bar.

• Mashed potatoes are a wonderful gift from the potato gods, but they need peeling, cutting, and boiling, followed by mashing. Don't tell anybody, but we almost always whip up instant mashed potatoes. They take less than 5 minutes and unless somebody sees you make them, they'll never taste the difference. Idahoan brand is hands-down our favorite instant potato maker.

• Store-baked pies or cheesecakes can be subdivided into clever individualized desserts by using a lightly greased 2-inch biscuit cutter to cut out individual round pieces. Top each with whipped cream or fruit. One pie can make 5 or 6 adorable little desserts. And guess who gets to eat the trimmings?

• The store-made guacamole you'll find in the produce department is always ripe, unlike buying green avocados and waiting for that 10-minute window of maximum tastiness.

- Bags of fresh salad mixes in the produce department cost about $2.50 and come with croutons, nuts, and dressing. You can't make it that cheaply or quickly, and your family will have no clue you didn't make it from scratch.

- Fried chicken tenders, from the deli section of your grocery or the drive-through window at Chick-fil-A, make a terrific complete meal when chopped up and used to top a bagged salad mix.

PREP SCHOOL

My shop teacher used to say, "Proper prior planning prevents poor performance."

- Before you start a recipe, scan it quickly so you can anticipate when to preheat the oven, boil the water, or bring something to room temperature—all of which take time.

- Like a contestant on Food Network, start with all the ingredients assembled in one spot.

- Chop the vegetables first, then the meat, so you can use the same cutting board without fear of cross-contamination.

- When chopping or cubing, the smaller the piece, the faster it cooks. If we're in a real hurry, because an asteroid is hurling toward Earth and we want a good meal on the way out, we'll use a box grater to shred some vegetables so they are done super-fast.

- Want a quick way to chop herbs? Roll a pizza cutter back and forth over them.

- An egg slicer slices eggs perfectly, but you can also use it on butter, mushrooms, strawberries, fresh mozzarella, bananas, and other softish things.

- Instead of brushing olive oil on something, we often use olive oil spray, which quickly covers everything you aim it at.

- If it works for the recipe you're making, measure dry ingredients before wet ingredients. If you do the reverse, ingredients often stick and cake onto spoons and cups, and we hate that.

- Measure and mix. When measuring several liquids, I'll use a large Pyrex cup so that I can put in all the wet ingredients and then mix them in the cup.

- Convection ovens shave about one-third of the time off cooking, so adjust your temperature and convect away. We often use a countertop convection oven, because it preheats faster and uses less energy, but more important, if we're making two recipes and one bakes at 325°F and the other is at 400°F, we can bake them at the same time and avoid a high-temp traffic jam.

- Air fryers and Instant Pots save time. If you have either one, you probably know how most of these recipes can be adapted.

- Watch the clock—*carefully*. If you overcook or burn something and have to start over, that's a terrible time-waster, so we always use an iPhone stopwatch or set the stove timer. If you're constantly opening the oven door to see if something's cooked, you lose a lot of heat and time. Set a timer, then check for doneness when it goes off.

- But . . . as the oven repair man told me, everybody's ovens and stoves vary heatwise, so if you've cooked something for the designated time and temperature and it doesn't look done, it probably isn't. Learn the quirks of your oven and stove—and use your judgment!

FIX FOOD FAST WITH HURRY HACKS

Here are some of our favorite little hacks for ingredients and quick bites:

• My current protein-rich breakfast is ready in less than 2 minutes. Crack one egg into a greased ramekin, add salt and pepper, stir it up, cover, microwave 45 seconds, turn it onto a plate, and top with a store-bought guacamole single. This keeps me full until lunch.

• Precook vegetables (like Brussels sprouts) in the microwave until they are half cooked, then finish on the grill or in the oven for great grilled or roasted flavor.

• For an easy, tasty breakfast or dessert, open a can of Pillsbury Cinnamon Rolls. Cook them one at a time in a waffle iron and top with the packaged icing, whipped cream, or ice cream.

• Homemade whipped cream whips up faster and easier when you use a chilled metal mixing bowl and beater.

• Peaches on the grill are a fast summertime treat. Place them cut side down until you have deep brown grill marks, flip and cook the other side, and serve with balsamic glaze or ice cream!

• For easy Arnold Palmers—our favorite summer drink—fill an ice cube tray with lemonade and freeze. To make one drink, place 4 to 6 frozen lemonade ice cubes in a tall glass, then fill with chilled iced tea. At our house it's the perfect ratio of tea to lemonade; experiment to see how you like them.

• We hate how melting ice cubes water down iced coffee, so we'll freeze an ice cube tray of coffee overnight and use the frozen coffee cubes in our iced coffee the next day.

1

SNACKS

STARTERS AND SMALL PLATES

WHEN WE WRITE A COOKBOOK, BEcause our names are on the cover, we work hard to make sure you can trust that the recipes are tasty, and that if you follow our instructions you'll wind up with something that looks just like the beautiful photographs in this book. We make everything ourselves in the Doocy test kitchen. Yes, it's a very big job, but luckily we each have an assistant. I am Kathy's helper and she is mine. Thankfully we also have a guy who goes to the grocery store to pick up everything we need, sometimes three times a day (pre-pandemic), and that guy is me.

Last week, ninety seconds into the store, I'd just turned down the aisle with the coffee pods when I saw a roadblock ahead. A woman's cart was taking up the entire aisle as she appeared to be memorizing the text on a box of Honey Nut Cheerios. I started walking flat-footed so she'd hear me and move out of the way, but she did not, so I stopped about two feet from her and politely paused, hoping she'd see me so I could get out of the store quickly.

I waited thirty seconds, but she never saw me. Finally, with a big smile, I said, "Ma'am?"

Startled, she apologized and pulled her cart aside, I picked up two boxes of Dunkin' Donuts hazelnut pods that she'd been blocking and I smiled broadly and said, "Thank you, ma'am, good morning." Expecting a smile in return, all I got back was a puzzled look. Oh well, that's Jersey.

Halfway down the next aisle it hit me. I'd said *good morning*—but it was 4:30 in the afternoon.

That, sadly, is an occupational hazard of doing a morning TV show and being sleep deprived all the time. When the red light goes on, my automatic response is to greet America with "Good morning!," which I do to Kathy's horror throughout the day and night.

I'm Steve Doocy, and I suffer from MSHTDCS (Morning Show Host Time of Day Confusion Syn-

Dinner's ready. Come and get it!

drome). Ask George Stephanopoulos—I bet he's got it, too.

Thirty seconds later I was in the soup aisle. I could feel somebody moving up on me and made sure I wasn't blocking the aisle. I turned as nonchalantly as I could, and it was the Honey Nut Cheerios lady. She still had that puzzled look, but now she was kind of staring at me like I'd sold her a hot Rolex. I smiled again.

"Steve?" she asked.

Oh no, I thought, she's somebody from one of the kids' schools or church or the gym or somewhere. Why wasn't Kathy with me? She is amazing at remembering everybody's name. In a jam, I said the only thing a person could in my situation: "It's nice to see you!"

"I thought that was you . . ." she said. Now she was smiling.

And so was I, because I was off the hook. We'd never met, and it was nice to see her, as I'd said.

"Listen, Steve, I see you in this store all the time and I just wanted to tell you, I love Kathy's cookbook with all of your stories."

Wasn't that nice! I thought.

"And, take a look at this!" she said as she handed me her electric bill envelope that had a penciled list on the back. Her handwriting was exactly like my mother's, so it was perfectly legible. It read:

Two pkgs Puff Pastry Shells, carrots, celery, onion, peas, chkn flav'd Better 'n Bouillon, rotisserie chicken.

"It looks like we're coming to your house for dinner," I announced.

"No," she said, a little surprised I didn't realize what I was holding. "These are the ingredients for your chicken pot pie!"

I looked at the list again. Yes, those were the exact ingredients for our friend Susan's chicken pot pie in our cookbook, the giveaway was the Better Than Bouillon, I should have caught that . . . doggone it!

"I've made it twice before, and we love it," she said. "Your grandma's goulash is amazing . . . but you know what our favorite is?" I shook my head. "Your mother's pot roast."

As that woman was telling me how much she loved mom's food, I stopped listening and started thinking . . . about my mom, who died on Christmas Day, 1997. And, for the first time, it occurred to me that there were tens of thousands of total strangers all over America who had never met my mom but had now made her pot roast and loved it.

My mom's legacy.

This cookbook is amazing!

People coast to coast now love Steve's mom's pot roast.

A viewer named Stephen Brake wrote to me to say, "The story of your wife making your mom's pot roast reminded me of my mom's, who I just lost in April. I wish I had more of my mom's recipes."

The favorite family recipes we grew up on aren't just delicious—they're time machines to a happy place that's very personal to us.

When I asked my TV couch-mate Brian Kilmeade what recipe made him happy, he said immediately, "My mom's meatballs."

Marie Kilmeade's recipe was challenging, but not because she'd forgotten how to make it; she made it exactly the same way for fifty years. The challenging part was that she'd never written it down. So I was her scribe. She sent me a general outline and I asked her dozens of questions. We went back and forth on every detail for weeks and I still remember the last thing we worked out. It was New Year's Day, 2018.

I'd written in the recipe to *roll the mixture into 24 meatballs, each the size of a Ping-Pong ball.* It's important in a cookbook to be as descriptive as possible.

"A Ping-Pong ball?" Marie said. "That's way too small."

Then how much bigger?

"Like an egg," she replied. But I told her cookbooks were very specific and there are many different sizes of eggs, medium, large, extra-large. What size?

"Let's try medium-egg size." So I prepped the recipe and wound up with eighteen beautiful meatballs. They were delicious.

"Nope, that's too many. It's perfect when the recipe makes fourteen meatballs . . ."

That meant a medium-size egg was the wrong size. So it was back to the Doocy test kitchen, and after balling up four and a half pounds of ground sirloin, I made a batch with exactly thirteen meatballs—close enough. How big did I roll the meatballs? The size of a *large* egg.

Marie sent me a thank-you note that signed off, "Good luck, Steve!"

A few months later, I got a call from a producer on the morning show. "Did you hear about Brian's mom?" I had not. Just a few hours earlier, Brian's mother had passed away suddenly. Three days later I was in the family church in Massapequa, Long Island, listening to Brian eulogize his mother with humor and great poise.

The day after the funeral mass, I got this text message from Brian:

"Thanks again for coming yesterday. Everybody loved seeing you. The girls want to cook my mom's meatballs tonight. And she never wrote down her recipe, except for you. Can you send it back to us?"

Fifty years of making these meatballs and I was the only one with the recipe.

Our *Happy Cookbook* had not come out yet, but I had a preview copy, so I turned to the page with Marie's meatballs, snapped pictures of the recipe, and sent them to Brian within two minutes. The recipe featured a beautiful photograph of a platter of the large egg–size meatballs. When Brian came back to work a few days later, he said of the cookbook photographs, "They look just like my mom's . . . thank you."

The Kilmeades are lucky; they have that recipe. But they almost lost it forever.

We all have foods that remind us of life growing up, or a special time in our lives. Sometimes we see that food on a menu or something prompts a memory that activates the Nostalgia Department in our brains, and it suddenly rushes back to us.

Pinterest might have 850 pot roast recipes, but not Aunt Astrid's, which involved a bottle of Dr Pepper and an all-day simmer in a Dutch oven in her little house at the end of the street. The crazy ways our memories work, you might see the name Astrid, or a Dr Pepper, or a Dutch oven, any of those things—and your mind just *click-click-clicks* back to that simpler time.

My mom didn't leave my sisters and me a single written recipe, but over fifty years, through the process of trial and error, we've been able to reimagine how my mom made our favorites. One recipe I loved growing up, and have made for years, always looked exactly as my mom made it, but didn't taste right. Then one day I had a bowl of Brunswick stew in Georgia, and it had that exact taste from my mom's goulash recipe. I asked what it was, and they told me . . . ketchup.

I'd finally found the missing link, and when we make that recipe now, that unique taste of ketchup takes me back to the mid-1960s, when my mom would stand at the back door of our house and holler, "Time to eat!" I'd climb down from my tree house, run in, and wash my hands. We'd all wait at the table until everyone was there, then bow our heads, pray over the meal, and eat, knowing that in half an hour we'd all be in the living room watching *The Ed Sullivan Show*. That was every Sunday night of my childhood. That memory makes me happy, and I'm smiling right now as I type it out.

My point is simple: Write down your recipes, or fifty years from now your grandkids may attempt to make your famous Dr Pepper pot roast, wondering all the while, "Who is this Dr. Pepper, anyway?"

Heaven help the person who thinks our appetizer Church Lady Ranch Dip requires an actual church lady.

SALLY'S SHAKA SHRIMP

MAKES 4 OR 5 APPETIZER SERVINGS

For our family vacation to Maui, Kathy booked Peter and me on a twenty-seven-mile bike ride down Mount Haleakala, an honest-to-goodness active volcano that rises straight up out of the Pacific two miles high. "Hey, chief," the tour guide said to me while looking at my paperwork. "You can't ride until you designate a next of kin." It wasn't until that moment that I realized there was an actual element of danger to this father-son bonding experience. When you ride the log flume at Six Flags, they don't make you fill out an organ donation form.

"Dad . . ." Peter nudged me. "I don't want your liver . . . just saying."

We took a long trip up the mountain in the dark of the early morning. When we saw the summit at dawn I realized we were above the clouds. That's when I knew I should have signed up for hula lessons in the hotel lobby instead.

"Let's ride!" Peter yelled, and we took off down the mountain. I tried not to look to the side of the road, because there was no side to the road, only empty space that went straight down into clouds! I never had to pedal; gravity pulled me down the steep road, fast. So I squeezed the hand brake the first three miles. Then I realized that the chase vehicle we'd ridden up in was five feet behind me. "Hey, chief," the tour guide yelled. "If you don't pick up the pace, we're going to miss lunch."

Two miles up, above the clouds.

Shaka Sally.

Miss lunch? We already *paid for lunch* . . . and with that, I realized I should relax. I was literally in paradise, and if something went wrong on my ride down the volcano, wasn't that where you'd want to check out, if you had the choice? So I released the brake, and by mile seven I'd zoomed past everybody. By the time Peter and I arrived at the famous Road to Hana, we were at the head of the pack.

Many nights of that vacation we ate a shrimp appetizer similar to this. We call our version Sally's Shaka Shrimp, because she was always making the shaka sign. It reminds me of one of this father's greatest days ever with his son. We saw the sun rise above the clouds, biked down an actual volcano, and, despite my occasional and terrifying vertigo, we didn't *Thelma & Louise* off the side.

Enjoy this speedy treat!

SAUCE
½ cup **Thai sweet chili sauce**
½ cup **mayonnaise (we use Duke's)**
¼ teaspoon **honey**
¼ teaspoon **Sriracha**

COATING
¾ cup **cornstarch**
¼ cup **all-purpose flour**
1 teaspoon **table salt**
½ teaspoon **freshly ground black pepper**

THE REST
1 pound **large frozen shrimp (31/40 count), thawed, peeled, deveined, and tails removed**
Vegetable oil, for deep-frying
2 **green onions, green parts cut into ¼-inch rings**

1. To make the sauce: In a medium bowl, whisk the sweet chili sauce, mayo, honey, and Sriracha until silky smooth. Set aside.

2. To make the coating: In a small bowl, combine the cornstarch, flour, salt, and pepper.

3. Rinse the shrimp with tap water and shake off any excess water. One at a time, press the shrimp into the coating and tap off any excess, setting them on wax paper as you finish. Let the coated shrimp sit for 3 or 4 minutes.

4. Heat 2 inches of oil in a deep saucepan over medium-high heat. You'll know it's hot enough when you stick the end of a wooden spoon in the oil and little bubbles percolate to the surface. Working in batches to avoid crowding the pan, fry the shrimp until they're a pale golden color *and cooked through*, 2 to 3 minutes per side. Set the shrimp on paper towels to absorb the excess oil.

5. To serve, place the shrimp on a serving platter and sprinkle the green onions on top. Park the serving bowl of sauce next to the shrimp. Serve pronto!

PROSCIUTTO AND PIMIENTO DIP

This past year our Florida friends, Kathy and Charles Theofilos, invited Kathy and me to join them for dinner at a place they're partners in. It's aptly named 1000 North, its street address on the legendary A1A that runs up and down the Atlantic in picturesque Jupiter, Florida. We accepted their dinner invitation for two reasons. First of all, Michael Jordan, one of the greatest sportsmen of all time, is a co-owner, and you never know, he might stop by the table and I can finally discuss the 1998 Bulls at Jazz, Game 6 of the NBA Finals. Okay, that's the dream sequence.

The second and main reason we accepted their invitation is that it's a private club/restaurant, and they'd have to pay!

When we got there, not only was it one of the most beautiful restaurants we'd ever seen, but the clientele looked like the dining room at ESPN *Sports Center*, with many famous faces lounging around—along with Michael Jordan, golfing superstars Ernie Els, Brooks Koepka, Justin Thomas, and Rickie Fowler all make appearances, because they're all partners in this place, which means they surely appreciated the Doocys running up their friends' bar tab. That's what friends are for.

What I remember most about that first visit was our hosts ordering the ham and cheese appetizer. I thought that didn't sound very swanky for this kind of place—but then it arrived, and it was so clever. The ham was fancy thin-sliced Italian prosciutto, and it topped a perfect-size portion of pimiento cheese dip, which we refer to at our house as Carolina Caviar—because we first fell in love with it in South Carolina.

It was so good that we started making our own version at home using the Doocy family recipe for pimiento cheese dip, which Paula Deen helped us perfect.

By the way, Michael Jordan *did* stop by our table one day, but we talked about food and golf, which means I may have to discuss that legendary Game 6 of the NBA Finals with Paula Deen.

(continued)

CHEESE DIP

1 cup mayonnaise (we love Duke's)
One 4-ounce jar diced pimientos, drained
1 teaspoon Worcestershire sauce
¼ teaspoon red pepper flakes
1 jalapeño pepper, seeded and minced
1 teaspoon finely grated green onion, white part only
Table salt and freshly ground black pepper
1 pound extra-sharp Cheddar cheese, coarsely grated

THE SANDWICH PART

1 baguette, cut into 12 slices ¾ inch thick
Olive oil
3 ounces thinly sliced prosciutto, cut into 2-inch squares
Balsamic glaze (we use Roland brand)

1. To make the cheese dip: For four-star reviews, make the dip at least 1 hour before it's served. In a medium bowl, combine the mayo, pimientos, Worcestershire sauce, pepper flakes, jalapeño, and green onion. Mix well, give a taste, and unless you think it needs some salt or pepper, leave it alone. Now add the Cheddar (Paula Deen says to always add the cheese last). Combine gently until smooth. Cover with plastic wrap and refrigerate for at least 1 hour.

2. To put together the sandwich part: Ten minutes before it's time to eat, preheat the broiler. Paint one side of each piece of bread with olive oil. Arrange the pieces on a baking sheet and place under the broiler until lightly browned, about 1 minute. Watch closely—they will burn quickly! (If you're BBQing, place the bread slices oiled side down directly on a hot grill until you get some nice grill marks on one side.)

3. To assemble, spoon a big tablespoon or two of pimiento cheese dip on the toasted (or grill-marked) side of each piece of bread. Next, snuggle a 2-inch square of prosciutto over the pimiento, so that the prosciutto fits the general shape of the toast.

4. Finally, give a zigzag squirt of glaze on top of each toast—and it's time to serve.

EASY STREET TACOS

The first time I met Kid Rock, he invited me to dinner—at somebody else's house. "My friends are having Taco Tuesday," he said on a Tuesday. "You want to go?"

"Absolutely!" I said. It sounded like fun, and it was. After I loaded up my plate with tacos, I walked past their powder room and I heard a little mechanical sound. I turned to see that a space-age toilet lid was magically opening. There were little blue lights on the side flashing and a robot arm was retracting.

"Is NASA missing a toilet?" I asked.

Kid Rock said, "You've never seen one of those?" Everybody laughed, because everybody at the table had one of these fancy space toilets—except the Doocys. Two weeks later, Kid Rock called me over to his place and presented us with one. Finally, we were fitting into the new neighborhood.

That's right, we went to Taco Tuesday and wound up with a fancy toilet. *Only in America!*

By the way, our hosts for Taco Tuesday, Kid Rock's friends Kathy and Charles Theofilos, have since become our great friends, too, and we love spending time with them, not only on Taco Tuesday, Waffle Wednesday, Thirsty Thursday, Fish Friday, Steak Saturday, Sundae Sunday, or Meatloaf Monday.

One 16-ounce bottle salsa verde
2 boneless, skinless chicken breasts, cut into 1-inch-wide strips
½ cup medium-diced red onion
1 cup chopped cilantro, plus more for garnish
2 limes, quartered
Table salt
1 medium tomato, sliced into ¼-inch chunks
1 avocado, halved and pitted
24 street taco–size corn tortillas
Sour cream, for topping (optional)

1. Pour half the bottle of salsa into a zip-top bag (the other half will be used as a topping). Add the chicken, seal, and marinate in the refrigerator for at least 2 hours—the longer the better.

2. About 45 minutes before dinnertime, fire up the outdoor grill to medium heat (around 350°F).

3. In a medium bowl, combine the onion and cilantro, squeeze in a tablespoon of lime juice, sprinkle in a few shakes of salt, and stir to combine. Set aside.

4. Place the tomato in a separate medium bowl. Scoop out the avocado halves and cut into chunks. Put them in the tomato bowl. Stir to coat the avocado in tomato, which will help to prevent browning.

(continued)

5. By now the grill should be at medium heat. Place the chicken strips in a grill pan and set it directly over the heat. Close the lid and cook for 5 minutes, flip the chicken, and grill until cooked through, 5 to 10 minutes longer. (Cut through a thick piece to make sure it's no longer pink.) Remove the chicken to a cutting board and cut it into ¼-inch chunks. Cover with foil.

6. Back on the grill, use tongs to heat up the mini tortillas (we use two on every taco). They can burn fast, so watch them, and once they have a little grill mark, they're perfect—remove *stat!*

7. To assemble a taco, double up the tortillas for the base, then add sour cream (if using), diced chicken, and whatever else you like: the cilantro/onion mix, the avocado/tomato salad, and very important, the extra salsa verde that was not used as a marinade. Garnish with lime wedges and cilantro and serve immediately.

Mary and Kid Rock playing all summer long.

GENERAL TSO'S 5-STAR CAULIFLOWER

When I was hosting a TV show based in New York in the early nineties and Peter was a little kid, we lived in a lovely apartment on the Upper East Side. The local restaurateurs really didn't want noisy children bothering the New Yorkers swilling the high-dollar highballs, and it didn't take a genius to figure that out, because 99 percent of the restaurants didn't have high chairs available.

Luckily a Chinese restaurant across the street did, and we were there all the time. Two-year-old Peter loved the lo mein noodles, and there was one dish Peter positively Hoovered like somebody on death row waiting for that eleventh-hour call from the governor.

"What is this chicken?" he'd ask, in his high-pitched voice, with most of his face covered in sauce.

It was General Tso's chicken.

What makes General Tso's chicken is the sauce, and when we later discovered it in the international foods aisle at our grocery store, we started trying it out on a bunch of different things. It's great on ribs and shrimp and, as it turns out, cauliflower! Our kids have been asking for more meatless options, and this is a crowd-pleaser.

Even better, you don't need a high chair to make it.

1 cup rice flour
1 tablespoon cornstarch
½ teaspoon table salt
¼ teaspoon freshly ground black pepper
¾ cup cold club soda or seltzer water
1 head cauliflower, cut into bite-size florets

Vegetable oil, for shallow-frying
Store-bought General Tso's sauce (we use Iron Chef brand)
1 tablespoon sesame seeds, for garnish (optional)
2 green onions, green parts only, sliced into little green rings, for garnish (optional)

1. First, let's make the batter. In a medium bowl, combine the rice flour, cornstarch, salt, and pepper. Now slowly add the *cold* club soda or seltzer, stirring all the while until it's as smooth as possible. It's okay if it's a little bubbly.

2. One at a time, dip the cauliflower florets in the batter. Park them temporarily on a piece of wax or parchment paper until they're all ready to fry.

3. Pour 1 inch of vegetable oil into a Dutch oven or deep skillet and heat over medium-high heat until it's sizzling but not smoking. Working in batches so they don't touch, add the florets and fry until softened inside and crispy and golden outside, turning with tongs to cook them evenly. The crispier they are, the more they resemble General Tso's chicken.

4. Drain the florets on paper towels, then place them in a serving bowl. Toss with just enough of the General Tso's sauce to coat them completely. If desired, toss on some sesame seeds and green onions.

5. Now you're ready for General Tso's Generally Fantastic Cauliflower. We serve it on a plate with toothpicks nearby for skewering, party-style.

GERRITYS' GREAT GRILLED ARTICHOKES

MAKES 8 SERVINGS

When Kathy was growing up in California, her family, the Gerritys, routinely dined on avocados, artichokes, and abalone. Three foods that start with an A—and three foods that I had never heard of growing up in 1970s Kansas. To me, abalone, pronounced *a-buh-LOW-nee*, sounded exactly like the sandwich I brown-bagged to school for years, made of sliced bologna, which we pronounced exactly like that exotic shellfish.

Steve, what's for lunch?

"A baloney sandwich—thanks for asking." I'll be here all week . . . try the artichokes.

Kathy had an avocado tree in her backyard growing up—they'd just pick one off the tree, cut it

in half, and eat it like most people eat an apple. How exotic. Artichokes are more work, but when her mother would boil up a batch, it was worth it.

Today we boil them as her mother did, but then we'll grill them on the Weber, a method we picked up at a local restaurant, which makes the second most awesome artichoke, after this one. This is Kathy's favorite California recipe. There's one way to really speed up the prep process, and that is to enlist the help of a grapefruit spoon; you'll be shocked at how fast it makes hay of that furry stuff in the middle.

And that's no baloney!

1 lemon
4 artichokes
8 tablespoons (1 stick) butter, melted
10 chives, chopped (optional)
Olive oil, for grilling
Table salt and freshly ground black pepper
Store-bought chipotle aioli (optional), for serving

1. Pour 2 inches of water into a large saucepan and set it over medium-high heat. Squeeze in the juice of 1 lemon and give a stir. Bring the water to a boil while you prep the artichokes.

2. First, using a vegetable peeler, remove the tough skin of the stem, then trim the bottom stem to about 1 inch. Next, use kitchen shears to remove the two rows of leaves closest to the stem. Clip the thorny tips from the leaves that remain around the middle of the artichoke. Cut an inch or so off the top of the artichoke, so it's flat. Turn the artichoke flat side down, so the stem is sticking up in the air, and carefully cut it in half vertically, right through the stem. Now let's do a little surgery on the center and remove all that furry stuff, which is the actual "choke." A grapefruit spoon works wonders; just dig in near the bottom, piercing the choke and then scooping it out. While you're at it, take out those purple-colored leaves in the center. Place the artichoke halves in the boiling water, cut side down, and repeat to prep the other artichokes.

3. When all the artichoke halves are in the boiling water, cook them for 20 minutes, until the hearts are tender when pierced with a fork.

4. While they cook, prep the melted butter for dipping. Add minced chives if you like.

5. Preheat the outdoor grill to medium-high heat (around 400°F).

6. Remove the artichokes from the water using tongs, giving them a squeeze with the tongs to help them drain, then give them a little squirt or drizzle of olive oil and a sprinkle of salt and pepper. Place them cut side down directly on the grill and let them get nice grill marks, about 5 minutes, then turn them over and grill the other side, another 5 minutes.

7. Remove from the heat and serve with melted chive butter or your family's favorite dipping sauce, such as a creamy chipotle aioli.

SEAN'S MAC AND CHEESE ROLLS

MAKES 12 ROLLS (WITH SOME LEFTOVER MAC AND CHEESE FOR SNACKING)

Every time I'm on Sean Hannity's show, I thank him for sharing his amazing corned beef and cabbage recipe in our first cookbook. And every time, he complains about the recipe being *waaaay* back in the book, on page 181—after all the other recipes from Fox hosts.

"If you want to be in front of everybody in the *next* cookbook," I told him, "don't do an entree, do an appetizer." Because apps come before main courses in cookbooks.

Fast-forward to a mutual friend's wedding, where I told Sean it was time to pick a recipe for us to include in this cookbook.

"So, what's your appetizer?"

"This right here," he said, brandishing a magnificent mac and cheese on a stick.

But the process of installing a working stick into the middle of mac and cheese is really hard, so we compromised and put Sean's delicious mac and cheese in an egg roll wrapper. They are actually faster, easier, and even better than the on-a-stick version.

Congratulations, Sean! You're ahead of all the other Fox News personnel in this book, and if you want to be any closer to the first page, you'll have to change your name to Table of Contents.

8 ounces elbow macaroni
3 tablespoons butter
2 ounces cream cheese, cubed (one-quarter of an 8-ounce package)
3 tablespoons all-purpose flour
1 teaspoon mustard powder
1½ cups whole milk
1 teaspoon table salt
1 teaspoon freshly ground black pepper
3 cups freshly grated Cheddar cheese (about 12 ounces)
12 large (6-inch) square egg roll wrappers
Vegetable oil, for deep-frying
Ranch dressing, for serving (optional)

1. Cook the macaroni to just al dente according to the package directions. Drain, rinse under cold running water to stop it from cooking, and set aside.

2. Meanwhile, in a large saucepan, melt the butter and cream cheese over medium-high heat, whisking them together. Add the flour and mustard powder and give it a good whisk. Slowly add the milk, letting it heat to just short of boiling, whisking constantly until smooth. Add the salt and pepper and fold in the Cheddar a bit at a time, whisking until fully melted into a nice creamy cheese sauce.

3. Mix in the drained pasta and stir with a wooden spoon for 3 to 5 minutes, until the pasta is coated and the sauce is thickened a bit (you don't want it too runny as an egg roll filling).

4. To assemble the rolls, fill a small bowl with water. Use a finger to wet the edges of an egg roll wrapper, then lay it out diagonally with a corner pointing at you. Place about ¼ cup of the mac

(continued)

and cheese in a little horizontal pile just below the middle of the square. From the bottom, roll the point up and over the filling, then fold the left and right sides toward the middle, making an envelope. Tuck everything in cleanly and roll until you have a tight log, making sure the edges are sealed (use another wet finger if needed). Set the roll aside and repeat to make the rest. (YouTube has videos on how to fill egg rolls, and most egg roll packages have diagrams, so don't let this process freak you out.)

5. Pour about 2 inches of oil into a Dutch oven or deep pan and heat over medium-high heat. You'll know it's hot enough when you stick the end of a wooden spoon in the oil and little bubbles percolate to the surface. Working in batches so that the rolls don't touch, carefully position them in the hot oil, seam side down. Keep an eye on them, and as they turn golden brown, rotate them gently with a fork until they are a perfectly uniform crispy and crunchy, about 5 minutes total.

6. Using tongs, carefully remove the rolls to paper towels to absorb the extra oil. Let them rest about 5 minutes; they will still be hot.

7. Serve with ranch dressing for dipping if you'd like.

On location with Hannity in New Hampshire.

PETER'S PARM CRISPS

MAKES 15 TO 18 CRISPS

When Peter worked at the Market Basket grocery store after high school, we developed a great affinity for a delicious snack they sold there. Those Parmesan crisps were so light and addictive that it was easy to start with one and wind up eating the entire package.

But here's the thing—a package was $9 for five ounces. That's more than printer ink!

So I decided to deconstruct it. I asked one of the guys who worked at the market how they were made, and he gave away the trade secret. "It's just baked cheese and a little salt."

Not exactly as complicated as the Colonel's secret KFC recipe.

So I bought a block of Parmesan to shred and embarked on a mission to break the $9 cheese crisp code. It took half a dozen batches to reach my current version of Parm perfection, as written below.

Peter loves them, and when you see him on TV, there's a chance he has a batch that his mom (who is famous for her snacks) made in his backpack. In fact, Peter showed up at the annual Congressional Baseball Game in Washington one year with a backpack, prompting then White House Press Secretary Sean Spicer to say, "What, did your mom pack that with snacks?" Mary Doocy, who was enjoying the game, turned to Sean and said, "Wait . . . do you know my mom?"

One 8-ounce block Parmesan cheese
¼ cup freshly shredded Cheddar cheese
Everything bagel seasoning (Trader Joe's is
  our favorite)

1. Adjust an oven rack to the highest position and preheat the oven to 400°F.

2. Shred the Parmesan on a box grater. The key is to shred it using the larger holes. In a large bowl, combine the shredded Parm and Cheddar.

3. Get out a large sheet pan, and if you have a silicone baking mat, set that on top. If you don't, line the sheet pan with parchment paper. You can make the crisps into any shape you like or just do them free-form on the pan, but we like to make them round. For this we use a 3- to 3½-inch biscuit cutter or silicone egg mold. Set it on the pan and place ¼ cup of the shredded cheese mixture into it, distributing it evenly. Repeat to fill the pan with cheese mounds, spacing them 1 or 2 inches apart. You'll be making more than one batch.

4. Season as many crisps as you like with a light sprinkling of everything bagel seasoning.

5. Set the pan on the highest oven rack and bake until the cheese is completely melted and starting to turn golden, 6 to 8 minutes.

6. Immediately dab the excess oil off the tops of the crisps with a paper towel, then let them rest on the pan for 1 to 2 minutes to firm up. (You can use this time to work on getting your next batch into the oven.)

7. Transfer the crisps to a paper towel to absorb oil from the bottoms, then dab the tops again. Extra oil makes them soggy!

8. That's it—they are ready to eat! They keep well a few days in a zip-top bag—although you probably won't have any leftovers. We never do!

CHURCH LADY RANCH DIP

MAKES 6 TO 8 APPETIZER SERVINGS

Growing up, I went to an honest-to-goodness one-room schoolhouse in Industry, Kansas. Hazel Lloyd taught all classes from kindergarten through sixth grade. There were only eleven kids in the entire school, and three were Doocys. Eventually the county realized the cost per child was too high, so they closed the school and bused us off elsewhere.

The schoolhouse then became a full-time community center. I remember helping my dad renovate the school by building the kitchen serving counters that I believe are still there today. Those counters held all sorts of delicious potluck foods our neighbors brought for the 4-H club, local basketball games, square dances, and box socials.

This dish was brought to many community events by a wonderful woman whose name I've forgotten in the last fifty years, but I remember her as the Church Lady. She'd make this with Miracle Whip instead of mayonnaise, which I don't think I ever tasted in Kansas back in the 1970s. Through the years we changed it up a little, eventually adding ranch dressing. And because the Church Lady lived on a large farm that some city slickers might call a ranch, it all works.

I love this recipe because it's such a vivid taste from a simpler time, when the farming families who grew the winter wheat that created millions of loaves of bread would park their combines and tractors for an hour or two and come together as a community, visiting with their neighbors and friends and doing what we loved so much . . . breaking bread together.

The Church Lady was a saint for sharing this with our family. It's delicious!

½ cup Hormel Real Bacon Bits (fastest) or
   6 slices bacon, cooked and crumbled
½ cup slivered almonds (lightly toasted
   in a dry skillet over low heat if you're
   ambitious)
6 green onions, dark green tops only, sliced
   into ¼-inch rings
1 cup mayonnaise (we use Duke's)
½ cup ranch salad dressing
One 8-ounce block Cheddar cheese,
   coarsely grated, or 2 cups shredded
   Cheddar (see Note)
Crackers, for serving (see Note)

1. In a medium bowl, combine the bacon, almonds, green onion tops, mayo, and ranch dressing. Mix well, then fold in the Cheddar until every piece is perfectly mixed.

2. Cover the bowl with plastic wrap and refrigerate for at least a couple of hours. It *always* tastes best the next day, so plan ahead and make it the day before if you can.

3. Serve with the crackers of your choice.

NOTE: *Paula Deen, the cookbook queen of Savannah, gave us a tip when making cheese dips. She said do not use preshredded Cheddar (unless that's all they've got), as it's fresher and much tastier if you shred it at home. Paula also told us, "Don't shred it finely. Go coarse." Use a cold block of Cheddar and the large holes on your box grater and it will be perfect . . .*

NOTE: *When I was growing up, this dip was always served with Ritz crackers (back when the only cracker choice was saltine or Ritz), but your favorite cracker or sturdy chip will doubtless taste like a million bucks.*

TODD'S HUMMUS, TWO WAYS

MAKES ABOUT 3 CUPS

My friend Todd the Car Guy knows more about cars than anybody I know. But he'd rather be Jacques Pépin because he loves to cook. Right now his specialty is homemade hummus.

The hummus is so good that it's always one of the first things to disappear at Todd and his wife Madeleine's parties. Madeleine is a nurse and started taking the hummus to the hospital. In fact, when one of her nurse colleagues went into labor, she had a craving—but not for pickles or ice cream. She wanted Todd's hummus—so he quickly made her a full batch and delivered it to the hospital. When the doctor said it was time to give birth, she asked if she could first finish off the hummus—a new one for that doctor. The laboring mom ate it directly out of the plastic container, then said, "I'm ready," and delivered the baby. It's that good.

She named the baby Chickpea.

Kidding.

Two 15-ounce cans chickpeas, drained (retain the liquid from 1 can)
2 garlic cloves, peeled
Juice of 2 lemons
⅓ cup tahini (stirred before measuring)
1 teaspoon sea salt
4 drops pepper sauce (we use Frank's RedHot)
Everything bagel seasoning (Trader Joe's is our favorite)
1 jarred roasted red pepper, drained and patted dry
Slivers of fresh red bell pepper, for garnish (optional)
Pita bread, pita chips, bagel chips, tortilla chips, cucumber slices, and/or carrot sticks, for serving
Store-bought tzatziki sauce, for serving (optional)

1. In a food processor, combine the chickpeas, garlic, lemon juice, tahini, salt, and pepper sauce. Pulse to puree to perfection; if it's too thick, add chickpea liquid 1 tablespoon at a time until you get the consistency you like.

2. Remove half the hummus to a serving bowl and shake everything bagel seasoning on top. Don't go crazy; a little goes a long way.

3. Add the roasted red pepper to the food processor and blend until it's perfectly creamy. Transfer the red pepper hummus to another serving bowl. If desired, garnish with slivers of red pepper (so people know what the flavor is).

4. Serve the hummus with dippers. Todd grills or toasts pita bread, then cuts it into triangles, and serves the hummus with a little bowl of tzatziki. right next to the hummus. A terrific taste and touch—and we agree!

BUFFALO CHICKEN TACOS

MAKES 10 TO 12 TACOS

When our girls are together with us at home, it usually takes at least half an hour to agree on a TV show or movie to watch. Some nights we'll go through Hulu, Amazon, Netflix, VUDU, and Pay Per View and not find a single thing everybody agrees they want to invest two hours in watching. That means I'll turn on *Below Deck* on Bravo—only to discover they're running the same episode we watched last time the girls couldn't decide.

Sometimes coming up with a dinner is almost as hard. Same family, same tastes, until they went away to college and everything went crazy.

Sally went to college in Texas and loves all things Tex-Mex. Mary went to school in Boston and insists that we have at least one food item that is coated with Buffalo sauce. So we started making these Buffalo chicken tacos—a perfect union of their food likes.

When we whip these up, it's a happy memory of when they worked so hard to get into great schools, then graduated and became amazing young women who can do anything they want in life—except agree on what to watch on TV. It doesn't matter to me; I usually fall asleep by the time the opening credits are done.

3 cups packaged coleslaw mix (from the produce department)
¾ cup blue cheese dressing (we use Ken's)
1 tablespoon olive oil
2 garlic cloves, roughly chopped
4 celery stalks, chopped
½ red onion, small-diced
1 pound ground chicken breast
Table salt and freshly ground black pepper
2 tablespoons butter
3 tablespoons pepper sauce (we use Frank's RedHot), plus more for serving
10 to 12 taco-size soft flour tortillas
3 green onions, dark green tops only, minced (optional)

1. In a medium bowl, combine the coleslaw mix and blue cheese dressing. Cover with plastic wrap and set aside in the fridge.

2. In a large skillet, heat the olive oil over medium-high heat. Add the garlic and swirl it around for about 1 minute to infuse the oil with the garlic. Use a spatula to remove the garlic from the pan and discard. Add the celery and onion and sauté for a few minutes, until the onion softens. Remove the vegetables to a bowl.

3. Add the ground chicken to the pan and cook, breaking it apart with the spatula, until it's completely cooked through, about 10 minutes. Return the celery and onion to the pan and add salt and pepper to taste. Reduce the heat to low, add the butter and pepper sauce, and stir to coat the chicken and vegetables with the butter sauce.

4. Warm up the tortillas according to the package directions.

5. Divide the meat mixture among the tortillas. Top with the blue cheese coleslaw and, if you like, garnish with green onions and/or a few drops of pepper sauce. You decide—that's the beauty of Buffalo . . .

6. Serve immediately, so you can get back to arguing about what to watch on TV.

That smile when they want something . . .

2

MORNING MEALS

HAVEN'T WAITED IN A LINE THIS LONG SINCE THE Marines!" a guy announced after standing in a three-hour line that led to a table where Kathy and I were signing copies of our cookbook. The funny thing was, half an hour earlier a woman had told us, "I haven't waited in a line this long since Rod Stewart!"

I can understand having to stand in line for the Marines, but three hours for Rod Stewart? Was there a car giveaway at the concert?

The turnout during our first cookbook tour was phenomenally gratifying, and I mention it as a way of saying thank you to the thousands of people we met. At one of our first stops at a Barnes & Noble, they sold out of copies of the book before we arrived for a Sunday afternoon signing, so the manager did an amazing thing—he told people to go down the street to the Walmart, where they still had some. It was like Santa in the movie *Miracle on 34th Street*, telling Macy's customers to go buy things down the street at Gimbel's.

In Canton, Georgia, there was such a Friday night crowd that FoxTale Book Shoppe moved the book signing from their landmark store to a giant church auditorium, and the crowd was standing room only. We signed books and happily smiled for selfies for five hours . . . on my birthday. What a wonderful gift!

In Naples, Florida, two women had bought the book earlier in the week and had already baked our Baseball Blueberry Buckle recipe and brought me a piece—which looked perfect. They handed me a fork and I immediately dug in, glad later that they'd read the recipe correctly and didn't include arsenic.

We saw lots of old friends and made new ones during our first cookbook tour.

All of the Doocy kids made appearances along the way, with Peter getting double takes acting as the greeter at Walmart Superstores in Franklin, Tennessee, and Birmingham, Alabama. Mary spearheaded our sales on Capitol Hill. Sally, who has a degree in marketing, helped us with . . . *marketing*. Late one night when Kathy, Sally, and I checked into an unusual hotel, we couldn't find Sally's bed, so we called the front desk and they told us to look in the kitchen. It wasn't really a kitchen, it was a bedroom, with a stove. They must have known we'd written a cookbook!

Kid Rock's mom, Susan Ritchie, had a chicken pot pie recipe in that cookbook, and we went to his new restaurant on Broadway in Nashville for a live TV show that made a lot of headlines, and then I drove over to the *Mike Huckabee Show* to chat with the governor, whose smoked pork butt secrets were shared in our book as well.

Paula Deen, the belle of Southern cooking, made our day when she said, "Steve, I have your cookbook on my counter at home." For a cookbook author, that's like having George Lucas say, "I love your home movies!"

In Palm Beach Gardens, Florida, a cheery woman named Sunny bought forty copies of the book! When I asked why so many, she answered, "You said on TV, 'Buy it for Christmas,' so I did." I should have said, "I'd love to find a new Mercedes convertible under the tree."

During our cookbook tour in 2018, a woman who was working our signing at Walmart had spent hours knitting Kathy a cozy pair of cashmere socks. She'd made them for her after hearing her tell a story on television that our family had never repeated in public.

Two years earlier, we were going to Florida on vacation and needed new prescriptions for sunglasses, so went to visit our eye doctor, who said Kathy had what looked like a freckle on the back of her eye. Come back in a few months, he said. It's nothing to worry about.

And we didn't. Months passed, and at her follow-up appointment our doctor took a look in Kathy's eye, left the room for a moment, and returned with a card that had the name and address of a retina specialist, whom he'd just spoken to; Kathy had an appointment to see him at 5 p.m. the next day. At 4 p.m. there was a white-out blizzard in New Jersey. We called to see if the office was closed, and they said they were waiting if we could make it, so we drove slowly and got there. The doctor spent about thirty seconds looking at the back of her eye with a gigantic magnifying prism that you'd associate with the Hubble Space Telescope. When he put it down, he looked at Kathy and said, "Can you go to Philadelphia?"

"Sure," Kathy said. "When?"

"Right now . . ."

The blizzard ended at midnight and we were on the road at 6 a.m. Nine hours later, Dr. Carol Shields at Wills Eye Hospital eyeballed her eyeball, then reviewed her charts after an exhausting day of tests.

"Kathy, you've got eye cancer . . ."

Anybody who's ever heard that knows that's when you stop breathing, and we did.

"But . . . I am going to save your life."

How can I have eye cancer? Kathy thought. *I don't have any symptoms. I just wanted a pair of sunglasses.*

Days later, Kathy was out of surgery, with an eyepatch covering an implanted radioactive plaque surgically stitched onto the back side of her eye. One night during recovery, she was wide awake, wondering, *What if it spreads?* She thought mainly about her three kids, who were at that moment asleep in a room next door. She thought about how they all gathered every night of their school lives at the dinner table for Kathy's supper, followed by an hour of family chattiness, with me doing the dishes.

Then and there, Kathy vowed that when she got home she would start writing down the recipes for the dishes Peter, Mary, and Sally grew up eating, so that if she didn't make it, they could make the recipes themselves if they ever had time, or, she joked, if GrubHub stopped delivering.

That's the story she told on TV the day our *Happy Cookbook* was officially released, and it opened the floodgates, with friends, family, and total strangers reaching out to us.

"Steve, I heard your wife's story today," a viewer named Edmund emailed me. "I was crying, driving down I-80. Very happy for you and your family."

The most poignant were cancer survivors who wanted to share their stories, with a surprising number telling us they'd gotten the exact same diagnosis, the exact same way. One day they heard, "It's probably just a freckle," and the next, "You've got eye cancer."

One woman wrote because her husband had just gotten the bad news and they'd never heard of this kind of cancer. They wanted to talk to Kathy directly—and they did. Some people made appointments to see Kathy's specialist, Dr. Shields, and others, like Dana Perino, who were blessed with great vision and had never had regular eye exams, were so concerned that a person could have cancer and no symptoms that they made an appointment to have their eyes checked.

Part of Kathy's intent in telling her story was to raise awareness of a disease that most people had never heard of—and she did it as nobody ever has.

A woman named Maya tweeted, "What an amazing story and such an inspiration your wife is." Maya, I agree with you completely.

In Tampa, the first person in a line of 500 was a woman named Virginia who had not left her house in 160 days for anything except chemotherapy because she could not be exposed to the general public. But she asked her doctor if it would be okay if she came to our event wearing a paper surgical mask. The staff put her at the front of the line to minimize her exposure to other people.

Virginia got up slowly from her chair and gave Kathy a warm embrace. "I just wanted to give you a hug," she said. She knew exactly what Kathy had gone through and wanted her to know she was not alone. Virginia wanted us to personalize her book with the phrase "Kick cancer's butt"—and we did.

So many cancer survivors came out to meet us because they just wanted to shake Kathy's hand and tell her they knew exactly how she felt. They'd had those sleepless nights, when it's dark and your mind starts to wonder, *What if I don't make it?* (By the way, Kathy has one bit of medical advice for anyone facing a health challenge. *Never* look at the Internet about any medical issues right before bed, or you'll never be able to fall asleep.)

That first book tour weekend, Peter Doocy, the Fox News correspondent who used to live upstairs at our house, was boarding a packed flight out of Reagan National in Washington to cover the midterm elections. As he headed to his seat in row 32, he was stopped momentarily in first class as a passenger up ahead struggled with putting a bag in the overhead bin. A woman recognized Peter and said to her husband in a stage whisper, *"Look who's here . . ."*

Peter turned to them and said hello, and they started chatting. They told him how much they enjoyed his reports and said, "We saw your mom's story on TV this morning. Is she okay?"

"After two years of treatment, she got the all-clear sign from her doctors—and she's cancer free."

"It was a miracle they caught it," the strangers said.

It was, Peter agreed. He shook their hands and was headed back to his seat when the man said, "Peter, can I get you a drink? I'll hook you up!"

No Doocy has ever declined an adult beverage after 5 p.m., and half an hour after takeoff that man from 1C walked from the swanky luxury cabin back to row 32, where he reached across two strangers to hand Peter an ice-cold Heineken.

They chatted a minute and then the man went back to the front of the plane. Upon landing, Peter recounted the entire story to Kathy and me on speakerphone, and we were both touched by that guy's uncommon kindness. I asked what his name was, and he said, "No idea . . . I never saw him again."

No name, Peter? Some great reporter . . .

When we first set out to write a cookbook, it was just a cookbook; we didn't even mention Kathy's condition to the publisher. But when Kathy decided to raise awareness about this very rare cancer, we never in a million years expected the kindness of all these strangers—who will never be strangers again.

Not long ago, I was waiting to board a plane in the Delta lounge at Palm Beach International when I heard, "Hey Steve." I turned to shake the hand of a smiling guy, who after a little small talk said, "By the way, I met your son Peter a couple weeks ago, and I bought him a beer."

Almost instantaneously a long-dormant neuron fired in my brain and I said, "*When* did you buy him that beer?"

"Couple weeks, maybe a month . . ."

Hmmmmm. "Was it a Heineken?"

A bigger smile crossed his face, and he nodded. I told him Peter recounted the entire story of the Traveling Heineken, and I had wanted to know the name of that guy—but Peter didn't know.

Now here he was in person! He introduced himself—Billy Green of Atlanta, Georgia.

"Billy, thank you for your kindness toward Peter and my wife," I said. "But I have some bad news. It wasn't a couple weeks ago you bought him a beer . . . *it was last year!*"

"Really?" he said, furrowing his brow. I counted out the months on my fingers, show-and-tell-style, and he started to laugh. "I've been kind of busy!"

Since the cookbook came out, when people come up to me in public they almost always say the same three things, in this order: We watch your show every day, we have your cookbook, and how's your wife?

And I answer: Thank you, thank you, and she's great.

Kathy's innocent-seeming eye freckle had turned out to be ocular melanoma, a very rare cancer, but now thanks to her story, millions of people know the importance of having an annual eye check. And while she had the world's best eye doctors, ultimately, the desire for a new pair of sunglasses saved her life.

It's a story with a happy ending, and the reason another one of our new friends from across the country spent hours knitting her a pair of socks. She wanted to make Kathy smile and let her know she will never be alone again.

Thank you.

GRANDMA BERNDT'S
HASH BROWN–CRUST QUICHE

MAKES 8 SERVINGS

Long before very convenient, super-efficient modern electric stoves, people cooked on giant cast-iron wood-fired stoves the size of a Buick. I have a distant memory from the 1960s of my great-grandma Berndt in Granada, Minnesota. "Stephen, I need some wood," she'd say, and I'd go outside to the stack and return with an armful of firewood that I'd put in the bin next to the stove. "It's hot," she'd say, to remind me to steer clear. Maybe my nose would melt off?

My primary memory of that house was the smell of wood burning. That stove burned all day, year-round, and it's a wonderful memory. Always parked on top of that wood-burning stove was the cast-iron skillet she used for everything, whether on the stovetop or in the oven. It was an amazing tool, and it cooked everything fast. Her daughter, my grandma Lilly, inherited her mother's kitchen skills and worked her whole life as a short-order cook.

This recipe makes me happy because it's a combination of two of my favorite of Grandma Berndt's breakfasts: hash browns and quiche. Making the hash brown crust takes a bit longer, but it's worth it. Now if I could just figure out how to make our modern dual-fuel oven smell like a wood-burning stove, I'd be right back at my great-grandma's house—hauling in firewood and worrying about my nose melting off.

One 30-ounce bag frozen shredded hash
    browns, thawed overnight in the fridge
1½ teaspoons table salt, plus more to taste
1½ teaspoons freshly ground black pepper,
    plus more to taste
2 tablespoons vegetable oil
1 tablespoon butter
Cooking spray
6 large eggs
1 cup half-and-half
2 cups shredded Cheddar cheese
One 7-ounce fully cooked ham steak, finely
    diced
3 green onions, green parts only, cut into
    ¼-inch slices

NOTE: *The cast-iron skillet used in this recipe will get very hot, so always use insulated kitchen mitts when you need to grab the handle.*

1. Preheat the oven to 400°F.

2. The first thing to do is to make sure the potatoes for your hash browns aren't damp (it varies from brand to brand), so they'll crisp up nicely. The quickest way to dry them out is to cut a 1-inch hole in one corner of the hash brown bag, turn the bag upside down over the sink, and squeeze it gently to drain it of as much liquid as possible. You can also place the hash browns on a large clean kitchen towel, gather the ends of the towel, and twist them *over the sink to* squeeze out as much liquid as you can.

3. Put the hash browns in a large bowl and season them with 1 teaspoon each of the salt and pepper.

4. Place a 10-inch cast-iron or other ovenproof skillet over medium-high heat (see Note). When

(continued)

it's good and hot, add the oil and butter. Swirl the pan to melt the butter. Take the pan off the heat and coat the sides lightly with cooking spray, then pour the hash browns into the pan. Use a silicone spatula to evenly coat them with the oil and butter and then spread them on the bottom and up the sides, making a nice crust. I like to use the flat bottom of a measuring cup to smooth it out.

5. Cook the hash brown crust over medium-high heat for about 10 minutes, until it slightly turns color. If you notice some shrinkage, use the spatula to move some of the potatoes around to patch any holes.

6. Remove the pan from the stove, lightly coat the hash browns with cooking spray, and place the pan in the oven. Bake until the hash brown crust edges are starting to turn golden, 10 to 15 minutes.

7. Meanwhile, rinse the bowl you used for the hash browns. Crack in the eggs, then add the half-and-half, Cheddar, and remaining ½ teaspoon each salt and pepper. Stir until evenly mixed. Set aside.

8. Carefully remove the pan from the oven and spread the ham and green onions evenly over the hash browns. Top with the egg and cheese mixture and rock the pan back and forth a moment to distribute the eggs and cheese evenly. Reduce the oven temperature to 350°F and bake until you can give the pan handle a shake and the middle does not jiggle, 30 to 35 minutes.

9. Let the quiche cool for at least 15 minutes before serving warm. Leftovers refrigerate and warm up easily. Take a picture and Instagram it. Thanks, Grandma.

A rare moment when Grandma Berndt was not cooking.

CARROT CAKE WAFFLES WITH MAPLE CREAM CHEESE

MAKES 5 OR 6 WAFFLES

When we lived in New York on East 54th, just down the street from Studio 54, there was a charming bakery on the corner that had the best carrot cake cupcakes. Never realized until we lived in New York, but carrot cake is a big deal in the Big Apple.

In Lower Manhattan, to celebrate the end of the Revolutionary War, they had a legendary blowout at Fraunces Tavern, three hundred years before the neighborhood was overrun with Panera Breads. According to historical documents, here's what they served George Washington, the future president: Fish House Punch, beef, ham, and vegetables, along with *carrot tea cake*. They also served tipsy squire, which is a custardy dessert, not a drunk guy in a triangle hat. Tipsy squire may have disappeared, but carrot cake survived.

A few miles uptown, one of New York's most recognizable institutions decided it would serve only one dessert on holidays: carrot cake. Who has the good taste to choose that item? Riker's Island, the city's main jail. Reportedly the inmate bakers make 2,500 cakes a year, each serving twenty people and weighing ten pounds (or perhaps that's from a file somebody smuggled inside).

You'll love this easy breakfast recipe—it's packed with carrot cake flavor, and the maple cream cheese on top is amazing. It reminds Kathy and me of the carrot cakes our moms made in the 1970s, but for others it may be a fond memory of their time in the joint.

4 ounces cream cheese (half an 8-ounce package)
2 tablespoons pure maple syrup
½ cup shredded carrot
1½ cups Krusteaz Light & Crispy Belgian waffle mix
1 large egg
2½ tablespoons vegetable oil
1½ teaspoons ground cinnamon, plus a pinch
⅓ cup pecans, finely chopped, plus more for garnish

1. In a microwave-safe bowl, combine the cream cheese and maple syrup. Cover the bowl and heat it in the microwave for 15 seconds. Remove and mash with a fork until smooth, then set aside.

2. Preheat a waffle iron to medium/medium-high heat.

3. In a medium bowl, combine the shredded carrot, waffle mix, ⅔ cup water, egg, oil, cinnamon, and pecans and give a stir until it's evenly mixed (do not overmix).

4. Pour ⅓ cup of the mixture onto the center of the waffle iron and close the lid. The waffles should be done when they stop steaming, but we want them crispier, so once they stop steaming or your waffle iron says *ready*, add another minute

(continued)

or so on the clock. Remove the waffles to a plate, cover to keep warm, and proceed to make the rest of the waffles.

5. When the waffles are almost done, add a pinch of cinnamon to the maple–cream cheese topping and give it a final stir.

6. Top each waffle with a big dollop of the maple–cream cheese topping. I like to smear it across the top so it fills in the little holes. Garnish with some extra pecans if you like.

I'm Sally Doocy and I approve this waffle.

10-MINUTE BEIGNETS

MAKES 32 BEIGNETS

In January 1997 Fox News sent me to cover Super Bowl XXI, in New Orleans. Our live truck location was set up just down the street from Café Du Monde, famous the world over for its chicory coffee and the amazing little squares of fried dough sprinkled with powdered sugar called beignets. That was my breakfast every morning for ten days. Fantastic!

Fast-forward to this year. One morning about 5 a.m. I was talking to Stephanie Freeman on our *Fox & Friends* producing team about this cookbook, and I asked her if she had any happy recipes that you could make in a snap, and she told me that when her family had a restaurant in Florida, they'd fry canned biscuits in the deep fryer, roll them in cinnamon sugar, and top them with icing. I said it sounded like a beignet and she agreed.

After that conversation I picked up a can of Grands! biscuits at the supermarket, heated some oil, fried each side a couple minutes, until they were Café Du Monde golden, and rolled them around in cinnamon sugar.

The entire recipe from start to finish took less than 10 minutes. Sally and I ate the whole can.

These will generate rave breakfast reviews, but they're also great as dessert. We like to slice them in half fresh from the fryer and fill them with ice cream for an amazing ice cream sandwich.

Vegetable oil, for deep-frying
½ cup sugar
1 tablespoon ground cinnamon
One 16.3-ounce can Pillsbury Grands!
   (we use Southern Homestyle) or similar
   canned biscuits

1. Pour 1½ inches of vegetable oil into a medium high-sided saucepan (the high sides mean you won't spend more time cleaning up oil splatters than you do making the recipe). Heat over medium heat.

2. As that's heating, mix the sugar and cinnamon in a small bowl. Open the can and separate the biscuits. Cut each biscuit into quarters and roll each quarter into a ball.

3. Test a pinch of biscuit in the oil to make sure it browns up quickly, then, working in batches so as not to crowd the pan, deep-fry the dough balls until golden brown on all sides, turning them with a chopstick or fork.

4. Use a slotted spoon to remove the balls from the oil, then park them on paper towels to absorb any extra grease. A minute later, roll the balls in cinnamon sugar to coat.

5. Eat these as soon as they're cool enough not to burn your mouth, and you can never go wrong with a hot cup of coffee on the side.

BLAST: BACON, LETTUCE, AVOCADO, SUNNY SIDE (EGG), AND TOMATO

MAKES 1 SANDWICH

In the late eighties, living outside Washington, DC, in suburban Virginia, almost every night I would wake up at 2 or 3 a.m. to the sound of an alarm going off. Of course I'd bolt out of bed, but as I followed the noise to the kitchen I'd realize it was the microwave beeping—again. It wasn't that a burglar had broken in and was making Cup O' Noodles on our Amana Radar Range, it was Kathy, very pregnant with Peter, making bacon. Some women crave pickles or ice cream, but Kathy's body was demanding the salty goodness of bacon, and she had that craving with all three of our children.

This is a BLT/fried egg sandwich version of the avocado toast our daughter Sally and I introduced to America on *Fox & Friends*. But fresh avocado is finicky—it's perfectly ripe for only about nine minutes—so we often use store-bought guacamole singles, which are always ripe and pretty darn tasty.

If Peter, Mary, or Sally ever does one of those genetic tests, it will undoubtedly show that the BLT is in our family's DNA. Who needs *23andMe* when you've got *Oscar and Mayer*?

2 slices thick-cut maple-smoked bacon
2 slices bread (nice oblong slices fit the toppings better)
One 2-ounce guacamole single (we use Sabra brand)
3 slices tomato, thick or thin, your choice
½ cup baby arugula, washed and patted dry
Table salt and freshly ground black pepper
1 teaspoon olive oil
1 large egg

1. In a skillet, cook the bacon over medium-high heat until it's as crunchy as you like it. Set it aside.

2. Meanwhile, toast the bread, then spread each piece with guacamole.

3. To assemble, start with 1 piece of the guacamole toast on the bottom. Stack the tomato slices on top, followed by the bacon, as much arugula as you like, and salt and pepper to taste.

4. Return the pan you made the bacon in to medium-low heat. We use the leftover bacon grease and a little olive oil, spreading it around where you're going to cook the egg. Crack the egg into a small cup or dish (this will help control the size of the finished egg), then carefully ease it into the pan as compactly as possible, sizing it to fit the shape of the bread.

5. Cover the pan and cook for 3 to 4 minutes or more, until the egg is the way you like. Sprinkle with salt and pepper, then carefully slide the egg onto your sandwich. Put the other guacamole'd piece of toast on top and enjoy the fact that you're having a BLT and it's not 2:30 in the morning . . . unless it is.

TEX-MEX MIGAS BREAKFAST

My mom, JoAnne, learned how to fry tortillas from our neighbor in Russell, Kansas, where my dad, Jim, worked in advertising and would occasionally run into Bob Dole downtown by his office. They'd shoot the breeze about whatever people talked about in the 1960s.

"Hey, Jim, how about that Bay of Pigs thing?"

When Sally went to school in Texas, at SMU in Dallas, she became our in-house resident Tex-Mex-ologist and exported many tasty recipes from the Lone Star state to Jersey. This is one of them. She and her then-boyfriend (now husband), Ali, would have migas at the Kozy Kitchen, their go-to joint in the Uptown neighborhood of Dallas. The key, Sally would tell me, is the crunch from the crispy tortillas.

One Sunday I promised to make these for Sally, and when I went to bed I knew we had a bag of tortilla chips, but apparently somebody stayed up the night before watching a Hugh Grant movie marathon and ate them all, so all I had to work with was a bag of zesty nacho cheese Doritos. Would they work? Yes, and they totally supercharged the recipe—try them if you're adventurous. Nobody has to know you're eating Doritos at breakfast . . . whatever happens in the breakfast nook, stays in the breakfast nook. But Doritos are a tough sell for Mrs. Doocy at breakfast. We report, you decide—pick your own kind of chip!

1 cup corn tortilla chips, plus more for serving if desired
8 large eggs
¼ cup half-and-half or whole milk
Table salt and freshly ground black pepper
1 tablespoon butter
1 tablespoon olive oil
½ cup chopped onion
1 medium tomato, seeded and diced
One 4-ounce can diced green chiles, drained
1 cup shredded Mexican-blend cheese
Tortillas, for serving taco-style (optional)
Salsa, for serving

1. First, let's do the prep work. Break the chips into 1- to 2-inch pieces and set them aside.

2. Crack the eggs into a medium bowl and add the half-and-half and salt and pepper the way you like your eggs (but remember that the chips are salty, too). Give a good whisk until the egg mixture is perfectly smooth. Set aside.

3. In a large skillet, melt the butter in the olive oil over medium-high heat. Add the onion and sauté until the edges start to soften and turn a little golden, 5 to 8 minutes. Reduce the heat to medium and add the tomato and chiles.

4. Now let's pour in the eggs and start scrambling them in the vegetables. Using a silicone spatula, gently move them across the pan as they firm up, cooking until they are scrambled the way you like them. Add the tortilla chips and lightly stir the works another 1 or 2 minutes, to coat and flavor the chips. Scatter the shredded cheese on top and stir gently until it's melted, another minute or so.

5. Plate it up, or make it a taco with a tortilla, then add your favorite salsa and enjoy!

LEMONY RICOTTA PANCAKES

When we took the kids to Walt Disney World they were fascinated by the rides and characters and general magic, but the enduring legacy of our first Disney trip was the pancakes. One morning at the now closed Disney Inn we ordered pancakes, and they arrived in the shape of Mickey Mouse's head!

The kids could not get over it, and I assured them I could make them exactly the same way at home, which I did. To make Mickey's head, all you do is pour a good-size round of batter and then add two small spoonfuls at the top, two or three inches apart. Voilà, mouse ears. Walt Disney was a genius.

I made these mouse-eared pancakes upon request right up until the kids went to high school, when they got up later and preferred a more caffeine-based breakfast.

This past year our girl Sally went to a very fancy breakfast place for brunch with her future husband, Ali, and had ricotta pancakes. When she came home she described them to me with great appreciation. I surprised her the next morning by making them exactly as she recounted.

"Dad, they're perfect!" she declared. It could have been the combination of lemon and almond that she remembered, or it could have been the fact that I made mouse ears.

Suddenly a brand-new recipe brought in a taste of her childhood. Old habits die hard. Make these pancakes any shape you want . . . I do.

3 large eggs
1 lemon
1 tablespoon almond extract
3 tablespoons vegetable oil
⅔ cup milk
¾ cup ricotta cheese
2 teaspoons baking powder
3 tablespoons sugar
2 cups Bisquick
Cooking spray
Store-bought lemon curd (we like Chivers brand), for serving
Whipped cream, for serving

1. Crack the eggs into a large bowl and whisk until a little frothy.

2. The lemon flavor is what makes this special, so let's focus on getting everything we can out of our lemon. First, the zest. Wash the lemon (super clean—never hurts). If you're good with a handheld zester, great—use it carefully. In a rush, we sometimes use a potato peeler to peel off very thin strips of the lemon zest (just the yellow part—not the white pith), then with a sharp knife we cut the zest into *very very* small pieces. But a good zester always works best. Anyway, zest the lemon and place the zest in the bowl with the egg, then slice the lemon in half and squeeze the juice into the bowl. We use a lemon press to avoid those pesky seeds dropping into the bowl.

3. Add the almond extract, vegetable oil, milk, and ricotta and whisk well, then add the baking powder, sugar, and Bisquick. Stir to combine, but don't overmix or the pancakes won't be as fluffy.

4. Coat a skillet or griddle with cooking spray and set it over medium heat. Give the batter one last stir, then use a ¼-cup measure to form rounds of batter in the pan or on a griddle. Cook until you see big bubbles in the center—you'll spot them after about 4, 5, or 6 minutes—then flip and cook until you have a perfectly golden pancake. Remove, keep warm on a plate covered with foil, and repeat to make the rest of the pancakes.

5. When serving, to make them amazing, smear with lemon curd on the top of each pancake, starting with a teaspoon and adjust according to your taste, then make it a work of art with a flourish of whipped cream.

The actual pancake I made for Sally that day.

ALI'S DALLAS DUTCH BABY BREAKFAST

MAKES 4 SERVINGS

In our first cookbook, we shared our recipe for Sally's Grab 'n' Go Bus Breakfast, a super-healthy and easy-to-make egg dish. But I have a confession: The recipe was actually a collaboration with Sally's future fiancé, Ali, whom she met at SMU in Dallas. When it was time to come up with a name for it, we decided to give Sally the solo credit, because if they ever broke up it would be hard to see in print the name of that loser who broke up with our angel.

But after almost seven years of dating, Ali and Sally got engaged, which is fantastic, because we love him and he's now a part of the family. So we're giving him a retroactive hat-tip on Grab 'n' Go, and a recipe of his own in this book.

One Saturday morning before the wedding I'd made my bacon Dutch baby before we went out to look at apartments for them, and I asked Ali how he would make that recipe for Sally when they were married.

"Well, in Dallas, they'd put salsa, avocado, and an egg on top," he said, so we started making it that way, and it's so much better—thanks, Ali!

So that's why we call it what we do. We didn't just gain a son-in-law, but an occasional cookbook collaborator, and it all happened *When Ali Met Sally.*

(continued)

Sally and Ali's engagement party in California.

5 slices bacon, cut into 1-inch pieces

3 large eggs

½ cup milk

½ teaspoon table salt

½ teaspoon freshly ground black pepper

¼ teaspoon garlic powder

½ cup all-purpose flour

2 tablespoons butter

Eggs, sunny side up, 1 per person

1 cup shredded Cheddar cheese, or your
favorite breakfast cheese

FOR SERVING (OPTIONAL)

2 green onions, green parts only, cut into
¼-inch slices

1 jalapeño pepper, seeded and cut into
¼-inch rings

Avocado slices

Salsa

1. Adjust an oven rack to the second-highest position and preheat the oven to 450°F.

2. In a small cast-iron skillet (we use a Lodge 10-incher), fry the bacon over medium-high heat to your level of crispy. Use a slotted spoon to remove it from the pan and park it on some paper towels. Immediately after the bacon is cooked, with the pan still hot, pour the bacon grease into a heatproof bowl and set aside.

3. While the bacon is cooking, make the batter. In a blender, combine the eggs, milk, salt, pepper, and garlic powder. Blend well, then add the flour

and blend again until super smooth. Have this ready to go when you remove the bacon grease from the pan.

4. Add the butter to the still-hot skillet, swirling to coat the bottom. It will melt and brown fast. Quickly but carefully pour the egg mixture into the skillet and set it in the oven. Bake until the edges of the Dutch baby are raised up and curled and the sides are turning golden brown, 18 to 22 minutes.

5. Meanwhile, prepare as many sunny-side-up eggs as you have people who want them. Our favorite egg-frying method is in a nonstick skillet over medium heat. Add the reserved bacon grease, then the eggs, keeping them separate so they don't touch, and basting the yolks with hot bacon grease as they cook. Remove them when they are done to your liking.

6. When the Dutch baby is cooked, carefully remove the very hot pan from the oven. Scatter the Cheddar across the center and crumble the bacon on top. Return the pan to the oven for a couple of minutes, until the cheese melts evenly.

7. To serve: Either top with a fried egg or two in the pan before you slice into portions, or slice and serve on plates, *then* top each slice with a fried egg. Garnish with your favorite combination of green onions, jalapeños, avocado, and/or salsa.

8. You can eat this with a fork and knife, but we'll pick it up and eat it like a slice of pizza.

FULL-HOUSE BREAKFAST CASSEROLE

MAKES 8 TO 10 SERVINGS

This is our favorite breakfast when the family is all under one roof, or as Kathy says, "All the chicks are in the nest."

On the rare occasions when this happens, Kathy and I sleep very soundly, because we don't have to worry about them being somewhere far away. We know they're right there across the hall, snug in the same beds they grew up in.

This has been our go-to Sunday morning brunch dish for a while. It's quick to whip up and stays warm, which is perfect, because even when the kids are all at home, that doesn't mean they're getting up at the same time. Which means it's also fine for lunch—if they sleep through breakfast and brunch. Sometimes we're like IHOP and serve breakfast all day.

Cooking spray
6 large eggs
1 cup half-and-half (fat-free works great) or milk
1 teaspoon table salt
1 teaspoon freshly ground black pepper
¼ teaspoon garlic powder
1 cup all-purpose flour
1½ teaspoons baking powder
One 9.6-ounce package Jimmy Dean Original Pork Sausage Crumbles or 2½ cups diced cooked ham
One 30-ounce bag frozen shredded hash browns, thawed overnight in the refrigerator
One 4-ounce can diced green chiles, drained
2½ cups shredded Cheddar cheese
Salsa, for serving (optional)
Sour cream, for serving (optional)

IMPORTANT: *Don't forget to thaw the hash browns! Place the bag in the refrigerator the night before you make this recipe.*

1. Preheat the oven to 350°F. Grease a 9 × 13-inch baking pan with cooking spray.

2. Crack the eggs into a blender, then add the half-and-half, salt, pepper, garlic powder, flour, and baking powder and give it a good medium-speed blending until smooth.

3. In a large bowl, combine the sausage crumbles, thawed hash browns, and green chiles. Add 2 cups of the Cheddar, then pour in the egg mixture. Gently stir with a rubber spatula until combined.

4. Pour that mixture into the prepared pan and rock it back and forth on the counter to evenly distribute any liquid on the bottom. Sprinkle on the remaining ½ cup Cheddar.

5. Bake, uncovered, until the eggs are set and a knife stuck in the center comes out clean, about 1 hour.

6. Let the casserole rest for at least 5 minutes, then slice into squares and spatula it up. The casserole is great served with your favorite salsa, sour cream, or whatever you like to add to your eggs to give them a little zing! And leftovers are great the next day.

3

SOUPS AND SALADS

ORD TO THE WISE, IF YOU'RE GOING to invite the president of the United States to your house for dinner, you really should tell your spouse.

Don't know if you've heard this, but a certain US president was a very big fan of my TV work. According to White House insiders, he watched me every day. Before he was president, he himself had been on TV, and according to sources inside the White House, I was one of his favorites who worked at his preferred TV channel.

Of course I'm talking about Ronald Reagan.

And you thought I was talking about . . . oh, never mind.

Let me explain: For much of the 1980s I was the feature reporter at the NBC-owned TV station in Washington, DC, and every day at the end of *Live at Five*, I'd have a lighthearted feature report about something amusing going on in our nation's capital.

Upstairs at the White House late one afternoon, President Reagan saw a funny feature I'd taped with a Reagan impersonator. The president knew his secretary would love to see it, but she was on her way home, probably in traffic, so he called the White House photographer's unit and asked them to get him a copy. But they had not recorded that newscast, so the chief photographer called me at my desk and told me POTUS saw my story and wanted a copy of the tape. He asked if I could help out the West Wing team, and of course I said I would.

As I hung up the phone, I thought to myself, the most powerful person in the world, a former governor and movie star who had famously played George Gipp in the Knute Rockne movie, telling Knute from his hospital bed to "win just one for

the Gipper,"—well, the Gipper wanted a copy of my story!

When I told the tape librarian I needed a copy of the story for the president, he said, and this is an exact quote, "Yeah, right."

A few days later, on my way home, I buzzed the Northwest gate at the White House and told the guards I was dropping off a package for the president. (They apparently had people dropping off packages for the president all day long, and I was one of the few not wearing a tinfoil hat.) Eventually I was sent to the press briefing room.

"Do you want to give the tape to the boss yourself?"

Of course I wasn't planning on an audience with Reagan, and I was dressed like a 1980s feature reporter, wearing a plaid madras shirt, no necktie, khaki pants, Top-Siders, and no socks. I was dressed for dropping a package off at the loading dock, not placing it in the in-box on the Resolute Desk.

"Give it to him myself? Why not!" I said, knowing I would never get that chance again. We turned past the famous blue curtain of the White House briefing room, and a pocket door slid open. I was led toward the Oval.

I did not know this at the time, but President Reagan had a rule that a man could not enter the Oval Office if he wasn't dressed properly in a coat and tie, because the room demanded respect. So as not to embarrass me, President Reagan excused himself from a meeting in the Oval and met me next to his secretary's desk, where there was no dress code.

"Well, hello there," President Reagan said, sounding exactly like President Reagan.

I immediately handed him the tape, in case the Secret Service realized a mistake had been made in

How about dropping by for dinner sometime?

admitting me and I was tackled by a bunch of burly guys.

"I really enjoy your reports," RR said. "I try never to miss them."

I didn't know if that was true; he was probably just being polite. But my head was spinning as I thought, *I am hanging out in the White House with the president, who enjoys my reports and tries not to miss them. Eat your heart out, Dan Rather!*

Suddenly I realized the president had stopped talking. He'd probably just asked me a question. I couldn't ask him to repeat it and I had to say something. Five minutes earlier I hadn't known I was going to be face-to-face with the guy who had the nuclear codes in his pants pocket, and I was suddenly on autopilot, trying to make small talk.

"You know, Mr. President, your motorcade goes through our neighborhood all the time; we're up in the Dove House on New Hampshire. If you're ever stuck in traffic, come knock on our door . . ."

He smiled, and I instantly realized that was a stupid thing to say, because if there was a traffic jam, it was created by his motorcade—his car is never stopped in traffic. Moving on to *anything* else, I went way out on that conversational limb with words I did not expect to come out of my mouth:

"If you'd ever like to sit down with an average American family, my wife, Kathy, would love to have you and the First Lady over for dinner sometime . . . she's a great cook!" I said enthusiastically, even though Kathy was still learning what all those knobs on the stove did.

To Steve Doocy — With appreciation, every good wish & Best Regards. Ronald Reagan

a handshake with the other. Then he turned and went back to running the country.

I showed that picture to my friends at work, and because DC is a very leaky town, one of the local papers called me the next day to ask about my chat with the Commander-in-Chief. That item ran the next day, and when Kathy read the story, her reaction was unexpected.

"Wait—when were you going to tell me you invited the president to dinner at our house?"

"He hasn't accepted—yet," I said.

"*Yet?*" And with that, Kathy started the just-in-case planning of a state visit to our one-bedroom walk-up condo.

"I don't know if you've noticed, but our plates don't match," Kathy started. "Our table seats two—where will you and Nancy sit? Look at this room—*we don't have curtains!*"

Word to the wise—always tell your significant other if you've invited someone to dinner, and that's especially important if they will arrive with an advance team, food tester, bomb dogs, and a nuclear football.

"Do we have to feed the Secret Service guys? What if he brings Kissinger and his wife? Isn't she a vegetarian? I need a new cookbook!"

Having the assets of NBC News at my disposal, I asked somebody in research for Reagan's favorite foods. Turned out he loved comfort foods, like meatloaf and soup, but his favorite seemed to be macaroni and cheese. Married less than a year, Kathy could make mac and cheese—from the blue box. At that point in history she was great at exactly one recipe—lasagna.

"Lasagna is kind of like mac and cheese," I remember she said. "Lasagna noodles *are* macaroni, and it's got cheese. So, I'm making lasagna. Now let's figure out an appetizer . . ."

"Well, thank you, Steve, that would be nice . . ."

"Mr. President, you're late for your next meeting," an aide stage-whispered, just loud enough for me to know that my time was up.

I quickly realized I could not leave without proof I'd been there.

"Mr. President, nobody at work is going to believe I was here. Could I get an autograph?"

His secretary pulled open a drawer, grabbed an 8 × 10 glossy and a Sharpie, and slid them in front of POTUS, who carefully wrote out, "To Steve Doocy—With appreciation, every good wish & Best Regards, Ronald Reagan."

He handed it to me as if it were a diploma at graduation, with the photo in one hand and

Kathy would make the lasagna and serve it with a green salad, crusty bread, and a white cake from Larimer's in Dupont Circle that she would personally festoon with his beloved Jelly Belly jelly beans to make a US flag on the top. He'd never know it was store-bought, because Kathy would be wearing her new apron.

Kathy was a former small business owner and brilliant TV producer and host and took the invitation as a personal challenge, and in no time she had the menu, a new dress, additional seating, and matching cloth napkins.

"I'm ready," she proudly announced.

So now it was only a matter of time.

By the time the ninth or tenth presidential motorcade closed the traffic in our neighborhood, with all the lights, sirens, motorcycles, ambulances, and fire trucks zooming past, it was clear that he might not be stopping by.

"Did he even ask for our phone number or address?" Kathy inquired. I shook my head.

It's probably a good thing they never stopped by, because I don't know that our young marriage could have survived a three-course evening of presidential small talk culminating with me saluting Kathy by saying *Hail to the Chef!*

On the bright side, we got drapes out of the deal.

Peter Doocy, future DC reporter, on first assignment at the Reagan White House with his parents.

ENGAGEMENT LASAGNA SOUP

MAKES 6 BIG BOWLS

One day after our daughter Sally had been dating her boyfriend, Ali, for six years, Kathy said, "It's time to learn how to make the lasagna." "The lasagna" is what Kathy baked on our first date when I said we'd be married someday. Then she asked me to leave. Would lightning strike twice? Two weeks after Sally made it, Ali proposed, and we switched our nightly TV viewing from watching *Tucker* to *Say Yes to the Dress*.

That lucky recipe, Engagement Lasagna, is in our first cookbook, and was the inspiration for this crazy-quick soup. You can have dinner on the table in a fraction of the time it takes to bake a lasagna, so when it's time to clean up you'll be happy to say *Yes to the Mess*.

2 tablespoons olive oil
1 large yellow onion, cut into ½-inch cubes
3 garlic cloves, minced
1 pound sweet Italian sausage, crumbled
½ teaspoon red pepper flakes
1 teaspoon table salt
1 tablespoon sugar
1 tablespoon Italian seasoning
½ teaspoon ground nutmeg
¾ cup red wine (Cabernet works great)
One 6-ounce can tomato paste
One 28-ounce can crushed tomatoes (San Marzanos are our favorite)
3 cups chicken broth
6 no-boil lasagna noodles (about 4 ounces), broken into 1-inch pieces (we use Ronzoni Oven Ready noodles)
½ cup shredded mozzarella cheese
¼ cup grated Parmesan cheese
½ cup ricotta cheese
¼ cup half-and-half

1. In a large soup pot, combine the olive oil, onion, and garlic and sauté over medium-high heat until soft, a few minutes. Remove the onion and set it aside, then add the sausage and sauté until cooked through. Season with the pepper flakes, salt, sugar, Italian seasoning, and nutmeg and pour in the wine. Cook, stirring, 3 to 5 minutes to infuse the meat with flavor.

2. Return the cooked onion to the pot and add the tomato paste, crushed tomatoes, and chicken broth. Give a thorough stir, then toss in the broken lasagna noodles and stir to combine. Simmer over medium heat for 20 to 25 minutes, stirring occasionally to blend the flavors and soften the noodles.

3. Meanwhile, in a medium bowl, combine the mozzarella, Parmesan, and ricotta and mash them with a fork. Cover the bowl with plastic wrap and refrigerate until it's needed.

4. Stir the half-and-half into the soup, then simmer for 2 to 3 minutes to smooth out the flavors.

5. To serve, divide the soup among large bowls. Top each with a big tablespoon of the cheese mixture and stir it in to melt it.

6. Serve it with a green salad, and wonder why it took you so long to start making lasagna soup.

WALDORF SALAD

When we were first married, we lived in Washington, DC, at 1740 New Hampshire Avenue, NW, in a stately redbrick mansion built in 1889. Divided into condos in the 1980s, it was a wonderful place to live, but there was no pool, and the DC summers were blazingly brutal. For relief, we got a summer pool membership at the nearby Washington Hilton Hotel, and it became our home away from home each summer in the city.

Whatever it cost, it was worth it, especially the summer that Kathy was pregnant with Peter, when heat records were being shattered every other day. She may have been pregnant, but Kathy, a former Ford model and California beach girl, wore a two-piece swimsuit to the Hilton, at a time when conservative Washington was wearing those one-piece full-length wool bathing suits from the 1920s.

One day a very famous US Congressman swam up to Kathy in the pool when she was cooling down and said, "You from Sweden?"

"No, Encino."

Almost every day that summer Kathy had a poolside Waldorf salad, often with our friend Maureen, a very successful sitcom director. To this day Kathy says she would not be surprised if a DNA test showed Peter as between 25 and 35 percent—Waldorf.

¾ cup mayonnaise
½ cup sour cream
2 tablespoons milk
¼ cup blue cheese crumbles
1 teaspoon freshly ground black pepper
2 small Granny Smith apples
2 tablespoons fresh lemon juice
2 cups diced cooked chicken (rotisserie or leftovers)
1 cup seedless red grapes, sliced in half
¼ cup finely diced red onion
3 celery stalks, chopped
Iceberg lettuce, for serving (arugula, romaine, and Bibb also work great)
⅓ cup roughly chopped pecans or walnuts

1. In a large bowl, combine the mayo, sour cream, milk, blue cheese, and pepper and mix until smooth.

2. Peel and core the apples and cut them into ½-inch cubes. Place them in a medium bowl, then quickly coat them with the lemon juice to keep them from browning.

3. Back in the big bowl, add the chicken, grapes, red onion, and celery. Next, add the lemonized apples and their lemon juice and give the whole works a tossing to coat all of the pieces.

4. Divide the lettuce among bowls, top with the salad, and sprinkle on the nuts.

"You from Sweden?"

RED, WHITE, AND BLUEBERRY SUMMER SALAD

MAKES 6 TO 8 SERVINGS

Our kids love Kathy's famous sugar cookies (found in our first cookbook), and when they run out of gift ideas for Mom, they'll wind up in the baking section of Sur la Table or Williams-Sonoma, buying her more cookie cutters. I just asked Kathy how many we have scattered all over the house and she said, "a couple hundred."

Here's the thing—she usually uses only three, the heart, the star, and the gingerbread man at Christmas. Which means we have a couple hundred we've never used. One day I ran across a gift bucket of cutters that had been jammed in a drawer and vowed I would use them right then . . . even though I wasn't making cookies; it was barbecue night.

Grilled vegetables and a fruit salad were on the menu, so I sliced the zucchini into strips and then cut out little shapes that were cute until I grilled them, after which they looked like a toenails with green edges. Onions, carrots, mushrooms—nothing else was cookie cut-able. But then I sliced the watermelon into thin cut-able slices, and I was looking at my canvas! I set to work cutting shapes out of the watermelon slices, ironically using the star, not one of the many unused cutters.

I tossed these perfectly juicy and delicious red stars on top of a bowl of blueberries and thought, *I have something red and blue; now I need something white to cookie-cut.* Kathy suggested we make stars out of thinly sliced mozzarella—and the dish looked like something out of a magazine.

Try it one night and people will think you're a smart cookie—*cutter.*

1 small seedless watermelon
1 cup fresh mozzarella pearls
1 pint blueberries
5 thin slices mozzarella
2 tablespoons shredded fresh mint
   (optional)
Balsamic glaze, for garnish

1. To make the watermelon stars, carefully cut the watermelon down the middle. Cut 3 or 4 rounds from the sliced sides, each about ½ to ¾ inch thick. A thicker slice is more stable. Now take a 2-inch star cookie cutter and cut as many stars as you can from the watermelon slices. Set the stars aside, then cut the remaining scraps, plus as much of the rest of the

watermelon as you like, into 1-inch chunks. Place the chunks in a large serving bowl.

2. Add the mozzarella pearls and the blueberries, reserving ¼ cup of the blueberries for later. Give the whole bowl a gentle stir and level out the top.

3. Next, use the 2-inch cutter to cut two stars from every mozzarella slice.

4. Artistically decorate the top of the salad with the red and the white stars, then sprinkle on the reserved blueberries and garnish with the fresh mint. Red, white, blue . . . and beautiful!

5. To serve, park the balsamic glaze next to the salad bowl so the diners can plate the salad and dress it to their liking.

ESTHER'S EASY LENTIL SOUP

Esther Ferris loved to make people happy. She volunteered as a Pink Lady at St. Joseph's Hospital in Elmira, New York, and was in the Women's Auxiliary at the Arnot Art Museum. Her garden made her happy, and others as well; she won first place at the Elmira New York Garden Tour at age eighty-eight. In the winter she'd shovel her sidewalk and the sidewalks of others—the ultimate sign of a good neighbor, because Elmira gets more than three feet of snow a year!

Esther was also a great cook who loved making the signature meals that her family grew up on. She would make this lentil soup for her kids on cold winter days—probably after she did some shoveling.

Esther passed away in 2019, but her daughter, Jeanine Pirro, says it's essential that she keep the tradition alive. She makes this recipe when she misses her mom, and it warms her body and soul, making her feel safe and secure and loved.

We love it because it's so easy and tastes great, with a bonus hint of cinnamon. It's perfect for a cold day when you need a warm soup.

1 tablespoon olive oil
1 yellow onion, small-diced
½ teaspoon table salt
¼ teaspoon freshly ground black pepper
¾ teaspoon ground cinnamon
1 quart unsalted chicken stock (or vegetable stock, for a vegan soup)
8 ounces brown lentils (half a 1-pound bag), rinsed and picked over
½ cup white rice (Jeanine likes jasmine)
3 or 4 escarole leaves, sliced lengthwise, then cut in half crosswise (optional)
1 lemon, for garnish (optional)

1. In a soup pot, heat the olive oil over medium-high heat. Add the onion and sauté until softened, 6 to 9 minutes. Add the salt, pepper, and cinnamon, stir to combine, and sauté for 1 minute. Add the stock, lentils, and rice.

2. Bring to a boil, then cover, reduce to a simmer, and cook until the lentils are tender, 30 to 35 minutes. Lentils are thirsty, so add water as they cook, 1 cup at a time, stir with each addition. We usually add 4 extra cups during the simmering and add more salt and pepper to taste.

3. That's the classic recipe, but Esther would sometimes switch it up a bit by throwing escarole in with about 10 minutes of simmering left, then squeeze a little lemon on top. If you like escarole, give it a try. Is this great or what? You be the judge . . . right, Jeanine?

GRANDPA PERINO'S SIMPLE RANCH SALAD

MAKES 4 TO 5 SERVINGS

Dana Perino's grandfather Leo Perino was the patriarch of their ranching family in Wyoming. As a teenager, Leo had dreams of one day traveling to see the world, and he did, as a Marine medic who served in the Pacific. After the war, he went back home—he'd seen enough.

On his first night back in America after the war ended, he went on a blind date with a nurse named Victoria, who was apparently taken with the young rancher, and three months later she left Philadelphia and moved to Wyoming to marry him. Leo and Vicky raised three boys and expanded the ranch. He was a proud county commissioner and held the yearly Perino Quarter Horse Sale for thirty-six years, drawing people from across the country. Dana's most vivid memory of him was how much he loved his wife, whom he referred to as Mother. Years later, when Dana was at a family cattle drive, she looked over and saw Leo and Vicky, well into their later years, sitting on a rock in the shade and holding hands.

Leo loved to make this dressing for salads made from his garden. Meals were special but not fancy. Not long ago, when Dana visited the ranch on vacation, her Aunt Donna made Leo's dressing. "One taste and I was right back at their kitchen table," Dana told me. This is one of her ultimate happy foods, one that instantly returns her to a time years ago when life was simple, and the White House was just a place you read about in the newspaper.

DRESSING
½ cup vegetable oil
½ cup distilled white vinegar
1 teaspoon table salt
1 tablespoon freshly ground black pepper
    (lots of pepper—that was his secret!)
1 teaspoon sugar, or to taste

SALAD
2 bunches green leaf or Bibb lettuce,
    shredded
2 tomatoes, diced
¼ cup medium-diced white or yellow onion
Other salad vegetables of your choice (but
    if you use cucumber, skip the sugar)

1. To make the dressing: In a medium bowl or screw-top jar, combine the oil, vinegar, salt, pepper, and sugar and whisk (or shake) to blend.

2. To assemble the salad: Place the lettuce, tomatoes, and onion in a large salad bowl. Add dressing to taste and toss well to combine. Now you're back on the ranch!

SHRIMP LOUIS WEDGE SALAD

MAKES 4 SERVINGS

In our early dating days, Kathy ate a lot of salads when we would go out to eat (which was every night), and I wanted her to think we had a lot in common, including our love of salads. This would require great acting skills.

In the beginning, I would order the exact same salad she'd order, and as we smiled at each other as newly dating people do, I would put a forkful of salad in my mouth, using mind over matter to imagine I was eating a plate of meatloaf. And you know what? It worked every time.

But then a funny thing happened on the way to a Lipitor prescription . . . I really started to enjoy salads. Occasionally she'd order a cheeseburger, and *I'd get a salad*! Especially one that combined tastes from my childhood, like this one does. The crispy-crunchy iceberg lettuce, Thousand Island dressing, and darn delicious shrimp are all simple flavors I could eat every day.

3 tablespoons olive oil

2 garlic cloves, sliced

1 pound large frozen shrimp (31/40 count), thawed, peeled, deveined, and tails removed

Table salt and freshly ground black pepper

1 pint cherry tomatoes, halved (different colors can be fun)

2 avocados, pitted, peeled, and cut into ½-inch cubes

1 head iceberg lettuce (the firmer the better)

Thousand Island salad dressing (we use Ken's)

2 tablespoons minced fresh dill

1. In a large skillet, heat 2 tablespoons of the oil over medium heat. Toss in the garlic and stir it around to infuse the oil. When the garlic slices have golden highlights, no more than 2 minutes, remove from the pan and discard. Add the shrimp in a single layer. Sprinkle on salt and pepper to taste. When the shrimp turns deep pink, 2 or 3 minutes, flip them over to cook the other side.

They're done when they're pink all over. Remove from the heat and drain on paper towels.

2. While the shrimp cool, in a medium bowl, combine the tomatoes and avocados and give a good stir, because the tomato juice will keep the avocados from browning. Add the remaining 1 tablespoon olive oil and a shake of salt and pepper, stir again, and set aside.

3. Trim the core from the iceberg lettuce and remove the outer leaves. Rinse and dry the lettuce. Cut the head into 4 wedges and place one on each plate.

4. Now let's build the salads. First, divide the shrimp so that every salad gets roughly the same amount and place them adjacent to each lettuce wedge. Next, be generous with the Thousand Island dressing over the shrimp and lettuce. Spoon the tomato and avocado mixture around the base of the wedge and, finally, garnish with the fresh dill.

5. Give a grind of fresh black pepper on the top and dig in!

KATHY'S CHEESY CARROT-POTATO SOUP

MAKES 8 SERVINGS

Shortly after Peter was born, a couple of our very best friends from New York wanted to visit and see the baby. That put a lot of pressure on Kathy, because she had not been cooking long and they were foodies before that was a thing. So Kathy decided on potato soup, which I told her I loved from my childhood. For her first batch, using a recipe she'd seen on TV, something distracted Kathy and she mistakenly added a shocking amount of salt. When it was served it tasted more like the Indian Ocean than my mom's Iowan potato soup.

Thankfully our friends brought a bottle of Champagne for dessert, which suddenly became lunch, and they forgot the attempted salt poisoning.

Next time she made the soup, it was perfect. Kathy would make this for our three children—who would never touch it if they knew it was full of vegetables, like broccoli and carrots. "What's in it, Mommy?" Peter would ask, and Kathy would answer, "Cheese," which is a dog whistle to kids. The first time Peter saw snow fall at eighteen months, he held out his hand to catch some flakes and announced, "Cheese," because it looked like the Jack cheese Kathy shredded for him.

Today, to save time, we chop the vegetables very small, with one of those "as seen on TV" choppers. They cook more quickly when chopped small, and that's why this is one of our favorite winter recipes—it tastes like it's been simmering on the stove all day, but it's done within an hour. Although you could skip the soup for chilled Champagne . . . if it's New Year's Eve.

2 tablespoons butter
2 tablespoons olive oil
2 large garlic cloves, minced
1 large yellow onion, small-diced
One 16-ounce package fresh carrot chips
1 teaspoon table salt
1 teaspoon freshly ground black pepper

3 medium white potatoes (about 2 pounds), peeled and cut into ½-inch cubes
6 cups low-sodium chicken broth
1 medium broccoli crown, cut into florets
1 cup chopped fresh dill
2 cups shredded Cheddar cheese

1. In a large stockpot, melt the butter in the olive oil over medium-high heat. Add the garlic and onion and sauté until they start softening, 6 to 8 minutes. Add the carrots, salt, and pepper and cook until the carrots start to soften, 3 to 5 minutes. Add the potatoes, stir to mix the flavors, and sauté 3 minutes or so.

2. Add the chicken broth and broccoli, bring to a boil, and cook for 5 minutes. Reduce the heat to a simmer and cook until the potatoes are firm-tender, 15 to 20 minutes. Remove from the heat and set aside to cool for about 5 minutes.

3. Stir-in the dill, then using an immersion blender, puree away until it's a little on the grainy side. (If you don't have an immersion blender, a regular blender will do; carefully transfer the soup out of the hot pot into the blender and then back into the pot, working in batches so you don't overfill the blender and splatter yourself with hot soup.)

4. Stir in the Cheddar—it should melt very quickly—and serve. If it's still really hot, wait a few minutes—it will be worth it.

4

CRUSTY THINGS

SANDWICHES AND BREADS

KATHY WAS ESCORTING OUR THREE KIDS to the A&P one town over from us after school one day, and you know what happens when kids are a little goofy, hopped up on the sugar of their after-school snack, combined with the extra endorphins from being sprung from the custody of the state until tomorrow at 8:05 a.m.? Over by a cheese case, eleven-year-old Peter spotted Polly-O ricotta cheese. He'd never seen it in person, only in the company's constantly running TV ad, which prompted him to belt out at full volume his personal interpretation of the cheese jingle.

Poooooooolllllllyyyyyy ooooooooooooo!!!!!

The star of the TV spot was an Italian woman joyously singing a kitchen opera that ended with a showstopping crescendo.

Rrrrrriiiiiiccccccotttttttttttttttaaaaaaaaaa!!!!!!!!!!

Peter mimed the singer's hand gestures and vocal volume and stretched out that "a" in ricotta for at least fifteen seconds. To the horror of his not-amused mother, Peter was like one of the kids from *Fame* who would occasionally just burst into song, until—

"Peter!" Kathy never really had to say much more than that.

"Sorry, Mom."

At the end of his performance, a grocery employee in a hairnet tapped the side of the cold case, as if to applaud Peter. Clearly it was a slow day over in the Gouda department.

Embarrassed, and trying her best to get in and out of the grocery as quickly as she could, Kathy left the cheeses and turned down the baked goods

Peter during his Polly-O period.

aisle. Thirty seconds later, a woman approached them at a pretty good clip, saying, "Excuse me, was that one of your kids singing?"

By the stern expression on the woman's face and the fact that she was well dressed, clearly she was part of the store management team, and that meant she was about to kick them out—never to return. Which would have been a tragedy because we loved their garlic knots.

"I am so sorry, *he's* just goofing off," Kathy said.

When she said *he*, the woman looked past Peter's sisters and stared directly at Peter, suddenly zeroing in on the supermarket songbird.

"Young man . . ."

When it starts with "young man," it's never good.

Then she turned to Kathy, who was ready to open her purse and surrender her check-cashing card.

"Ma'am," she said in Kathy's direction, "your son has a gift."

A gift? This was not the chewing-out that Kathy was expecting.

"I heard him over in dairy and I had to see who it was," the stranger continued. "He has the most beautiful voice. The voice of an angel. Has he had training?"

"Training?" Kathy was puzzled.

The woman introduced herself and extended her hand to shake Kathy's. She said, "I'm the musical director for the boys' choir at [she gave the name of a New York City school that most kids only get into if their parents have a Gulfstream] and your son is exactly what we're looking for—someone who can project, someone with *flair and personality.*"

Peter had a gigantic smile, primarily because he was not in trouble, but also because he was being recognized as having a skill. Until that moment we didn't realize he had any, aside from being a human food vacuum.

"Our school would love to have you audition, young man," she continued, then turned to Kathy. "Of course we have scholarships—so you won't ever have to worry about the cost of your son's future education . . . ever!" The woman's excitement made it sound like prep school, high school, and college were suddenly done deals because Peter had sung a song about cheese. Kathy glanced around to see if the Candid Cameras were rolling, because Peter was no singer and she was late making dinner.

"We'll think about it," Kathy said, but she knew Peter's dream was to be a pitcher for the Yankees, and that his road to the Bronx did not start with ricotta.

"Let me give you my card," the woman said, and Kathy put in her jacket pocket. "Wonderful meeting you all."

The woman turned to resume her shopping, but first she gave Peter a little wink, which was probably a secret signal from the elite school. Next time she'd show him the secret handshake. If there was a next time . . .

"Voice of an angel . . . ," she proclaimed as she pushed her cart toward canned goods.

"Mom," Peter asked when everybody was back in the car, "am I going to change schools?"

"No," Kathy said, knowing in her heart of hearts that while Peter had a lot of personality, he didn't really have any singing ability. He'd never once been asked to sing a solo in any school production, although we do have video of him and a choir of fifteen other middle school boys singing "Wells Fargo Wagon."

Kathy should have known he had talent, because when Peter was two years old, I was hosting a show in New York and a TV producer heard Peter perfectly sing a song on the stage in front of two hundred people. The producer asked whether we'd consider having him on a sitcom that the producer knew was looking for a three- or four-year-old. "Peter would be perfect!"

"Peter is only two!" Kathy told the producer. We weren't interested, because showbiz is a tough business, and it's especially hard for children. Besides, if Peter had done that sitcom, he would have had less of a chance to have a normal childhood. Which he did.

Fast-forward to 2019, and we were at an engagement party for our daughter Sally and her fiancé, Ali, in Orange County, California. As is the case when two families get together and try to learn more about the new family they're marrying into, there were a lot of "remember the time . . ." tales.

Somehow the table topic of conversation shifted to music, and Peter said, "Of course there was the time I was discovered in the cheese aisle at the grocery . . ."

Ali said, "I've gotta hear about that . . ."

Peter told the Polly-O story, and at the end of that Sally said, "Peter, sing it!"

He didn't really want to, but she was borderline begging, and it was her big party, so he agreed to do it. Of course by this time he was a prominent TV network news correspondent, and the last thing he needed was a silly video being leaked to TMZ. So he performed an updated, more restrained version at 15 percent of its original volume, but it was so lackluster that people at the other end of our table could barely hear him.

I don't blame him for not going full Adam

Levine volume, as we had a prime table in the middle of a landmark Newport Beach Mexican restaurant, and he was clearly trying hard not to scare off our new in-laws.

"Come on, Peter, do it the right way, like in the commercial—really loud!" Sally said.

By this time, Ali's mother, Sholeh, who was hosting the party, was curious about these singing Doocys and joined Sally's request. "Yes, Peter . . . please sing it . . ."

Peter told me later that he did a calculation: In a very noisy restaurant that's known for its margaritas, people probably broke into song all the time, and besides, he was three time zones from home and odds were that nobody would know who he was. "All right," he said, to gleeful applause from Sally. He pushed his chair back a few inches so he could stand, and then he sang exactly the same lyrics from twenty-some years earlier. But this time he was not a boy soprano, he was a baritone—and it was impressive.

Pooooooollllllllyyyyyy oooooooooooo
Heads swiveled around in the fancy Mexican restaurant, busboys stopped clearing, and conversations ceased as all wanted to see who was singing with such gusto about queso.

Rrrrrriiiiiiccccccottttttttttttttaaaaaaaaaa!

Just like the original commercial, Peter's song lasted thirty seconds. The crescendo was beautiful, and he stretched out the final "a" in *ricotta* to full fortissimo. And as he finished, he took a deep, dramatic bow toward his sister, the bride, and said, "*Grazie*, Sally!"

There was a one-second pause, and then the room burst into applause—two tables actually stood and clapped. One table shouted, "Nice job, Peter!" Apparently the Fox News Channel had a lot of fans in Orange County, California.

So twenty-some years after being discovered in the cheese department, Peter finally passed his audition.

Our waiter, who'd been standing tableside for the entire song, turned to Peter and said, "That was nice. Can I make the guacamole now?"

And he did—it was delicious.

SUMMER SALAD PIZZA ON THE GRILL

MAKES 6 TO 8 SERVINGS

During our 2001 summer vacation with Kathy's brother Rob's family, we had to travel from London to Paris, which meant we would have to cross the English Channel. Some fly, some boat; we traveled the thirty miles *under* the water via the Eurostar train through the Channel Tunnel, or Chunnel. Our kids loved their first train ride—and it was catered!

Looking at the menu, they were fascinated by a British dish called bubble and squeak, served with a rocket salad. Didn't matter what it was, they ordered it—because *bubble, squeak,* and *rocket* all sounded funny. Like the time Peter ordered sweetbreads, thinking it was a pastry of some sort rather than the thymus gland of a cow. Nonetheless, he ate it all without complaining, proving that in his teenage years he was the closest thing we had to a garbage disposal.

As for the bubble and squeak (boiled potatoes and vegetables), the kids thought it was just okay. But they really liked the rocket salad. Rocket is arugula. It was big in Europe that year, and they ordered it a number of times, because they thought ordering a rocket salad was hilarious. When we got back to the USA, arugula was tough to find, so I started growing it in the garden. But the deer liked it just as much as the kids. Thankfully it's now widely available in stores, and this recipe always recalls that fun trip.

While that was Sally's first ride on a train, today she often takes the New York City subway, which doesn't have much in common with her first train. The subway does not serve *bubble and squeak,* and if you've ever taken it, you know it isn't a *rocket.*

2 tablespoons all-purpose flour
One 16-ounce bag store-bought pizza
    dough, at room temperature
Olive oil cooking spray
1 cup shredded mozzarella cheese
2 cups baby arugula
Olive oil, for drizzling (optional)
Table salt and freshly ground black pepper
¼ pound thinly sliced prosciutto, cut into
    strips
½ cup shaved Parmesan cheese (optional)
10 grape or cherry tomatoes, halved
Balsamic glaze, for garnish

1. Clean the grill grates and preheat the grill to medium heat.

2. Back in the kitchen, flour the counter and the pizza dough ball, then carefully stretch the dough with your hands (don't use a rolling pin) to ½ inch thick and as round as you can make it. It's not going to be perfectly round, but that's okay—it's going to be delicious.

3. Coat the dough on both sides with olive oil cooking spray, walk it over to the grill, and place it directly on the grate. Close the lid and grill for about 5 minutes, until that side of the dough is nicely baked and you have some awesome-looking grill marks. Use a very large spatula (or two) to flip the dough over, then scatter the mozzarella on the top of the grilled dough, leaving an outside

(continued)

edge. Close the lid again and grill until the cheese is melted and the bottom crust is baked to your liking, 3 to 6 minutes more.

4. Place the crust on a flat serving platter and top it with the arugula. Drizzle olive oil on top if you like and lightly salt and pepper the arugula to taste. Now toss on the prosciutto, shaved Parmesan, tomatoes, and my favorite, the balsamic glaze. Serve pronto, but that shouldn't be hard—it's pizza!

The Doocys with cousin Dane on the Chunnel train.

BUFFALO CHICKEN TACODILLAS

We may look like a lovely family—but we're a family divided. Everybody pretty much ate the same things and rarely strayed from Kathy's classic cooking, until the kids went to college.

Peter went to Philadelphia and fell in love with Pat's cheesesteaks.

Mary went to Boston and got hooked on Buffalo sauce.

Sally went to SMU in Dallas and had authentic Mexican cuisine.

So when the kids come home and we want to make one dish that calls back to their college days, it's this one, combining Buffalo chicken with cheese in this stuffed taco, grilled like a quesadilla courtesy of the Doocy Food Dorm!

1 pound ground chicken
½ teaspoon table salt
¼ cup Frank's RedHot sauce, plus more for drizzling
6 burrito-size flour tortillas
1 cup shredded Cheddar cheese
About 2 tablespoons creamy blue cheese dressing
2 cups shredded lettuce (we use iceberg)
1 large tomato, small-diced
3 or 4 green onions, green parts chopped
¼ cup blue cheese crumbles

1. In a large nonstick skillet, cook the chicken over medium-high heat until it's thoroughly cooked through, usually up to about 10 minutes, breaking it up as it cooks. Season with the salt. Remove from the heat and stir in the hot sauce. Set aside.

2. For each serving, place a tortilla on a large plate. Sprinkle 1 or 2 tablespoons of the Cheddar in a line down the center, then top it with a little more than ⅓ cup of the Buffalo chicken. Lightly drizzle with about 1 teaspoon of blue cheese dressing.

3. Top with lettuce and tomatoes. Toss on a few green onions and a few blue cheese crumbles, drizzle about 1 teaspoon of hot sauce on top, and finally top with another 1 tablespoon shredded Cheddar.

4. Now let's fold up this package burrito-style. Starting on the bottom side of the large tortilla, lift up the edge and fold it over the center. Then fold the right and the left sides toward the middle, and then fold the remaining side up and over.

5. Holding the top closed, place it seam side down in a medium nonstick skillet over medium heat. Don't be in a hurry; if the pan is too hot it will burn the tortilla. After a few short minutes it should be golden. Use a spatula to gently flip it to the other side and cook until golden. Remove it from the pan to rest for a few minutes before eating.

6. Continue making the rest of the tacodillas!

SWEET POTATO BISCUITS
WITH MAPLE BUTTER

MAKES ABOUT 12 BISCUITS

When Kathy knows that our entire family will spend time together, she pulls out all of the stops, so when the kids arrive at the house they grew up in, she makes sure they have all of their tasty foods and snacks from their childhoods plus whatever is important to them these days. Back in 1999, if they'd requested we stock the refrigerator with White Claws, we would have gone over to Red Lobster, but today we know it's sold at the liquor store, and we'd better have at least two flavors.

Kathy just wants the precious time when they are home to be like a trip in the Wayback Machine, when everybody was younger and life was simpler. I wouldn't be surprised if she bought the girls some of the Lisa Frank coloring books they'd loved working on in summers past, but after a couple of White Claws, it's hard to stay inside the lines.

As for me, I love having the kids home, but sometimes I really need Peter in particular, because he can help me lift heavy stuff I can't manage alone anymore. This last trip he helped me hoist the ladder to fix the motion lights, we moved the couches, and we carted off an old NordicTrack—ironic, because the only exercise we ever got from it was taking it to the curb.

Once the chores are done, we'll adjourn for a family meal, and these biscuits often make an appearance. It's a special taste for a special time, when we're all together. My kids can eat an entire batch once we start the meal, which is as soon as they help me put the ladder away.

MAPLE BUTTER
8 tablespoons (1 stick) unsalted butter, at
 room temperature
1 tablespoon pure maple syrup

SWEET POTATO BISCUITS
1 large sweet potato (about a half-pounder)
2 cups all-purpose flour
1 tablespoon baking powder
¼ teaspoon baking soda
2 tablespoons light brown sugar
1 teaspoon table salt
1 stick very cold unsalted butter
½ cup whole milk

1. Adjust an oven rack to the center position and preheat the oven to 425°F.

2. To make the maple butter: In a medium bowl, mix the softened butter and maple syrup until perfectly creamy and smooth. Transfer to a small serving dish and smooth the top for attractive serving. Place the butter in the refrigerator to firm up. You will remove it from the fridge to soften for about 10 minutes before serving.

3. To make the sweet potato biscuits: Puncture the skin of the sweet potato with a sharp knife half a dozen times and microwave it until cooked through (press the sides; they should give), 6 to 7 minutes. Cut down the middle like a baked potato and set it aside to cool.

4. In a large bowl, combine the flour, baking powder, baking soda, brown sugar, and salt.

5. Next, take the cold stick of butter, pull back the paper to expose one end, and grate it on the larger-size holes of a box grater directly into the flour bowl. Don't do the last inch of the stick; it's too close to your fingers. Use the end of the butter to grease a baking sheet.

6. The halved sweet potato will be cooled down by now, so scoop it out into a medium bowl. Add the milk and use a fork to really mash the potato and mix with the milk until blended pretty smoothly. Add the sweet potato mixture to the flour mixture and stir with a rubber spatula just until combined, creating a grainy orange dough.

7. Place the dough on a piece of plastic wrap or wax paper and knead it with your hands until it's a smoother consistency. Flatten it with your hands into a 1-inch-thick slab.

8. Use a 2¼-inch biscuit cutter (or similar round cutter) to cut out as many biscuits as you can, then fuse the scraps together and cut out more biscuits. Place them on the prepared baking sheet about 2 inches apart. Bake until golden and gorgeous, 13 to 18 minutes.

9. Serve them immediately with the maple butter.

CRUSTY CUBANO CALZONE

We spend a lot of time in Florida, and a sandwich staple there is the Cubano. You can get one almost anywhere. Over a one-week vacation we noticed the Cubano was not only on every restaurant menu, you could find them premade and stacked in the cold case at the Publix grocery store; a gas station had them chilled next to the cashier; and in a bait shop I had the choice of nightcrawlers, salmon roe, wax worms, or Cubanos.

At our house we bake a lot, and this recipe was our invention to broaden the appeal of our beloved Cubano to our kids, who love all things in a pizza crust. This is a great recipe for leftover ham and or pork loin, and if you have neither, the deli guy will slice it up for you. To us this is a taste of so many vacations down South, and as soon as we taste it, it reminds us of those happy family vacations in Florida, of the kids wearing mouse ears as we watched the clock waiting for 5 p.m.—official wine time for America's parents on vacation with multiple noisy children.

With this Cubano calzone, you'll think you died and went to Havana.

1 refrigerated unbaked pizza crust (we love Wewalka brand crusts)
All-purpose flour, for dusting (optional)
¼ pound deli-sliced roast pork loin or Spanish pork roast
¼ pound deli-sliced honey ham
4 slices deli Swiss cheese
Sliced dill pickles
Mustard, Dijon or yellow
Olive oil or olive oil cooking spray

1. Adjust an oven rack to the center position and preheat the oven to 425°F.

2. First, unroll the pizza crust. (We like the pizza crusts that are packaged on parchment paper, such as the Wewalka brand or Pillsbury Best classic crusts. If your pizza crust does not come on parchment, roll out the dough on a lightly floured surface.)

3. Now you'll be making a giant calzone! Arrange the pork slices on the bottom half of the pizza crust, leaving a 1-inch border free along the bottom. Top with the ham and cheese and a few pickle slices. Drizzle or spread mustard to taste over the ingredients, still leaving that empty edge.

4. Time to close up the calzone! Dip your finger in water and run it around the edges of the crust (this will help the two sides stick together). Carefully fold the top half of the crust over the bottom, lining up the edges. Give the entire calzone a little pat down to remove any air bubbles that might be lurking. With a fork, crimp the edges as you would a pie crust. Cut a couple steam vents on top, then brush or spray the entire surface lightly with olive oil.

5. Place the completed Cubano calzone on an ungreased baking sheet and bake until it has a deep, even color, 20 to 25 minutes. Remove it to a serving plate.

6. Let the calzone rest at least 10 to 15 minutes before serving—the pickles are hot! Slice into wedges and serve.

BUILT-IN CHEESEBURGERS

When I was growing up, my family loved cheeseburgers, so that's what my mom made. Two things made them unique: First, she used the same Lipton onion soup mix, as in her magical pot roast, and second, she put the cheese inside the burger.

She was born in Minnesota, and when she was growing up back in the 1950s, there were places where they put the cheese inside the burgers and called them Juicy Lucys. Of course, instead of making Juicy Lucys, JoAnne Doocy made Juicy Doocys. This is that recipe.

NOTE: *You'll need a stainless-steel grill pan or other setup to keep the burgers intact on the grill!*

1½ pounds ground beef (80/20 or 85/15)
½ packet Lipton onion soup mix (shake to mix before opening)
¼ cup shredded Cheddar cheese, or 4 deli Cheddar slices, or four 1 × ½-inch Cheddar blocks
Cooking spray
4 hamburger buns
Butter (or more cooking spray), for the buns
Hamburger fixings—whatever you like!

1. In a large bowl, combine the ground beef and Lipton onion soup mix until thoroughly mixed.

2. Divide the meat mixture into 4 balls and slice each ball in half. Press 4 of the halves into patties about ½ inch thick. Place cheese in the middle of each patty, one of three ways: 1 tablespoon of shredded, 1 slice that's been cut into quarters and stacked, or 1 small solid block. You choose your cheese.

3. Press the remaining 4 burger halves into patties and set them on top of the cheesy patties, then use your fingers to completely seal the edges of each patty stack by pinching them together. If someone were to walk into your kitchen right now, they'd have no idea there was cheese hidden in your burgers. Set the patties on a platter and refrigerate them for 20 to 30 minutes.

4. As they're chilling, let's warm up the grill. On half of the grill, crank up the temperature to high, 425° to 450°F. The other half of the grill stays off, because we'll need indirect heat later.

5. If you put the burgers straight on the grill, they will usually disintegrate, so we'll use a stainless-steel grill pan. Place it over the hottest part of the grill. As that heats up, at a safe distance from the grill give each of the patties a light coat of cooking spray. Place the patties on the pan and sear each side for 3 to 4 minutes, before they start burning. Then, drag the grill pan to the side of the grill that is not turned on and close the lid. Cook the burgers via indirect heat for 5 to 10 minutes, until done to your liking. Let them rest for about 5 minutes because the cheese will be molten hot.

6. Open the buns and butter the cut sides (or give them a light coating of cooking spray). Place them over the heat on the grill for a light toasting, watching them carefully.

7. Serve up promptly with whatever you like on your burger. Remember, you won't need onions, because they're already built into the burger—just like the cheese!

PETER'S CHICKEN TIKKA WRAPS

MAKES 5 WRAPS

In Peter's sophomore year of high school, his cousin Dane and he applied and were accepted to a summer study abroad program at Oxford University, in England. Yes, Oxford.

We bought him a seat in coach, but apparently a supervisor saw an unaccompanied kid with a backpack and fanny pack, so he was moved to a place where they could keep an eye on him—*first class*. He was the only passenger on the top deck of a Virgin Atlantic 747—just Peter and three flight attendants. Somehow he left from a New York–area airport but wound up in an Austin Powers movie.

At the end of the summer we flew to Oxford to pick him up. We'd seen pictures of the campus many times and even in the movies. Warner Brothers filmed the Harry Potter movies in Peter's dining hall; during our tour I made Sally return the souvenir fork she tried to pinch. Then we entered a lecture hall and watched our young man, clad in a prep school blazer and khakis, take part in a very high-minded economics discussion about something that made no sense to us.

For lunch we didn't get to eat in the Harry Potter cafeteria, famous for the floating candles and magic wand hijinks. Instead, Peter took us to the place he'd gone every day for lunch: an Indian food takeout place.

"Mr. Peter!"—the guy behind the counter announced when we walked in. He was a wonderful man, and we had a nice chat about how Peter and his cousin ordered the same thing every day: the chicken tikka wrap. "He's a very polite young man," the guy said, and then surprised us with, "Peter's also a very good tipper." Good tipper? He must have gotten that from his mother.

That lunch was delicious, and Peter still loves it because it reminds him of the summer he went to Europe. Some think of Oxford as the oldest university in the English-speaking world, but Peter thinks of it as the institute of higher education where he learned to speak tikka.

Try it . . . it's tasty!

2 tablespoons olive oil
1 pound boneless, skinless chicken breasts, cut into ½-inch cubes
One 15-ounce jar tikka masala simmer sauce
2 tomatoes, cut into ½-inch cubes
½ red onion, thinly sliced
5 burrito-size flour tortillas
2 cups shredded iceberg lettuce
Store-bought tzatziki sauce (we like Clark's cucumber garlic dill flavor)
Cooking spray

1. In a large skillet, warm the olive oil over medium-high heat. Add the chicken and cook, turning occasionally, until thoroughly cooked, with no pink showing, 8 to 12 minutes. Pour in the tikka masala sauce, mix, reduce the heat to medium, and simmer for 15 minutes, stirring occasionally so that the sauce doesn't burn.

2. Meanwhile, in a medium bowl, combine the tomatoes and onion. Mix and set aside.

(continued)

3. Divide the chicken among the tortillas, placing it right down the middle and leaving plenty of empty room at the ends for folding later. Spoon a little extra sauce over the chicken. On one side of the chicken, place some tomato-onion mixture, and on the other side, place some shredded lettuce. According to your own taste, spread 2 to 3 tablespoons of tzatziki sauce over each. Tightly roll up the tortilla burrito-style.

4. Working with one wrap at a time, in a clean skillet coated with cooking spray and placed over medium-high heat, set a wrap seam side down. Cook for a few minutes, until it's a deep golden, then flip. You can wrap each one in foil while you cook the rest if you like. Serve immediately.

Harry Potter ate here!

Peter at his Oxford tikka takeout spot.

If you build it, we will cook.

FLAKY HAM AND CHEESE IN A HURRY

MAKES 4 SANDWICHES

There are certain things that if you do once, you'll never do them again. I will never again squeeze ketchup straight from the bottle onto a hot dog without first shaking—because it always comes out watery. I ordered haggis in Scotland without asking what haggis was . . . never again. Then there's the ultimate—we remodeled our kitchen. Please, as public service, let me warn you . . . don't even think about it.

Don't get me wrong, it was time. We had to replace our 1980s pickled pine cabinets and worn-bare laminate flooring. So we bought a bunch of kitchen magazines, tore out the ideas we liked, and found a guy who could turn those paper scraps into our new kitchen. A contract was signed, and that started the clock on two months of torture. The dust, the noise, those construction people looking at us wondering why we weren't leaving. Hey guys, we weren't leaving because *this is our house!*

In the beginning of the construction, it was kind of fun having takeout from the best places in our town, but after a month we were ready to find a way to cook something in our house. But the oven was in a landfill, the stove was in the garage, and all we had access to was a microwave and a waffle iron. A microwave can't make anything crispy, but a waffle iron can, so we turned our attention to the Cuisinart Classic Round Waffle Maker—which was worth its weight in gold. And we put plenty of gold griddle marks on sandwiches—especially when we used croissants instead of Wonder Bread, so they'd be extra flaky and delicious.

3 tablespoons mayonnaise (we love Duke's)
1 tablespoon Dijon mustard
Freshly ground black pepper
4 large croissants (the wider the better),
**   halved horizontally**
⅓ pound sliced deli ham
⅓ pound sliced provolone cheese

1. Preheat a waffle iron to medium heat.

2. In a small bowl, mix the mayo and mustard. Add a grind of pepper.

3. Spread the mayo-mustard mix on both cut sides of each croissant. Next, roll up a piece or two of ham and bend it into a curve. Set it in the bottom of a croissant, then top with provolone. Make sure that the top croissant piece covers all the cheese; if it doesn't, snuggle the cheese a little further inside the bread or cut it a bit smaller. Otherwise it'll leak out (and waffle irons are tough to clean). Now that the sandwich is built, place it on a microwave-safe plate and microwave it for 30 seconds, to get the cheese melting inside. Meanwhile, fill the rest of the croissants.

4. Place the sandwich on the waffle iron and lower the lid. Push the lid down a bit to squash it a little, then release and let the sandwich cook for 3 to 5 minutes, until the croissant is crispy and the filling is hot (if your waffle iron has an alarm, it should go off). Remove the sandwich and let it cool for 3 to 5 minutes. Repeat to cook the rest of the sandwiches.

ALDO'S AMAZING CHEESY TOAST

MAKES 12 SLICES

Everybody knows that Aldo's in northern New Jersey is one of the best Italian restaurants in the Tri-State area. It's where Peter developed his love of chicken Parmigiano, and where Sally and Mary got hooked on Bolognese. Kathy and I love their chicken capricciosa. Over the last twenty-five years, we've spent thousands of dollars on delicious meals at Aldo's, when sometimes we really just had a hankering for the free cheesy bread Aldo serves as you wait for the meal to come out.

For years Kathy made a pretty good knock-off version, and it was close but never exactly right. Then one night this past year, Aldo came over to our table to say hello. I told him we were writing another cookbook about foods that made us happy, and nothing made us happier than his cheesy bread. He shocked us when he said how easy it was.

"It's three things," he said, revealing the holy grail of toast secrets. While he did not give exact amounts to use, we turned to the Doocy test kitchen and figured out this almost-perfect home version of Aldo's appetizer.

8 tablespoons (1 stick) butter, softened at
    room temperature for 30 minutes
½ cup grated Pecorino-Romano cheese
½ cup grated Parmigiano-Reggiano cheese
1 loaf Italian bread, cut on an angle into
    12 slices

1. Adjust an oven rack to the highest position and preheat the oven to 450°F.

2. In a medium bowl, mash the butter with a fork. Add the two cheeses and work them into the butter with a fork until it forms a paste. Keep mashing! It will look like mashed potatoes when it's perfect.

3. Spread a layer of cheese paste at least ¼-inch thick on each bread slice and set the slices on an ungreased baking sheet.

4. Set the baking sheet on the top oven rack and keep a close eye on the toasts. As soon as the cheese has even golden edges, remove from the oven. This can happen quickly or take a little bit of time, so watch carefully. Serve immediately!

TOM'S TERRIFIC SAUSAGE AND PEPPERS

MAKES 5 SERVINGS

About a month after we first moved to New Jersey, the church down the street from us was having a Christmas fair, with booths selling food and holiday items. It was not our church, but we wanted to be good neighbors, and because it was a fundraiser we bought a wreath and some other lovely handmade things. But we brought home something else that's permanently memorable—and that is the love of sausage and peppers.

Clearly we'd lived sheltered lives. We'd never had them before, and with just one bite Kathy and I gave each other that *eyes rolling into the back of our head* look when you taste perfection.

Fast-forward twenty-five years, and a new neighbor, Tom DiSarno, told us he'd figured out how to make them even better. And he's honest; he cheats—he uses his mom's recipe.

Tom's mother, Bridgetta, came through Ellis Island, and somehow the paperwork or handwriting was misunderstood and the Italian-speaking matriarch had her name officially changed by the US government to Patricia, which is how she ended up being known for the rest of her life. An amazing cook, she passed her secrets of the sausage to her son, Tom, who now fires up the grill and makes these for special events in our neighborhood.

This is mainly Tom's recipe, but we do add tomatoes, which is how they made them at the Christmas fair down the street.

"*Così buono!*" Tom says. I say, "Eat up!"

5 Italian-style sausages, mild or hot, your choice
1 tablespoon olive oil
1 red onion, sliced in half, then cut into 1-inch pieces
1 green bell pepper, cut into ½-inch-wide strips
1 yellow bell pepper, cut into ½-inch-wide strips
1 large garlic clove, minced
One 14.5-ounce can diced tomatoes (optional)
½ teaspoon table salt
½ teaspoon freshly ground black pepper
¼ teaspoon red pepper flakes
5 sub or hoagie rolls, split open

1. This recipe starts in the kitchen and finishes on the outdoor grill. Pour 1 inch of water into a large saucepan or Dutch oven and set it over medium-high heat. Place the sausages in the pan and bring the water to an even rolling boil. Cook for 20 minutes, flipping halfway and adding more water if you run low. Remove from the pan and set aside covered with foil. They'll finish cooking later on the grill.

2. Preheat the grill to medium-high heat.

3. Meanwhile, in a large skillet, heat the olive oil over medium-high heat. Swirl it to coat the pan bottom, then add the onion and bell peppers and cook for 3 or 4 minutes, breaking the onion sections apart with your spatula. Throw in the garlic and stir it around for 1 or 2 minutes to flavor the onions and peppers. Add the diced tomatoes (if using). Add the salt, black pepper, and pepper flakes and give the mixture a good stir. Reduce the heat to medium and cook, stirring, until the tomatoes are warmed through. Remove from the heat and cover.

4. Now it's time to grill! Grill the sausages and turn often for about 15 minutes. They're done when they've got a good charred look to them (cut into one to make sure it's done). Toast the rolls on the grill as well to warm them up.

5. To serve, place a sausage on each roll and scoop some of the peppers and onions mixture on top. So delicious—thank you, Bridgetta! I mean Patricia . . .

5

HOT POTATOES!

WHEN PETER, MARY, AND SALLY ARE IN residence at their ancestral home, Kathy spends a few days gathering and preparing their childhood favorite foods, the ones they can't get anyplace else on earth, because they know nobody makes them better than their mom.

Peter adores every form of chicken Parm, and Sally is the same with cheeseburgers. Mary has the most exotic tastes, because during our overseas vacations, Mary fell in love with everything about Europe: the architecture, the history, and of course the food. If you go to our refrigerator *right now*, there are *two* packages of Citterio brand prosciutto di Parma, as an enticement to get Mary to take the train home to Jersey for the weekend. Yes, it's a food bribe, and it works remarkably well.

When Mary followed in Peter's footsteps and attended Oxford in England for summer high school studies, the first thing we reviewed was the dining situation. Meals would be served in the same Oxford dining hall that Peter had experienced—the one where they filmed the Harry Potter movies with the floating candles and scary gargoyles. For an English major who stood in line with her dad at Costco on the days all the Potter books were released, that would be a dream come true.

One time when Mary was five, she and Kathy were at the local library at 5 p.m., and when they heard a message over the public address system that the library would be closing in five minutes, Mary turned to Kathy and said, "Mommy, wouldn't it be great if we got locked in here all night and we could do research?" To this day Kathy has no idea what research Mary would have done. She was in kindergarten.

That summer Mary's plan was to expand her academic horizons while keeping an eye out for

Lady Mary Doocy on the quad.

then-single, super-dreamy bachelor Prince Harry. The prince would fall in love with Mary, the funny, charming American, which is like the story line from every Hugh Grant movie, and by the end of the summer Mary's face would be on the five-pound note and I would get a cushy job as a marquess. (Note to self: Google how much a marquess makes.)

I booked her air travel online at Virgin Atlantic, and when I was entering her name into the reservation, I noticed that it asked for her title. The options were Miss, Mrs. Ms—the standard—along with some very British titles, such as Baroness, Dame, and Viscount. Then I got to Lady, and Mary's always a Lady to me, so I clicked on that. What a nice way for a father to honor his daughter! (Actually, I thought that somebody at the airline might see that title and bump her up to the front of the plane, but that scam didn't work.)

When Kathy found out, she was close to popping one of those important arteries in her forehead and insisted I change it. I tried, but apparently TSA and Homeland Security restrict access to that, so Mary's title is official, according to an airline database. In fact, we still get correspondence addressed to Lady Mary.

This would not be the first time we'd planned for Mary to travel internationally at a tender age.

For her sweet sixteen birthday, Kathy planned a trip for the Doocy girls to go to Paris and spend their afternoons lunching on croque-madames at the Louvre.

On departure day, the international story was that the suburbs of Paris were on fire—there was a full-blown riot, with looting, violence, and general chaos. Kathy called the airline and, by the luck of the draw, got a sympathetic agent who was also a mother of a teenage girl and agreed with my wife that the only thing that should be torched on a sweet sixteen were birthday candles.

A new trip was booked, and that afternoon they flew to southern California instead. They stayed at the famous Shutters on the Beach in Santa Monica, and while at the gym there they worked out next to Jude Law and Pamela Anderson. Fancy!

Fast-forward a few years, on the day Mary was ready to fly to Oxford, a terrorist rammed a Jeep Cherokee loaded with propane tanks into the glass doors of a UK airport.

Time to scrap another trip? Where could she go? Where was Pamela Anderson?

Kathy and I decided that because of the attack an hour earlier, Heathrow and other UK airports were at that moment probably the safest in the world, and we decided she would go. Mary put on her brave face and walked through security backward so she could see us every step until she disappeared behind a Panera Bread. From that point we were trusting the uniformed personnel of the TSA to keep her safe between Newark and the Land of Austin Powers.

When Kathy and I got home, I logged onto the Virgin Atlantic website, which read *Hello Lady Mary* at the top. Then I tried to get her flight status, but it would not load, so I switched to another online tracker and got a message I'd never seen before.

Call the airline.

I knew it was nothing; the fact that there was an international terror attack earlier that day was pure coincidence. I reloaded the page thirty times in thirty seconds.

Call the airline. Call the airline. Call the airline. Call the airline. Call the airline.

She was fine; I knew it. I just couldn't verify it with my own two eyes, or two flight trackers.

The second-guessing started instantly. Why didn't she go to a summer camp in Maine, where the only worry was mosquitos the size of chihuahuas? I finally took the advice of the online prompt and I called the airline,

"Due to an unusually high call volume, your call will be answered by the next operator in approximately twenty-three minutes."

Why was there unusually high call volume? *Because thousands of paranoid parents like me were probably calling to see if the plane had taken off on time and was in the sky, and if it wasn't, where the hell was it?*

I was a terrible father. I should have flown to London with her.

Call the airline. Call the airline. Call the airline. Call the airline.

Twenty-one minutes into my agonizing phone wait, the website changed its message for her flight: *Taxiing for takeoff.* Five minutes later: Altitude—50 feet, which was too close to the ground for my money, so I kept refreshing the page and watched that plane climb until they were at 35,000 feet. I went downstairs, and Kathy was watching a TV show.

"Don't you think if something bad happened, it would have been on the news?" she wisely observed. As somebody in the news business, I knew she was right, but it's hard to be a helicopter parent when your kid is on an airliner.

A dozen hours after *Call the airline*, our landline rang.

"Hi, Dad!"

"Mary—you took off late . . ."

"Really? Didn't notice. It's pretty here today . . ." I could hear kids laughing in the background, and

for the first time that day a feeling of relief washed over me. But then her cell phone cut off.

"Mary?"

I called back and Mary didn't answer. Instead, I got a recorded message: "Hi, this is Chuck Norris . . ."

Yes, Chuck Norris, who's so tough, he can make a fire by rubbing two ice cubes together. When Chuck had made a TV appearance on *Fox & Friends* promoting one of his projects, during a commercial I asked him to record Mary's answering machine message, to the envy of her class. He was happy to oblige.

"Mary Doocy can't come to the phone right now because we're out fighting crime," Chuck read in his no-nonsense Chuck Norris voice. "Leave your message at the sound of the beep." *Beeeeeep.*

When Mary returned at the end of the summer, Kathy flew to Oxford to pick her up. As luck would have it, they were experiencing the worst flooding in decades, and because the bus from the airport wouldn't drive through the standing water, Kathy had to wade through it. When they eventually got home, I'd laid out a beautiful buffet of prosciutto and mozzarella—and as soon as Mary saw it, she knew she was home.

Kids hope that whatever they do and wherever they go, somewhere someone wants to know they got there safely. I called my mom like that until I was thirty—and the only reason I stopped was that I started calling my wife, who would then call my mom.

Mary had an amazing educational summer in Oxford, and she's okay with the fact that she did not become the American girl who married the Prince; that was Meghan Markle. If that Hugh Grant-y plot line had happened for Mary, she never would have finished college, gone to law school, or become a high-powered lawyer. In fact, the little girl who wished she'd be trapped overnight in the local library eventually wound up with a job in the Capitol across the street from the Library of Congress, where a copy of every book published in America is stored. When Mary gave me a tour of Capitol Hill, she pointed toward the Library of Congress and said, "Dad, look, it's my Graceland!"

So she has this big job in the big town working for big famous powerful national figures, but to us, she's still our little girl, who knows that between her mom, brother, sister, me, and Chuck Norris, she's never really alone.

Now that the kids are on their own, maybe Kathy and I will finally one day go on our own European trip. We got a glossy catalog of vacation spots from one of the airlines today. It was addressed to Lady Mary Doocy.

First day, and Mary is ready to learn.

Future Supreme Court Justice Lady Mary Doocy.

FULLY LOADED CHEESY FRIES ON THE GRILL

MAKES 10 SERVINGS

When I told Kathy I was going to make French fries on the grill, she gave me that look she gives me when she knows I've just said something out loud that I should have kept to myself. "Won't they fall through the grate?" asked my wife, the comedienne.

"They would," I said, channeling Captain Obvious, "but I'm using a cast-iron skillet."

Our giant frying pan is identical to the ones my grandmas had parked on the top of their stoves, waiting to make something delicious and voluminous for their starving loved ones.

When I made this live on *Fox & Friends*, it got more comments than any food item we've ever prepared. But what's not to love? It's French fries, bacon, and cheese, all crispy and served hot.

This recipe uses frozen fries, which is a big time-saver, and my daughter Sally insists that I make this every time we fire up the grill. I just love that I can make French fries outside on a BBQ grill—and they don't fall through the grates.

6 slices bacon, cut into ¾-inch pieces
4 green onions, cut into ¼-inch rings, white and green parts kept separate
2 pounds frozen French fries (we use crinkle cut)
Table salt and freshly ground black pepper
¼ teaspoon garlic powder
1½ cups grated Cheddar cheese
Jalapeño slices (fresh is great but jarred pickled are faster; optional)

1. Preheat the grill to high heat and place a large cast-iron skillet on the grates to preheat, too.

2. When the skillet is nice and hot, add the bacon, separating the pieces and stirring occasionally. As the edges start to turn golden, add the white parts of the green onions and sauté until the bacon is browned. Remove the bacon and onions to a plate and cover with foil, leaving the bacon fat in the pan.

3. Slowly and carefully ease the fries into the skillet, sprinkle on salt and pepper to taste, add the garlic powder, and mix well but gently. It's very important to make sure all the fries are coated with the bacon grease so they crisp up properly.

4. Grill until the fries start turning golden on the bottom, about 5 to 8 minutes, then use a spatula to flip them. Repeat that flipping every couple minutes until the whole pan is your level of crunchy.

5. Reduce the grill temperature if you can, then sprinkle on the Cheddar and stir gently. Add the bacon and onions and the green parts of the green onions. If you're adding jalapeño slices, toss them on now. Close the lid and cook for 3 to 5 minutes to melt the cheese.

6. The skillet will be way too hot to put on the table to serve, so transfer the fries to a large bowl.

CRISPY CRUNCHY TATER ROLLS

MAKES 10 TO 12 SERVINGS

How many ways do you make potatoes? My mom either mashed, baked, or boiled them. Kathy generally mashes, bakes, or boils them or makes home fries or potatoes au gratin.

Considering that many of us have potatoes at every dinner, that's not much variety.

This is a tater recipe unlike anything you've ever had, and once you've had it, you'll wonder why you've never made it before. You might be thinking, egg roll wrappers look too complicated! That's what I thought before I started doing it, and now it takes me less than thirty seconds to roll one up, and when you taste it you'll wonder, *Where have you been all my life?* This is *by far* my favorite potato side dish. I'll make a dozen and heat up the leftovers the next day in the oven.

2 cups leftover mashed potatoes or instant mashed potatoes (we use Idahoan Buttery Homestyle in the 4-ounce size)
1 cup shredded Cheddar cheese
½ cup cooked bacon pieces (we use Hormel Real Bacon Bits)
4 green onions, dark green parts only, chopped
¼ teaspoon table salt
¼ teaspoon freshly ground black pepper
10 to 12 large egg roll wrappers
Vegetable oil, for frying
Thai sweet red chili sauce, for serving (optional)

1. This recipe can be made with leftover mashed potatoes or instant (we actually prefer instant; you'll see why if you try them). If you're using instant, prepare the potatoes according to the package directions and place them in a medium bowl. If you're using leftover mashed potatoes, place them in a medium microwave-safe bowl. Give a stir, cover with a lid and microwave until they are at serving temperature. Either potato method brings us to the next step.

2. Add the Cheddar, bacon, green onions, salt, and pepper and stir it to a nice consistency. Set aside.

3. To assemble the tater rolls, fill a small bowl with water. Use a finger to wet the edges of an egg roll wrapper, then lay it out with a corner pointing at you. Place about ¼ cup of the filling in a little horizontal pile just below the center of the square. From the bottom, roll that bottom point up and over the filling, then fold the left and right points toward the middle, making an envelope. Tuck everything in cleanly and roll until you have a tight log, checking to be sure the edges are sealed. Set the roll aside and repeat to make the rest. (YouTube has videos on how to do this, and most egg roll packages have diagrams, so don't let this process freak you out.)

4. Pour 1½ to 2 inches of oil into a deep skillet and heat over medium-high heat. You'll know it's hot enough when you stick the end of a wooden spoon in it and little bubbles percolate to the surface. If there are bubbles everywhere before the spoon is inserted, it's too hot; remove the pan and reduce the heat. Working in batches so as not to crowd the pan, position the rolls in the hot oil, seam side down. Keep an eye on them and rotate them with a fork as they turn golden brown on the bottom, until you have perfectly uniform crispy crunchy crackling tater rolls, 4 to 5 minutes.

5. Remove the rolls to paper towels to absorb the extra oil. Let them rest about 5 to 10 minutes before serving. They are delicious as is when served with dinner, but when we make them as an appetizer, sometimes we'll serve them with Thai sweet red chili sauce for a little extra pizzazz.

Don't worry. It was 5 o'clock somewhere . . .

HASSELBACK SCALLOPED POTATOES

My great-grandparents on my grandpa Sharp's side lived in a big limestone house in the center of Algona, Iowa, and for special family gatherings we would go to their house, because Great-grandma was a great cook but more important, they had more chairs than any other branch of our family tree, so they hosted everything based on seating capacity.

Great-grandma Sharp wanted to make sure nobody ever went home hungry. For a predinner snack she'd put out a beautiful buffet of things most five-year-olds wouldn't touch, such as pickled herring, sardines, and smoked oysters. I guess I was starved, because I loved them all then, although I haven't touched them since Nixon was in the White House.

But there was one dish served at Great-grandma Sharp's big dinners that we serve all the time these many years later, and that's her scalloped potatoes. Our kids adore them, and what's not to love? It's potatoes and cheese. When America started Hasselbacking everything, we created this version, which shaves about an hour off Great-grandma's recipe, which means I have more time to get reacquainted with pickled herring—*not!*

6 medium russet potatoes
4 tablespoons (½ stick) butter, melted
Table salt and freshly ground black pepper
One 10.5-ounce can condensed cream of celery soup
½ cup whole milk
1 cup shredded Cheddar cheese

1. First, you'll cut the potatoes into thin slices, but not all the way through. To do that, set a potato on a cutting board and place a wooden spoon along each side. The spoons will keep you from cutting all the way through the potatoes. With a sharp knife, make a series of vertical slices ¼ inch apart across the potato from the top down to the wooden spoons, leaving about ¾ inch at each end. Repeat to cut all the potatoes.

2. Preheat the oven to 400°F.

3. The speedy trick here is microwaving before we bake. Microwave the potatoes for 12 minutes—just set them directly on the revolving tray. Carefully remove the potatoes from the microwave and arrange them in a medium baking dish. Usually the microwaving opens up the slices, but if not, fan them open a bit by hand. Pour the melted butter over the potatoes and season with a little salt and pepper. Bake for 15 minutes.

4. Meanwhile, in a small saucepan, combine the soup and milk and warm over medium heat, stirring often.

5. Pour the soup mixture over the potatoes, especially aiming to get the sauce in between the cuts, then scatter the Cheddar on top.

6. Return to the oven to bake until the potatoes are tender and the cheese is melted, 10 to 15 minutes or even more. A friend loves to turn on the broiler at the very end for a few minutes and slightly crisp and brown the tops—your choice.

LISA'S LEGIT HASH BROWN CASSEROLE

I still remember the day back in the mid-1960s in Russell, Kansas, when my mom did something totally radical, different, and unlike my mom. She bought potatoes that were already cut up—in a bag! When she brought home the bag of hash browns from the grocery store, I remember thinking, *Why wasn't she chopping up the potatoes herself?*

I'll tell you why. It's because *it was five p.m., her five kids were screaming, and she was tired!* So she fried up the store-bought hash browns with a yellow onion and seasoned them with salt, pepper, and garlic powder (as she seasoned everything), and when I tasted them I thought they were, dare I say, better than Mom's? Actually, I dare not, so let's just describe them as a gift from the potato gods.

Served next to a great Kansas sirloin steak and a side of green peas, it had me thinking, *This is living!*

This fantastic hash brown recipe is from my sister Lisa, who works at one of the finest restaurants in Kansas, the Brookville Hotel in Abilene. And every time I taste it, I remember the time our mom made hash browns for dinner, when we were all still together and life was simple and oh so happy.

One 8-ounce package cream cheese, at room temperature
One 10-ounce can condensed cream of chicken soup
1 cup sour cream
1½ teaspoons freshly ground black pepper
1½ teaspoons table salt
½ teaspoon garlic powder
One 30-ounce package shredded frozen hash brown potatoes, thawed
4 green onions, dark-green parts only, cut into ¼-inch rings
2 cups shredded Cheddar cheese
Cooking spray

1. Adjust an oven rack in the high position and preheat the oven to 350°F.

2. In a large bowl, use a wooden spoon to stir up the cream cheese a little, so that it's easier to mix with the rest of the ingredients. Add the soup, sour cream, pepper, salt, and garlic powder and stir until smooth. Fold in the hash browns, green onions, and Cheddar and stir until all the potatoes are coated.

3. We always make this in individual custard cups or ramekins for dinner that day, then bake the rest in a medium baking dish for leftovers. Give each of the custard cups or ramekins a coating of cooking spray, then fill each to the brim with the hash brown mixture, plus some extra mounded on top. Use a rubber spatula to smooth it out and create a little dome, like a snow cone. Use a paper towel to remove any excess that spilled down the side of the cups. Neatness counts!

4. Bake them, uncovered, parked on a sheet pan on the top oven rack until golden brown, 50 to 60 minutes. (Timing on your extra dish will depend on the size and quantity.)

5. Let the ramekins rest a few minutes, then serve them up individually. They will be very hot and will stay toasty the entire meal. Any leftovers warm up great the next day.

PUMPKIN-SPICED SWIRLED SPUDS

MAKES 14 SERVINGS

Peter Doocy has a great smile, but for a very long while he never smiled . . . because he couldn't. For close to four years, Peter had braces on his top and bottom teeth, and to make it more challenging, they were rubber-banded together . . . all the time. That made smiling tough—and eating tougher.

Meanwhile, he was also going through a growth spurt, and because he could barely get any food past all that hardware, it would take him close to an hour to eat a ten-minute meal. So rather than continue to make him his favorite foods, which were torture for him to try to eat, Kathy just focused on mashed potatoes. They were a snap to eat, as he could handily Hoover them from his fork through the bands and down the hatch. Kathy made plenty of extras every night, and when you saw her boiling vats of potatoes you'd think we were having the defensive lineup of the New York Giants over to eat. Nope— just Peter, growth spurt, braces.

About that time he was also in the Boy Scouts, and while he never won the Pinewood Derby, he brought home the first-place ribbon every year for carving—pumpkins!

(continued)

Peter's perfect pumpkin project. (Say that three times fast.)

This recipe showcases Peter's love of both mashed potatoes and pumpkin.

Many of us make mashed potatoes all the time, and to be honest, while they're delicious, they can get a little boring. Take a couple extra minutes to add a swirl of orange pumpkin to your snow-white potatoes. Not only does it look amazing, but it tastes like something Starbucks would dream up in their pumpkin spice latte lab.

And it all got started with those awful braces that kept Peter's mouth shut. Fast-forward to today, and as a network TV reporter, Peter's actually paid to open his mouth. What are the odds?

One 15-ounce can unsweetened pumpkin puree
2 tablespoons butter
½ teaspoon pumpkin pie spice
Two 8-ounce packages instant potatoes, prepared according to the package directions (we use Idahoan Buttery Homestyle; see Note)
Hot gravy and/or butter, for serving

NOTE: *Because this is a cookbook of speedy recipes, we save time by using instant mashed potatoes. You can also use 8 cups of leftover mashed potatoes; just heat them up to serving temperature and go from there.*

1. In a medium microwave-safe bowl, mix the pumpkin, butter, and pumpkin pie spice. Cover the container and microwave for about 2 minutes, until warmed through. Stir again.

2. Spread the hot mashed potatoes in a shallow serving dish, then spoon the pumpkin mixture onto one side of the mashed potatoes. Artistically swirl the pumpkin into the mashed potatoes— think a swirly tornado pattern. There is no wrong way to do it as long as you don't overmix into one color! You want to see a distinctive swirl of orange and white.

3. We serve these with whatever gravy we've got going that day, or butter, of course.

GRANDMA LIL'S SWEDISH POTATO PANCAKES

MAKES 8 TO 10 SERVINGS

My grandma Lillian was a terrific short-order cook who made great things for anybody who walked in the door at a roadhouse joint on the north side of Algona, Iowa, called Frank & Em's.

She made American classics like meatloaf, pot roast, and sky-high pies, and she taught my mom and her sister how to cook—and cook well. My mom used to make us Grandma's potato pancakes, but it wasn't until Kathy and I took the kids to the Swedish Crown restaurant in Lindsborg, Kansas, that I realized I'd been eating Swedish potato pancakes all those years.

We've had other countries' versions of potato pancakes—boxty in Dublin and German *Kartoffelpuffer*—and they're also very tasty. But, for my money, this recipe is the best of the bunch and reminds me of my "Gunga," as I called her, because "Grandma" was too hard for me as a little kid.

Before we left Lindsborg that day, we stopped by a souvenir shop, put the kids on top of a giant Swedish Dala horse for photos, and had them paint a smaller version that said *Doocy*, which we placed on the side of our New Jersey house for more than ten years. It's common for people of Swedish descent to have them, proudly announcing that Swedish pancake is spoken there.

Grandma Lil with my mom and sisters.

1 large egg
¾ cup whole milk
½ cup all-purpose flour
1 teaspoon table salt, plus more to taste
½ teaspoon freshly ground black pepper, plus more to taste
½ teaspoon garlic powder
2 pounds russet potatoes, peeled and cut into medium shreds on a box grater or in a food processor
½ medium yellow onion, small-diced
Corn oil, for cooking
Ketchup, for serving

1. To make the pancake batter: In a large bowl, combine the egg, milk, flour, salt, pepper, and garlic powder. Mix until nice and smooth. Add the potatoes and onion and mix gently until every morsel is coated with the batter mixture.

2. You can't pour out this batter like regular pancake batter, so use a ½-cup measure to scoop out a scant ½ cup of the potato mixture. Place it in your hand and form it into a pancake patty,

squeezing out the juice and making it as flat as you can. Set it on a baking sheet and proceed to form the rest of the pancakes. Set aside.

3. Pour a thin layer of corn oil into a large skillet and set over medium heat. When the oil is hot, add the pancakes to the pan, working in batches so as not to crowd them. Salt and pepper the tops, just for a little extra flavor. Fry until one side is a deep gold, 3 to 5 minutes, then flip with a spatula and cook until the other side is golden and the potatoes are tender inside, usually about another 3 to 5 minutes.

4. Remove the pancakes to a plate covered with paper towels to absorb any excess oil. Serve immediately (or cover the plate with foil to keep the pancakes warm).

5. My great-grandma would serve these with lingonberry jam or cranberry sauce, but as a salute to my grandma who worked in the diner, today we serve them with a squirt of good old American ketchup.

Swedish horsing around.

PICNIC POTATO SALAD

Shortly after we were married, Kathy spent half a day making her first batch of potato salad with a recipe from *The Silver Palate Cookbook*, and it was beautiful. She asked me to carry it to the table, which I did, but only after I made a detour and did what my mom always did to her potato salad: shake an obscene amount of red paprika on the top, making it easily visible from the then-still-circling Skylab.

When Kathy saw it, she actually screamed, "What happened?" She was pretty angry at me for a couple days, and I'm sure she wondered why she'd married me and not that handsome guy who gave her a Saab.

Over the years she's branched out into other varieties of potato salad that are harder for me to vandalize with the red stuff. This recipe has an amazing flavor, thanks to the fresh tarragon, which we use a lot in the summer, and guests always say, "That's good, what is it?" But fresh tarragon is sometimes hard to find, in which case we'll use dill.

This is our favorite potato salad recipe to bring to a picnic or outdoor buffet, where unrefrigerated things sit out in the sun. You won't have to worry about that with this recipe, which is refreshingly mayonnaise- and paprika-free.

2 pounds small Red Bliss potatoes, quartered, each quarter cut in half
Table salt
⅓ cup olive oil
2 tablespoons white wine vinegar
1½ tablespoons grainy mustard (Dijon also works fine)
Freshly ground black pepper
¼ cup finely chopped fresh tarragon or dill
4 green onions, dark green parts only, chopped

1. Place the potatoes in a large saucepan and fill with salted cold water to 1 inch above the potatoes. Set the pan over medium-high heat. When the water comes to a slow boil, start a timer and boil for 10 minutes. Test a potato with a fork to see if it's just tender. Keep cooking and testing every couple of minutes until the potatoes are done. Drain the potatoes and set aside to cool.

2. Meanwhile, to make the dressing, in a medium bowl, combine the olive oil, vinegar, and mustard. Whisk, taste, and add salt and pepper to taste; it should have the balance of a good vinaigrette.

3. Place the potatoes in a large bowl and pour over the dressing. Scatter the tarragon or dill and green onions on top and toss until well coated.

4. Transfer to a clean serving bowl, then cover and refrigerate for at least 1 hour, or until ready to serve—the colder the better.

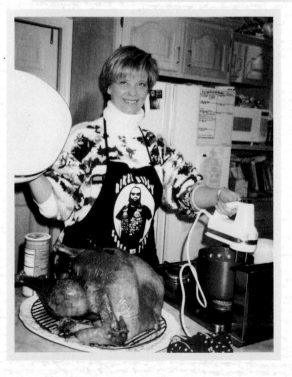

6

ONE-DISH DINNERS

SALLY DOOCY WAS THREE YEARS OLD AND tasked with the very prestigious flower girl job at my sister's wedding. After she'd executed her duties—flawlessly—I was taking the official wedding photographs and Kathy was running our 8mm video camera. That's when I heard Sally make a muted kind of coughing sound. It was a weird noise, kind of a barking cough, and that's why I turned toward her, right as she did it again.

AAAAhhhhhhhhkkkkkk!

"Did you eat one of the flowers?" I asked her, because she looked like she'd done something she wasn't supposed to. Sally didn't answer me, then she made that coughing bark thing again. It sounded a little wheezy.

"She's choking!" Kathy screamed.

Sally just stood there with her mouth closed as her face turned gray. One of my cousins said, "Heimlich her!" The priest dashed toward the rectory to call someone.

Kathy and I had taken a baby CPR class years earlier, and we both knew the drill: A-B-C, Airway, Breathing, Circulation. I opened my mouth as big as I could, right in Sally's face, one of those monkey-see, monkey-do things dads are known to do in hopes that she'd do the same. She did, but there was nothing blocking her airway that I could see. I turned her around and started giving her firm slaps with the heel of my hand between her shoulder blades. Every time I'd hit her and nothing happened, I'd make the next one harder. Tears started streaming down her face and she was crying, without making a crying sound.

I heard one of my aunts saying a prayer behind us, on the tenth or twelfth back blow, Sally *hack-hack-hacked* up something like a cat coughing up a furball. It went flying straight out of her mouth

Sally the flower girl.

and landed under one of the pews. What was it? A quarter. It landed heads up—lucky.

Sally was painfully quiet the rest of the day, and every time somebody asked *How are you?* she'd answer, "Don't eat da money."

The next day at breakfast my father picked her up in his arms and held her tightly, then, looking right into her deep-blue eyes, he famously said, "Sally, can you cough up another quarter? Grandpa wants to buy a newspaper!"

That broke the tension and we all laughed. But Kathy and I knew that what had happened was really serious and almost terrible, and that Sally's first wedding was almost her last.

Sally would grow up to have a very happy childhood. Every Friday I'd take her to the Dairy

What is the flower girl eating now?

Queen down the street from the Jonas Brothers' boyhood home, she got good grades, she was the captain of her high school swim team, she got into college early decision, and while at SMU in Dallas a handsome young man she struck up a conversation with told her the first time they ever spoke that she was the most beautiful girl in the world. And Sally would later tell her parents that Ali looked like a Disney prince. *Meet cute.*

See where this is going?

After seven years of dating, Ali Sadri proposed to Sally Doocy. She thought he was kidding, but she immediately accepted—just in case. Sally was shocked, but we weren't, because Ali had come from his job in Dallas to our house months earlier to ask for her hand in marriage. I wasn't home at the time, and Kathy, who was making dinner, didn't quite understand why he was pacing back and forth in the kitchen like a NASA mission specialist during a moonshot.

While she was dishing up some chicken and pasta, Ali started to talk about how long he and Sally had gone out, saying that he really loved her, and that it was time to get married—if Sally's mom and dad approved.

Kathy had no idea that was coming. She took

a minute and carefully considered what to say. "Ali, Sally really likes her job in New York City. I don't know if she wants to move to Dallas . . ."

Ali immediately answered, "Then I will get a job in New York."

Exactly the correct answer. Kathy said, "In that case, you have my blessing." That was the good news. Then she gave him the bad: "Ali, Mr. Doocy is going to give you a really hard time."

The next day, Ali had asked if he could go with me to my gym to work out, and afterward I asked him if he'd like a beer (it was noon somewhere; just not there). We sat at the bar waiting for a couple of Coors Lights and I was wondering, *What's taking him so long?* Of course Kathy had spilled the beans, so I knew it was killing him, but it was killing me, too. *Come on, kid!*

As soon as they served the beer—it wasn't even off the coaster—he asked me, "What would you think if I was going to ask Sally to get married? I wouldn't ask her if you or Mrs. Doocy objected." Had to hand it to him—it was an excellent pitch to a very overprotective father about his younger daughter.

I paused a moment, then I gave him my verdict. "Are you kidding me, Ali?" I said in a scary, loud, and firm voice. If I could have a do-over I would have made it 75 percent less scary, loud, and firm. Too late—I was on a roll. "Sally's only twenty-five; that's way too young. . . . No!"

He was stunned as I turned my *how dare you* stare back to my beer, where I took two meaningful sips, torturing him. I glanced over briefly, and Ali looked a lot like Sally did twenty-three years earlier when she was turning blue.

Okay, the Alpha Dad was done messing with his future son-in-law. "Ali, you know I'm kidding!" and I gave him a big hug. "Welcome to the family."

Yeah, the Addams Family, Ali was probably thinking.

Ali never finished that drink; it was just an excuse to hang out. Wish he would have told me he didn't really want that beer, because it cost me $6.

As the father of the bride, over the next year I learned a lot about the current price of weddings, remembering fondly that when Kathy and I got married in a park in Kansas City (on the hottest damn day of the year), the total out-of-pocket cost was $284. Not a misprint—less than three hundred bucks! Thankfully my brothers-in-law paid for the dinner at a beautiful restaurant, and to save us money my parents brought the wedding cake (as I wrote in our first cookbook, it melted in the trunk of the family K-car). Today weddings cost more than a car; the only question is: How fancy a car do you want to not buy in order to have a party?

Kathy had asked Ali if he needed help with the ring, and he said, "No, I've got a good idea what Sally would like." He saved up and sketched out his idea and showed it to a jeweler, who made it exactly to his specifications. It was gorgeous, and he thought she'd love it, but he was freaked out that somebody was going to steal it before he gave it to her, so he kept it "on his person" for a month and a half. That's how Ali described it: *on his person.* Don't know exactly what that meant, and I don't think I want to.

Ali's plan was to pop the question during their annual ski trip to Deer Valley. The first night in Utah, he had arranged for a picturesque horse-drawn sleigh ride before dinner. Sally loved the idea. As they got settled under heavy blankets in the back of the sleigh, a woman approached and said she was a photographer-trainee there at the Stein Eriksen Lodge and asked if she could hitch a ride with them, to take practice stock pictures of the sleigh ride up the mountain. Why not, Sally and Ali said, and the student photographer climbed up front next to the driver. Off they went.

About ten minutes into the ride, near the top of the mountain, the photographer said, "This would make a great shot," and asked the sleigh driver if he could stop. Sally was surprised, because after all it was Sally's sleigh ride, not the photographer's. The photographer jumped off and said she wanted to get some wide shots. "I'll get some shots of you guys, too," she said.

When the photographer was at least one hundred feet away, she called Sally and Ali to look over at her camera, and they did. Just then Ali started digging around in his pockets. Sally assumed he was looking for his gloves—she'd told him to wear them or he was going to freeze. Then he appeared to lose his balance and took a knee. "Ali, what are you doing?"

"Will you marry me, Sally?"

Caught off guard, Sally paused for a moment, then she looked into his eyes and said, "Really?" Ali smiled and she screamed, "Yes!"

The student photographer was really a professional whom Ali had hired through the resort concierge weeks earlier. Her photos were stunning—a perfect surprise.

Kathy and I also had a part in the proposal—we had to make sure that Sally's hands looked nice so that they looked great in the close-up photos. A couple days before the trip, Kathy announced to Sally, "Let's get manicures, and Dad will make dinner." Which I did. Ali was happy about that, but then stipulated that if Sally chipped a nail after their trip to Natural Nails, we had to come up with a creative way to repair the polish. To minimize the chance of a nail disaster, I did all the dinner dishes and coal mining that week.

Yes!

Suddenly engaged, plans were discussed, the wedding industrial complex was employed, and a date was set: May 2, 2020. Forty days before the wedding, the Centers for Disease Control and Prevention announced that any gatherings of fifty people or more would not be allowed because of the global coronavirus pandemic. So Sally and Ali changed their date to later in the summer, which gave me several more months to think about how our family was changing. That's when it hit me that Sally, who had lived at home for a couple years after she returned from college, would finally officially move out of our house forever.

The clock was ticking, and I had to maximize our remaining time together.

When our daughter Mary was leaving for college, I asked her what a fun dad and daughter activity we could do was, and she did not hesitate. "Mani-pedis!" Didn't see that coming.

My first mani-pedi did not feel good. A very capable woman was in charge of my procedure. After squirting some stuff on my feet that actually burned, she picked up the same kind of sanding block I use on the rough ends of dimension lumber and ground down my feet for probably three agonizing minutes. I was relieved when she stopped, only to realize she was just pausing to change gizmos! She picked up one that worked much like a vegetable slicer and she started lopping off foot parts that I had spent the previous decades growing.

As we left, Mary gave me the biggest grin, which didn't take a mind reader to know it meant, Thank you, Dad, that was fun. But it was worth being out of my comfort zone, because shortly after that Mary went to Boston College, then Villanova Law School, then moved to Washington, DC, for a rewarding career in public service. She never moved back home again.

Now it was Sally's turn to leave forever, so I asked her how we could spend more time together before the wedding. Two days later, she announced we'd be doing father-daughter Pilates!

We went to the local Pilates place and took an introductory class. I was the only man, and got plenty of side-eye glances that I interpreted as, What's that guy doing here? Didn't care; this was my time with Sally, and it was kind of fun. At the end they asked if we wanted to sign up for more classes. Sally's eyes were telling me she'd love to join, but I said, "Not today." They knew I would never ever be back to that place. Pilates was not my thing.

Over dinner that night, Sally and I shared stories with Kathy about what we did and the funny looks I got. Then I said something surprising: "Sally, I'm gonna sign us up tomorrow."

"*This is going to be so much fun, Dad!*" You could hear the italics in her voice.

I did some research. When Joseph Pilates opened his first studios in New York about a hundred years ago, 60 percent of his clients were men. That was then and this is now, so as we started our first father-daughter fitness class, once again I was the only man in the studio. "I'm Every Woman" was blasting from the speakers as Sally and some of my classmates sang along with Whitney Houston. To show I really wanted to fit in, I joined them on the last song as we all belted out "It's Raining Men."

Workout-wise, the Pilates machine called the reformer is good for your back, hips, glutes, abs, and arms; and great for posture, balance, and stability.

As a bonus, I was doing some unusual things for the first time in my life. At sixty-something I had never curtsied, so the curtsy lunge was a little challenging. There was one side effect I had not expected; after a few months, I was visiting my doctor and asked him what an odd lump was. He examined it and gave me the news: "Steve, I don't know how to tell you this, but you have . . . triceps."

Months before the wedding, Sally was wedding-ready when it came to fitness, and we were playing tennis and our score was tied. We played some more and were still tied, but by this time we were also completely exhausted, so I made Sally a bet. Our contract with her wedding venue was for *premium* drinks—which I thought was the absolute best. Silly me—*premium* was topped by *top shelf.*

So here was the bet: If Sally could beat me, I'd pay for top shelf.

What a motivator! You'd think Vince Lombardi had given her a half-time pep talk. I hadn't seen her play with this much heart since I was her soccer coach and promised a dollar to the first kid who scored a goal. It worked every time.

Wouldn't you know it, Sally won.

As we were walking to the car after the match, I thought of her upcoming wedding and I had a flashback to a scary time twenty-three years earlier when the flower girl turned blue.

I stopped in my tracks, grabbed her hand, looked directly into her eyes, and said, "Sally, can you cough up another quarter? Daddy needs to buy top shelf liquor for your wedding."

HOLLYWOOD CHICKEN STROGANOFF

Kathy's mom was always looking for a good deal, especially at garage sales. She knew the best garage sales in the world were just over the mountain from their Encino home, so she loaded up the car and she'd head to Beverly . . . Hills, that is. Swimmin' pools, movie stars.

Once she stumbled upon a prominent church in Beverly Hills having a bazaar. This was a good way for the rich and famous to offload things they didn't want anymore instead of posting a garage sale sign in front of their mansions.

"Look at this," she said as she pulled a white mink stole from a bag, bragging to Kathy when she returned home. "It was Liz Taylor's!" And with that jaw-dropper, she opened it up to show the label, and there was *Liz* monogrammed inside. Kathy knew it could have been any *Liz*, but her mother insisted it was Liz Taylor's to justify whatever it cost—which was way too much, according to Kathy's dad, who inspected it later that night.

She bought one other item of note. At that time in Hollywood one of the biggest movie stars in the world was Vincent Price, and when he wasn't scaring the living daylights out of people in his movies, he and his wife, Mary, wrote bestselling cookbooks. At that bazaar was an autographed first edition Vincent Price cookbook, which Kathy's mom bought and promptly presented to Kathy, who was in high school and just learning to cook.

The recipes were way past Kathy's home ec skill level, but whoever owned it before had taped into the book scads of recipes clipped from newspapers, and Kathy found a beef stroganoff recipe that she's made for years. This chicken version of that recipe reminds Kathy of her childhood near Hollywood, where you never knew when you'd run into a movie star at the Rexall drugstore (where she met John Wayne), the car wash, or the church bazaar, where Liz Taylor might have donated her mink stole.

Curious about what she paid for that autographed first edition cookbook? One dollar. Not bad, *Price-wise.*

(continued)

2 tablespoons olive oil

2 pounds boneless, skinless chicken breast, cut into ¾-inch chunks

2 teaspoons freshly ground black pepper

One 12-ounce bag egg noodles

1 large yellow onion, medium-diced

One 10-ounce package button mushrooms, stems trimmed, halved

One 10.5-ounce can condensed cream of chicken soup

1 packet Lipton onion soup mix

1½ cups low-sodium chicken stock

2 teaspoons all-purpose flour

4 ounces cream cheese, cubed, at room temperature

1. In a large skillet, heat the olive oil over medium-high heat. Add the chicken, season with 1 teaspoon of the pepper, and sauté until all the pink is gone and the chicken is cooked through, about 10 minutes. Remove to a plate and set aside.

2. Meanwhile, in a large pot of boiling water, cook the egg noodles according to the package directions. Leave the noodles in the water until ready to serve.

3. Add the onion and mushrooms to the skillet, return the heat to medium-high, and cook, stirring often, until the onion is softened and the moisture from the mushrooms disappears, usually about 10 minutes. Return the chicken to the pan. Add the cream of chicken soup, onion soup mix, stock, flour, and remaining 1 teaspoon pepper and stir well. Cook, stirring often, until bubbles form around the rim of the pan, then simmer for 2 or 3 minutes so it's nice and hot.

4. Remove from the heat, stir in the cream cheese, and let the cheese melt. Give another good stir and it's ready! Drain the noodles, plate them, and ladle the stroganoff on top. Hooray for Hollywood church bazaars!

SAVORY SKILLET CHICKEN POT PIE

MAKES 8 SERVINGS

Like many families in the 1960s, the Doocys lived paycheck to paycheck, and with five kids my mother was an expert buck-stretcher. Biggest bang for a buck was when the Dillons grocery store in Salina, Kansas, had Swanson pot pies on sale, ten for a dollar. Mom would spend three bucks and fill the freezer. Generally Mom tried to buy all chicken pot pies, because we all liked chicken, but an occasional beef pie would show up in the cart if the store was short on poultry. If they ran out of chicken and beef that meant we were in the danger zone and she'd buy tuna pot pies. At that stage in life we'd go to bed hungry rather than finish that tuna pie after we'd eaten off the crust. What kid doesn't like pie crust, once the tuna is scraped off?

This is my mom's recipe, and it makes me happy today because our kids adore it. Kathy and I have been making pot pies for more than thirty years. They're a good way to use up leftover chicken or turkey, so we always make them the day after Thanksgiving, after we've returned from an early morning at Walmart, where we've been known to sprint to the rear of the store to try to snag a deeply discounted flat-screen TV.

NOTE: *This recipe calls for an ovenproof skillet. We use a 10-inch Lodge cast-iron skillet and it's perfect. But the handle will be very hot, so have a mitt ready.*

Cooking spray
2 tablespoons olive oil
1 tablespoon butter
1 yellow medium onion, medium-diced
One 6.5-ounce can sliced mushrooms, drained
½ teaspoon table salt
½ teaspoon freshly ground black pepper

¼ cup all-purpose flour
One 10.5-ounce can condensed cream of chicken soup
½ cup half-and-half
Breast meat from 1 rotisserie chicken or 2 to 3 cups leftover cooked turkey
One 15-ounce can peas and carrots, drained
⅔ cup milk
1 large egg
2¼ cups Bisquick

(continued)

1. Preheat the oven to 400°F.

2. Lightly coat a 10-inch ovenproof skillet with cooking spray, then preheat it over medium-high heat for a couple minutes. Add the olive oil and butter, then immediately add the onion and sauté until it starts to soften, 2 to 3 minutes. Add the mushrooms and cook, stirring, to warm them up for a minute or two. Add the salt, pepper, and flour and stir to combine.

3. Working quickly, add the canned soup, half the soup can of water, and the half-and-half and stir until combined. Add the chicken and peas and carrots and bring the mixture to a boil. Use a silicone spatula to stir the mixture and remove the pan from the heat.

4. Now let's make the topping. In a medium bowl, whisk the milk and egg until smooth, then add the Bisquick. Use a fork to create a sticky dough. Because it is *soooo* sticky, I use a butter knife to drop the dough in small portions onto the pot pie. When the pie is mostly topped (with a few holes of the chicken and vegetables peeking out), put the pan into the oven (use an oven mitt—it's hot!) and bake until the biscuits on top are golden, 20 to 30 minutes.

5. Let rest 10 minutes before serving. This isn't a traditional pot pie and there's no bottom crust, so just scoop out the top crust and filling with a spoon. Enjoy!

KATHY'S CAJUN SHRIMP AND SAUSAGE SKILLET

MAKES 5 SERVINGS

I was in New Orleans the night before the 1997 Super Bowl, working with TV producer Gary Schreier, and we decided to go to Paul Prudhomme's world-famous K-Paul's Louisiana Kitchen. We didn't have a reservation, I had never been there, and when we arrived, there was a line out the door and down the street. This was the toughest ticket in town—on the busiest night in years.

"I'm friends with Mr. Prudhomme," I told the hostess, which was exactly what everybody says when they're not really friends with Paul Prudhomme and need a table on the busiest nights. But it worked and she seated us . . . one hour and fifteen minutes later.

Parked at a big table with total strangers, next to the kitchen door, I mentioned to the hostess, "Can you tell Paul I'm here?" She gave me that nod she gives every nonregular customer who drops the boss's name. After we were seated, I asked the waiter and busboy as well. To them, I was simply an out-of-towner who'd seen the owner on TV and was trying to leverage his celebrity for a free appetizer.

After we ordered dinner, as we were complaining to the strangers at our table about the noise from the kitchen, the hostess urgently approached us. "I'm so sorry to interrupt, but Paul would like you to join him at his personal table upstairs." I turned toward the busboy and shot him that "Told you . . ." look.

"Stevie Boy!!" Paul shouted above the people lined up to get their cookbooks autographed. "This is my old friend Steve!" he announced proudly to the room.

A few years earlier, when I had hosted a TV show at NBC, Paul would fly to New York every week to share his Creole and Cajun dishes. He was one of the first American celebrity chefs.

"Sit down, I'm ordering," he said that night, as one of the greatest meals of our lives was presented course by course. When my curious producer Gary asked the secret to the amazing flavors, Paul said, "Well, I have been known to cook with a little butter . . ."

To which I added, "Paul—everything's delicious . . . when there's a stick of butter in it."

A big laugh, and then an "Amen to that!" Paul hugged us both on the way out. When I got home I described the jambalaya to Kathy, who came up with her own version, which was flavorful and yet didn't contain any butter. Paul would have loved it.

Did you know he was my friend?

(continued)

2 tablespoons vegetable cooking oil

1 pound large frozen shrimp (31/40 count), peeled and deveined, tails off

1½ teaspoons Creole seasoning (we use Tony Chachere's original)

One 12- or 14-ounce package fully cooked andouille sausage

1 small yellow onion, finely chopped

2 large carrots, finely diced

3 celery stalks, finely diced

One 10-ounce can Ro-Tel diced tomatoes and green chilies, drained

One 14.5-ounce can stewed tomatoes, drained

2 cups cooked rice

1. In a large skillet, heat the oil over medium-high heat. Add the shrimp and shake ½ teaspoon of the Creole seasoning on top. Cook until both sides are a bright pink and cooked through, about 3 minutes per side. Remove to a plate and set aside.

2. Remove the sausage from the casings and cut it into ½-inch rounds. Add to the pan and sauté until a bit browned and warmed through, 2 to 3 minutes. Remove to the plate with the shrimp.

3. Add the onion, carrots, celery, and the remaining 1 teaspoon of Creole seasoning. Sauté until the vegetables are tender and start to turn golden, 5 to 7 minutes. Add both cans of tomatoes and cook, stirring, until hot. Return the shrimp and sausage to the pan and warm them to serving temperature, 2 to 3 minutes. Add the cooked rice, stir to combine the flavors, and serve.

ROSEMARY-LEMON CHICKEN AND POTATOES

MAKES 4 SERVINGS

Early in our marriage, Kathy had perfected two entrées: lasagna and a Betty Crocker chicken casserole. So she had meals for two nights a week covered, unless we had leftovers, which added up to four. But what about the other nights? Kathy's friend Maureen, a sitcom director, shared her recipe for a super-easy, very juicy baked chicken that she'd made one night when we were at her house for dinner.

Maureen's secret was a jarred marinade, which Kathy bought and used until that company went out of business—so Kathy experimented until she found the perfect proportion of lemon juice and spices. She'd start baking the chicken at 3:30 and it would be done when the kids came home from school. You might think 5 p.m. seems a little early for dinner, but when her husband hosts a morning TV show, she has to work fast before I fall asleep in the chair watching Martha.

Since we've been married, closing in on thirty-five years, I would guesstimate that 80 percent of our home-cooked meals have been chicken-based. When we'd go out, Kathy would say, "I don't care what it costs, I'm ordering a steak! We've had so much chicken that I'm gonna grow feathers."

Chicken also dominated young Peter's public performances. He had a joke book written especially for grade-schoolers, and there were two food-themed jokes that he'd roll out when we had company over for dinner.

"Why did they let the chicken in the school band?" he'd ask, and we'd pretend we didn't know. "Because he had his own drumsticks!"

If somebody laughed, Peter would leave them with one more . . .

"What do you call a scary chicken?" He'd pause a beat. "A *poultrygeist!*"

How Peter wound up a TV journalist and not the Tuesday opening act at Dangerfield's baffles me sometimes.

We still eat a lot of chicken, and this is in our current recipe rotation. It's a streamlined version with the taste of Kathy's early-bird special.

1 cup all-purpose flour
1 teaspoon table salt
½ teaspoon freshly ground black pepper
Leaves from 4 rosemary sprigs, finely chopped, plus a sprig or two for garnish if desired
4 thin-sliced chicken breast cutlets (4 to 6 ounces each)
3 tablespoons olive oil

One 1½-pound bag microwaveable new potatoes, such as Steamables
4 tablespoons (½ stick) butter
2 shallots, finely chopped
One 10-ounce package mushrooms, trimmed and halved
Juice of ½ lemon

1. In a large shallow bowl or pie plate, combine the flour, salt, pepper, and one-quarter of the chopped rosemary. Mix until the spice flecks are evenly distributed.

2. One at a time, dredge each piece of chicken in the flour mixture. Park them on a piece of aluminum foil.

3. In a large skillet, heat the olive oil over medium-high heat. Add the chicken and cook 5 to 7 minutes, or until about half done, then flip, and cook until perfectly golden and cooked through, 5 to 7 minutes longer. Cut into the meat to make sure there's no pink. Remove the chicken to a plate. Set aside and cover with (new!) foil to keep warm.

4. Meanwhile, microwave the potatoes according to the package directions. Set aside and keep warm.

5. In the empty skillet, melt 2 tablespoons of the butter over medium heat. Add the shallots and fry until they are a little tender, about 2 minutes. Add the mushrooms and cook until the liquid releases and reduces and they are caramelized, 5 to 10 minutes. Add the remaining chopped rosemary, the remaining 2 tablespoons of butter, and the lemon juice and stir for 1 minute to warm them through.

6. Add the potatoes and stir to coat and warm them for a few minutes. Move the mushrooms and potatoes to one side and return the chicken to the pan to warm up, using a spoon to coat it with the sauce.

7. Serve in the skillet, with a rosemary sprig or two as a garnish if you like.

EASY SLOW COOKER CARNITAS

There was a place not far from our house in Virginia that had a fall-off-the-bone tender platter of carnitas, and I always ordered it and would pretty much lick the plate clean. Sidenote: They also had a margarita that could make you lose the feeling in your toes.

This is one of those happy recipes that reminds us of going out to eat with our small kids, who grew up with a wonderful appreciation of the foods of Mexico. When they got older, one by one they turned from our dining companions to our designated drivers, on nights when Dad had that drink with the salty rim and stopped feeling his lower extremities.

One 3- to 4-pound boneless pork shoulder
One 1-ounce package Old El Paso slow
    cooker seasoning mix for pork carnitas
3 tablespoons olive oil
One 16-ounce jar salsa verde (we use
    Herdez brand)
Tortillas, flour or corn, crunchy or soft, your
    choice

OPTIONAL TOPPINGS (PICK 2 OR 3)
Mexican crema or sour cream
Monterey Jack or Cotija cheese
Fresh guacamole or diced avocado
Small bag fresh shredded cabbage mix (we
    use Fresh Express Angel Hair Cole Slaw)
Limes, quartered

HAPPY IN A HURRY TIP: *Using a disposable slow cooker liner makes cleanup a breeze. If you don't use a liner, give the bottom of the cooker a coating of cooking spray. It's not needed with a liner. I like the liner because it speeds the cleanup. Kathy prefers not to use a liner . . . because I do the cleanup.*

1. Rub the pork shoulder with the carnitas seasoning mix. Really work the mixture into the meat.

2. In a deep skillet, heat the olive oil over medium-high heat. Add the pork and brown it on all sides, about 10 minutes total.

3. Meanwhile, pour 1 cup of the salsa verde into the slow cooker.

4. Transfer the browned meat to the slow cooker, fat side facing up. Pour the remaining salsa verde over the meat. Cover and cook on high for 4 to 6 hours, until the meat is fully cooked and separates easily with a fork.

5. When you're ready to serve, place the pork in a large bowl. Use a couple forks to shred it. Add a little of the sauce from the slow cooker to moisten and season the meat.

6. Now it's taco time! Serve the pork with tortillas and your favorite toppings. There are a million variations . . . all delicious!

7. There will probably be plenty of leftovers, so tomorrow you can have carnitas burritos or carnitas bowls. You decide!

GRANDMA'S SWEDISH MEATBALLS

MAKES ABOUT 3 DOZEN 1½-INCH MEATBALLS

My sisters and I grew up with the sure knowledge that because my father was 100 percent Irish and my mother was 100 percent Swedish, we were all half Irish, half Swedish. There was never any question, until my dad, Uncle Phil, and I went to Dublin to trace our roots, and workers at the Irish government archives told us they could not find our family name in the official records.

Years later I did a DNA test and discovered that I am indeed Irish—a whole 19 percent!

The rest of me is Scandinavian. I guess it's not a shock, since I'm blond, I've driven a Volvo since 1982, and I have an inexplicable urge to visit IKEA on family holidays. That can't be a coincidence, right?

This is a faithful version of the meatballs my mom and grandma made when I was growing up. I believe they're very authentic, and I would know. I've got very deep Swedish roots—I'm not an *artificial Swedener*.

I've been waiting fifty years to use that joke.

Enjoy the meatballs—they're wonderful. We serve them with egg noodles, but they're also great with Grandma Lil's Swedish Potato Pancakes (page 108).

¾ cup panko bread crumbs
¾ cup milk
Olive oil, for frying
1 yellow onion, small-diced
1½ pounds meatloaf mix (½ pound each ground pork, veal, and beef)
1 large egg, whisked
½ teaspoon table salt
¼ teaspoon freshly ground black pepper
Pinch of ground or grated nutmeg (optional)
One 12-ounce package egg noodles
One 10.5-ounce can condensed cream of mushroom soup
1 packet Lipton onion soup mix
1½ cups chicken stock
½ cup sour cream

1. In a small bowl, combine the bread crumbs and milk and let sit while the all milk is absorbed.

2. Meanwhile, in a large skillet, heat 1 tablespoon olive oil over medium-high heat. Add the onion and sauté until it starts to soften and brown, 2 or 3 minutes. Remove the onion to a plate to cool. Remove the pan from the heat but leave the oil in the pan.

3. Grandma used her meat grinder for this recipe, but we use a food processor. In a food processor, combine the softened bread crumbs, cooled onion, meatloaf mix, egg, salt, pepper, and nutmeg (if using). Process until the mixture is a consistent pink color.

4. Grandma would run two plates under the water so the meatballs wouldn't stick. We use wax or parchment paper to park them on. Shape the meat mixture into 1½-inch meatballs and set them aside on the wax paper or parchment. Small meatballs cook faster!

5. In a pot of boiling water, cook the egg noodles according to the package directions. Leave them in the water to keep them warm if they are done before you're ready to serve.

6. Meanwhile, to cook the meatballs, pour a thin layer of olive oil into the skillet and set it over medium-high heat. Working in two batches, fry the meatballs until nicely browned and cooked through, 10 to 12 minutes per batch. Slice one open to make sure it's done. Remove the meatballs to a plate and cover them with foil to keep them warm.

7. Wipe out the pan and again set it over medium-high heat. Add the cream of mushroom soup, the onion soup mix, and the stock and whisk until smooth. When the mixture comes to a boil, reduce the heat to medium, add the sour cream, and stir to mix it in completely. Add the meatballs and let simmer for a couple minutes to warm them through.

8. Serve over the egg noodles.

Swedish grandma Lil on my parents' wedding day.

AMY'S ARTICHOKE CHICKEN CASSEROLE

MAKES 6 SERVINGS

When he was a single man covering the Pentagon for Fox News, Bret Baier had a friend who tried to set him up on three blind dates, and each "ended horribly." Undeterred, Bret's friend told him, "I've got one more..." Bret made it clear that this was the last setup, and he'd never again listen to that joker about women.

Bret met Amy Hills at a Rolling Stones concert in Washington. She'd flown in from Chicago on this one-chance-in-a-million date, and by the end of the weekend, Bret had called the matchmaking friend to say, "I'd like to see her again." The friend was obviously relieved to hear this. Then Bret dropped the bomb: "By the way, I'm going to marry her someday."

For a year they had a challenging long-distance relationship. Amy would fly to DC to visit Bret, and he was racking up airline miles to visit her in Chicago. Amy's mom, Barbie Hills, would often make this chicken casserole for him at family meals, because every mother knows that the fastest way to a man's heart is through his stomach. The recipe had been a family favorite for years, and it was Barbie's secret weapon.

Bret says, "This recipe reminds me of Amy's family and the first time I ate with them. She has three brothers, and they were there and their kids were running around and it was great. It's one of those taste-good meals that a family passes around."

I'd love to be able to say that this casserole led to Bret's proposal, but that isn't true. It was because Amy is a wonderful, amazing person and he couldn't live without her. Today, after fifteen years of marriage, Amy makes this recipe all the time, and they both told me that when they walk in the kitchen and smell it cooking, it makes them happy because it's a taste of home.

Today Bret and Amy have two handsome young boys and she somehow makes sure that their Christmas card is the first one to arrive each season. It always features a wonderful family photo that shows us how tall Paul and Daniel have grown since the last Christmas and it's signed "The Four Baiers." Unlike in the "Three Bears" fairy tale, Amy's meals are never served too hot or too cold, they're always just right.

So next time you see Bret anchoring *Special Report* on TV, and you wonder what he's having for supper after his show, just know, if he's lucky, it's this.

(continued)

Cooking spray

4 tablespoons (½ stick) butter

6 thin-sliced chicken breasts (about 6 ounces each)

1 teaspoon table salt, plus more to taste

1 teaspoon freshly ground black pepper

16 white pearl onions, jarred or thawed frozen

One 29-ounce can small whole potatoes, drained, or 20 very small fresh potatoes

Two 10-ounce packages frozen artichoke hearts, thawed

1 cup chicken broth

Juice of ½ lemon

1. Preheat the oven to 325°F. Coat a 9 × 13-inch baking dish with cooking spray.

2. In a large skillet, melt 2 tablespoons of the butter over medium heat. Season the chicken with the salt and pepper. Working in batches if necessary, add the chicken to the pan in a single layer and cook until the chicken is a deep golden brown and cooked through, 5 to 7 minutes per side. Place the chicken in the prepared baking dish and set aside.

3. Clean out the hot skillet with paper towels. Add 1 tablespoon of the butter to the pan, set over medium heat, and add the onions and potatoes. Cook until golden on all sides, 8 to 10 minutes, rolling them around to coat with butter. Add the artichoke hearts and sauté for 2 minutes. Transfer the vegetables to the baking dish and spread over the chicken.

4. Add the chicken broth to the skillet and increase the heat to medium-high. Bring it to a quick boil, then pour it over the chicken and vegetables. Sprinkle the lemon juice evenly over the casserole and give it a light shake of salt. Cover with foil and bake until bubbling and beautiful, about 1 hour.

5. Serve the chicken with the vegetables on the side.

CAULIFLOWER GNOCCHI BOLOGNESE

Peter Doocy was picking up some groceries in a Trader Joe's in Arlington, Virginia, one night after work when he noticed a man in workout clothes who was being shadowed by a security detail. When he got a good look at the guy, he realized it was former Texas Governor Rick Perry, who was then Energy Secretary. They chatted by the checkout for a few minutes, then Peter looked down into Perry's basket and saw his dinner: a spinach salad and granola.

"Mister Secretary," Peter observed. "You were the longtime governor of Texas. Shouldn't you have a big ol' steak in there?"

Perry nodded and said, "Peter, my daughter has me eating this stuff."

I know exactly what he's talking about. When Trader Joe's unveiled their now famous cauliflower gnocchi, which look like Tater Tots, my daughter Mary read about it and immediately added it to her recipe repertory, because she's always looking for healthy alternatives to pasta. She told us to try it, and we all fell in love with it.

But after a while the gnocchi prepared simply topped with marinara sauce got a little boring for us, so as a family we came up with this Bolognese recipe. My mom used to make a gnocchi-like pasta dish with hamburger, so we added a pound of beef. Sally thought a little cream and cheese would smooth out the red sauce, so that's in. And when Kathy first told me about Trader Joe's, it was a story of appreciation about how they could sell a bottle of vino for less than a cup of coffee, so we added some red wine as a hat tip to their notoriously famous and cheap Two Buck Chuck. The result? We say it's more delicious than a spinach salad and granola . . . sorry, Governor.

Two 12-ounce packages cauliflower gnocchi
    (Trader Joe's is our favorite)
3 tablespoons butter
1 pound ground beef
½ teaspoon table salt
½ teaspoon freshly ground black pepper
¼ teaspoon garlic powder
½ cup red wine (or beef stock)
½ yellow onion, finely diced
2 garlic cloves, minced
One 4-ounce can mushroom pieces and
    stems, drained
One 24-ounce jar marinara (Rao's is our
    favorite)
½ cup heavy cream or half-and-half

Ricotta cheese, for serving
Grated Parmesan cheese, for serving

1. Set a large nonstick skillet (that has a lid) over medium heat and add the cauliflower gnocchi. They need to be a single layer deep, with a little space between them, so work in batches if you need to; otherwise they will get gummy. Add ½ cup water and cover the pan. When the water has cooked off, 5 to 8 minutes, quickly remove the lid, add the butter, and swirl the gnocchi in the pan so they are buttered and not sticking. Cook for up to 10 minutes, until browned and

(continued)

fried on all sides, turning them with a spatula every couple minutes.

2. Meanwhile, in a large saucepan, combine the ground beef, salt, pepper, and garlic powder. Brown the beef thoroughly over medium-high heat, stirring often. Add the wine (or beef stock) and cook for a few minutes. Add the onion, garlic, and mushrooms and sauté until the onion starts to soften, 3 to 5 minutes. Add the marinara, stir in the cream, and bring to a simmer to heat up the sauce.

3. Add the gnocchi to the pan with the sauce and stir to coat. Serve up in bowls and garnish with ricotta and Parmesan.

Meet our cauliflower gnocchi-ologist.

BUFFALO CHICKEN MAC AND CHEESE BAKED SKILLET

MAKES 6 SERVINGS

On page 52 I told the story of the time I invited Ronald Reagan over to a family dinner. What would have been on the menu? His favorite—mac and cheese.

Like most parents, we made our kids mac and cheese, a lot, but because we were busy parents just trying to make it to 6 p.m. when it was okay to have a glass of wine, we took the easy way and served the boxed version you'd add milk to and quickly stir up on the stove. Our kids adored it.

Fast-forward to thirty years after Reagan left Washington, Kathy and I were throwing a thirtieth birthday party for our daughter Mary literally one thousand feet from the White House at P.J. Clarke's. It was a lovely sit-down dinner for forty of her closest friends. She may have been turning thirty, but Mary was still a kid at heart, which meant when she selected the menu she chose their mac and cheese, served in adorable little ramekins.

These days we like to riff on the classic mac and cheese with this one-hour version, with Buffalo chicken and pancetta baked in a skillet. It always takes me back twenty-some years earlier. standing at the stove in our kitchen stirring up a box of mac and cheese and thinking to myself, *Someday when I have more time, I'm going to make an amazing version of this stuff*. This is that recipe.

Cooking spray
8 ounces elbow macaroni
3 cups shredded cooked chicken (rotisserie works great)
¼ cup Frank's RedHot sauce
¼ cup panko bread crumbs
1 teaspoon olive oil
3 tablespoons butter
2 ounces cream cheese (one-quarter of an 8-ounce package), cubed
3 tablespoons all-purpose flour
1 teaspoon mustard powder
1 cup whole milk
½ cup ranch dressing
2 cups shredded Cheddar cheese
One 4-ounce package pancetta, small-diced
⅓ cup blue cheese crumbles

FOR TOPPING (OPTIONAL)
2 green onions, green parts only, cut into ¼-inch slices
2 celery stalks, cut into ¼-inch slices

1. Preheat the oven to 375°F. Coat an 8 × 8-inch baking dish or 10-inch cast-iron skillet with cooking spray.

2. Cook the macaroni in a large pot of boiling water until just al dente according to the package directions. Remove from the heat but leave the noodles in the water.

3. Meanwhile, in a medium bowl, combine the chicken and Frank's and stir to coat.

4. In a small bowl, combine the panko and olive oil and stir to coat the bread crumbs evenly.

5. In a large skillet, melt the butter and cream cheese over medium heat, whisking them to combine. Whisk in the flour and mustard powder; it will thicken like a roux. Quickly add the milk and give it a good whisk until smooth. Bring to a boil and immediately remove it from the heat. Fold in the ranch dressing, then the Cheddar, and stir until it melts. Mix in the sauce-coated chicken until evenly combined.

6. In a small nonstick skillet, fry the pancetta over medium heat until it just starts to brown and renders some fat, 3 to 5 minutes. Pour the pancetta and its oil into the cheese mixture and stir well.

7. Drain the noodles and add them to the cheese mixture. Stir to coat the noodles evenly.

8. Pour the cheese-and-noodle mixture into the prepared baking pan or skillet. Sprinkle the oiled bread crumbs on top, followed by the blue cheese crumbles.

9. Bake until golden, about 20 minutes.

10. Let it rest for at least 5 minutes. If desired, top with green onions or celery to add some tasty freshness. I love this recipe!

Pop, fizz, happy birthday, Mary!

Mary and Peter, the Doocys of DC.

RED WINE INSTA-POT ROAST

MAKES 6 SERVINGS

One year our big vacation was a trip with our young kids to Disney World. The kids could not wait, and after months of planning and looking for deals, we landed in Orlando during one of the worst rainy seasons they'd had in decades. In the dream sequence, somebody at the airport would have said, *"Here are five free airline tickets home—come back when it's sunny!"* But of course that's not how the world—or Disney—operates.

Like Clark Griswold in the *Vacation* movies, I reminded the kids that a little rain never hurt anybody, so we would make the best of a bad situation. First, we bought Mickey Mouse ponchos and suddenly the kids were giggling because we were in costumes!

The next day it did clear up, and we discovered that EPCOT had great restaurants that represent the classic cuisines from the four corners. We hadn't been to a French restaurant *with cloth napkins* since we'd had kids, and were shocked we could get a reservation at Chefs de France. "Will you need a high chair?" Yes! we told them, and were thrilled because we were used to New York restaurants, which commonly limited the number of high chairs to cut down on the number of pint-size patrons. This place was wall to wall with them! And at this French restaurant we didn't have to worry about our fussy kids bothering the other diners, because they had their own fussy kids who were bothering everybody. It was wonderful!

I ordered a red wine beef dish and gave Kathy a taste. I asked her if she could make it when we got home, and she did. She found a recipe that was just okay, so she decided to add more vegetables, because vegetables are good for you, and more wine, because . . . well, it's wine.

You can make it on the stovetop, but today we make it in the Instant Pot, which is like a Crock-Pot on steroids. And it's much faster than waiting on the line to Space Mountain.

One 3- to 4-pound beef pot roast
1 teaspoon table salt
1½ teaspoons freshly ground black pepper
Olive oil, for frying
3 large potatoes, peeled and quartered
2 cups beef stock
2 cups red wine (we use Cabernet Sauvignon) or beef stock (a great nonwine substitute)
One 6-ounce can tomato paste
1 large yellow onion, quartered
One 1-pound bag baby carrots
One 12-ounce container small white mushrooms, stems trimmed
4 garlic cloves, minced
2½ tablespoons all-purpose flour

1. Season the roast with the salt and 1 teaspoon of the pepper. Pour 2 tablespoons of olive oil into your Instant Pot (ours is a 6-quart pot) and add the roast (if it's extra wide, I'll cut it in half for an easier fit). Press Sauté and brown the roast on all sides, 2 or 3 minutes per side. Transfer to a plate.

2. Put the potatoes in the Instant Pot cut side down and sear them a few minutes on a couple sides to give them some nice brown marks that help keep them from getting mushy. Remove the potatoes to a plate.

3. Add the beef stock to the Instant Pot and bring to a boil. Use a wooden spoon or silicone spatula to deglaze the pot and scrape up any stuck food (or you may wind up with the dreaded BURN message). Once the bottom's clear, add the wine and tomato paste and stir until all the tomato paste is dissolved. Hit Cancel.

4. Return the roast to the pot. Top with the potatoes, onion, carrots, mushrooms, and garlic. Put the lid on top, lock it, make sure the valve is set to Sealing, and program 60 minutes on High Pressure.

5. When the hour is up, allow it to depressurize naturally for at least 20 minutes. When ready to open, carefully turn the top valve from Sealing to Venting. Once it's released any remaining pressure, open the lid. Remove the roast and vegetables and arrange deliciously on a platter.

6. To make a gravy to go with your meat feast, cover the platter with foil for a moment. Transfer 3 cups of the cooking liquid to a skillet. In a small sealable container, like a Tupperware bowl, combine the flour, remaining ½ teaspoon pepper, and ¼ cup cold water. Seal and shake it until it's completely mixed. Set the pan of cooking liquid over medium-high heat, and as it heats up, slowly stir the flour mixture into the drippings. Heat until the mixture boils and thickens, whisking away the whole time. When the lumps are gone and the gravy is to your desired consistency, ladle it up into a gravy boat and serve with the meat and vegetables.

PAPRIKA CHICKEN UNDER A BRICK

Thirty years ago, Kathy came home one day, pointing to an amazing recipe she wanted me to try. I thought it looked odd, because the chicken was flat as a pancake. It looked like it was run over by a Buick. Was it a roadkill recipe? Nope, it was called Chicken Under a Brick, and she wanted me to go to Home Depot and get some bricks so we could try it. So I did. I bought the cleanest construction bricks they had, then brought them home and wrapped them in tinfoil.

We followed the recipe and the chicken was, as advertised, very moist and delicious, but I always wondered whether regular house bricks were safe for home cooking. Did they emit toxic fumes? Does the Department of Agriculture monitor brick production? No. So we stopped making the dish, because Williams-Sonoma didn't offer bricks for sale.

Fast-forward thirty years, and our friend Kevin Kohler at Café Panache in Ramsey, New Jersey, had Chicken Under a Brick on his menu. I asked him where he got the bricks, and he said he used a heavy frying pan instead of bricks. Eureka!

We now make this at our house all the time, because we love the crispy skin and juicy meat, and the fact that it takes a fraction of the time to cook a whole chicken.

I'm also saving a lot of foil because I'm not wasting it wrapping bricks. Instead, I can use it to make a tinfoil hat to keep the extraterrestrials from listening to my thoughts. They wouldn't understand anyway.

1 whole chicken (3 to 5 pounds)
Table salt and freshly ground black pepper
2 to 3 tablespoons smoked paprika, to taste
3 tablespoons canola oil
Cooking spray
One 1½-pound bag microwaveable
    fingerling or new potatoes, such as
    Steamables
2 tablespoons butter

NOTE: *This requires two large, heavy ovenproof skillets, preferably cast-iron. If one pan is larger than the other, the larger one will hold the chicken and the smaller will go on top of the chicken.*

1. Place the chicken breast side down on a work surface. Now, to remove the backbone so that the chicken will cook flatter, take a pair of kitchen shears and, starting near the tail, cut straight up along the side of the backbone until you get to the top, opening the chicken all the way from top to bottom. Repeat on the other side to remove the backbone altogether. Remove any extra fat down around where the tail was. Now look for the center breast bone that runs from the top to the bottom inside the chicken. Carefully snip that bone the whole way up, but don't cut all the way through; the breast meat on the other side needs it to hold it all together. Now the chicken will open like a book.

2. Flip the bird skin side up and season the skin all over with 2 teaspoons salt, 2 teaspoons pepper, and the smoked paprika.

3. Preheat the oven to 425°F.

4. Set the "bottom" skillet over medium heat and add the canola oil. When the oil is hot, swirl the pan to coat the bottom, then place the chicken in the pan breast side down. Coat the "top" skillet on the bottom with cooking spray to keep it from sticking to the chicken, then press the bottom of the pan down onto the chicken to flatten it as much as you can. Let the chicken cook for 5 minutes. Slightly move the chicken to make sure it has not stuck to the bottom pan; if it has, use a spatula to gently break it free. Cook the chicken for another 5 to 10 minutes, or until you get a good crisp on the skin.

5. Now it's time to take this whole setup and place it in the oven. Because the handles will get extra hot, rotate the handle of the top skillet 45 degrees toward the back, so that when you reach for the bottom handle the top handle won't burn you. Bake for about 30 minutes, until a thermometer stuck into the thickest part of the bird reads at least 165°F and the juices run clear if you poke the chicken with a knife or skewer.

6. Remove from the oven and let the chicken rest for 10 minutes with the pan on top.

7. Meanwhile, microwave the potatoes according to the package directions (about 10 minutes). Place the potatoes in a large serving bowl and toss them with the butter and salt and pepper to taste.

8. Park the chicken on top of the potatoes, skin side up, and carve it to serve, along with your perfectly timed taters.

MOM'S MAPLE AND MUSTARD CHICKEN

MAKES 6 SERVINGS

For Christmas one year, Janice Dean, the meteorologist on *Fox & Friends*, gave me the most beautiful bottle of real maple syrup I'd ever seen, imported from Canada. It was one of the best gifts I got that year—so thoughtful, and full of Janice's Canadian pride and delight in showing off one of Canada's national products. Because the bottle was so fancy, I was determined to only use it on *important* recipes, not Sunday morning pancakes . . . but what would fit the bill?

A few days later, Kathy and I were in Juno Beach, Florida, eating at Ke'e Grill, and I ordered the maple and mustard salmon. It was delicious—and also seemed distantly familiar. Then it hit me, like a ton of maple trees—my mom used to create this exact taste. Like some sort of sensory archaeologist, I'd just unearthed a happy taste memory from decades in the past. But my mom didn't make it with fish; in fact, the only fish we ever ate was tuna in a can or catfish that Grandma caught in the East Fork of the Des Moines River.

Back in the 1960s and 1970s, my mom had combined these flavors to make a great chicken recipe. But as I recall, she didn't use pure Canadian maple syrup; she opted for our favorite pancake syrup and she paired it with the very international sounding *French's* mustard, which is not actually from France but is today made in Springfield, Missouri, at 4455 East Mustard Way.

As for that amazing bottle of Canadian real maple syrup—thank you, Janice, for the gift that jogged my memory and added another happy recipe to our cookbook!

Cooking spray
1 pound very small new potatoes
2 tablespoons olive oil
Table salt and freshly ground black pepper
1 tablespoon chopped fresh rosemary, plus more sprigs for garnish if desired
½ cup Dijon mustard
¼ cup pure maple syrup
6 boneless, skinless chicken thighs

1. Adjust the oven racks to the center and top positions and preheat the oven to 375°F. Coat a 9 × 9-inch baking dish with cooking spray.

2. Place the potatoes on a sheet pan. Drizzle with the olive oil and season with salt and pepper to taste and the rosemary. Stir to coat the potatoes in the oil and seasonings.

3. In a small bowl, combine the mustard and maple syrup. Place the chicken thighs in the prepared baking dish, unrolling them if they come rolled up so they cook more quickly. Salt and pepper the chicken, then spoon about three-quarters of the maple-mustard sauce on top, nice and thick.

4. Put the sheet pan of potatoes on the top rack and the baking dish of chicken on the center rack and bake for 30 minutes.

5. Flip the potatoes with a spatula and use a spoon to baste the chicken with the rest of the sauce. Bake until the chicken is cooked through and the potatoes are crispy on the outside, delicious on the inside, another 20 to 30 minutes.

6. Place the chicken on one side of a serving platter and spoon the pan sauce on top. Place the potatoes on the other side of the platter and garnish with rosemary sprigs if desired.

MAIN EVENTS

ENTREES

O CELEBRATE A JOB PROMOTION EARLY IN my career, my parents said, "Let's party—we're going to Mars!"

Mars was Mars Chinese Restaurant on the west side of Salina, Kansas. I remember their food was such an exotic taste for somebody like me, raised on red meat and potatoes, but apparently some hearty Kansans did not care for the portion size and had complained that they were hungry shortly after they'd eaten there, because every time we went to Mars, at every table next to the soy sauce would be a stack of about ten pieces of Wonder bread. Go figure.

After that celebratory meal at Mars, the waitress slid the bill in front of my dad, who glanced down and then struck up a conversation about how another customer in the restaurant reminded him of a guy he'd served in the army with in Germany thirty years ago. The story just went on and on, and I was thinking, *Let's go, Dad, pay the bill.* He glanced at the bill a couple times but didn't pick it up, which was so unlike my dad. Then it finally dawned on me! He wanted me to pay—something I had never done.

Why not? I thought. It was a good way to start to repay my parents for a lifetime of giving, so I picked up the bill, smoothly slid my VISA card into the brown folder, and motioned for the waitress, who picked it up.

"What are you doing?" my mom asked.

"I'm treating, Mom."

"Put that credit card away, Stephen. Your father has money." She reached for the bill.

"He's got a good job—if he wants to pay, let him," my dad observed, declaring he was off the hook for this single meal.

Dining out with the Doocys.

The waitress came back, and I was ready to sign and dash out to end this family disagreement. But then she announced, "Your card has been declined."

All four of my sisters and both of my parents turned to the bearer of bad news, who added, "This card is stolen."

Wait, what? My parents gave me that suspicious look, as if to ask, *What exactly do you do in the big city, Stephen James?*

As it turned out, the day before at the rental car desk at Kansas City International, at the end of the transaction the desk attendant had returned a VISA card to me, just not mine. Of course we didn't figure this out until the end of a half-hour call to the card company, during which we ate most of that stack of Wonder bread, and my dad paid.

I was trying so hard to be a grown-up and pay my parents back a little for all they'd given me, but it's hard to be a good son when you're about to be charged with grand theft auto.

My first job was at a grocery store, working as the cashier, when I was twelve.

In high school, I got the best job a high school kid could have in Clay Center, Kansas, working at Summer's Menswear.

All clothing stores have to look into their crystal ball and figure out what their customers will want to buy six months from now, and in order to do that, they go to "market" and see what the future of fashion holds. Because I'd been hired to give a teenager's perspective to the operation, the bosses invited me to go along to the market in Kansas City, an adventure 185 miles from home, staying in a nicer hotel than I'd ever seen in my life.

My bosses had made our first appointment for before breakfast, and luckily the first vendor served some brunchy food, including an item the boy from the flatlands of Kansas had never seen in his seventeen years on earth: a bagel.

Les Legler, the main sales guy for our store, said, "Kid, try one, you'll love it."

Did you cut it up and eat it with a fork? Why was there thin-sliced fish and a toaster parked next to it? Knowing that whatever happened in Kansas City, stayed in Kansas City, I threw caution to the wind, picked one up, and started to take a bite.

Les barked at me, "What the hell are you doing?"

Okay, I guess it was a fork item. Les took the bagel out of my hand and said, "This is the good part," as he slathered something creamy and white on the top. "Now you're ready."

I took one bite. It was one of those *eyes rolling to the back of your head* moments that changed everything. Where had this been all my life?

"This is amazing—what is it?"

"Cream cheese, kid," Les said. Then he started to giggle, motioning for me to look in one of the full-length mirrors. Cream cheese filled the gaps between every one of my teeth, and it looked like I'd just had an instant mouthful of caps installed.

From that moment, and for decades to come, whenever I had a bagel it was always slathered with cream cheese—right up until my New York City cardiologist said somebody my age had eaten enough cream cheese in his life and prescribed Crestor. Party pooper.

Life is so much more interesting when we try new foods, and usually it means we have to leave the house and let somebody else do the cooking. Sometimes this requires a road trip to Kansas City, or beyond.

When my mom died, my parents had been planning on taking the trip of a lifetime to Hawaii. But my dad said he couldn't go without her, and never used the tickets. Later that same year, I asked my dad whether there was any other place on earth he'd like to visit, and after he said, "No," I stunned myself by saying, "I'll pay," sounding like a dot-com billionaire who'd bought Amazon at a nickel a share.

Eventually he said, "Ireland. I've always wanted to go back to the old country," and we started making plans. A couple days later he called and said, "Phil wants to go, too, and you're going to pay for him . . . right?"

My dad never asked for anything, and it would mean a lot to him. Besides, my uncle Phil, who was also my godfather, was a very prominent deacon in the church, and if I took him on this trip of a lifetime, I'd wind up in the E-ZPass lane to eternal salvation. "Happy to pay for Phil," I said.

It turned out that the best way for the three of us to travel to cover the most territory quickly was a bus tour. A month later, my father, uncle, and I hopped a red-eye from Newark to Shannon, and as we wandered off the overnight flight into the blinding blaze of an Irish sunrise, we found a luxury motor coach parked at the curb. According to the brochure, this trip would include world-class cuisine and accommodations. But because it was based on double occupancy, dad and Phil would get the beds, and the person paying for their trip would spend the week on a rollaway bed.

I didn't sleep right the whole time—a combination of jet lag and the cheap bed—but the food was terrific. Breakfast was biscuits or scones with whipped cream and jam, or better yet, *whiskey butter*. Lunches were sandwiches built with nutty Irish brown bread we'd dunk in a steaming soup. And the day would wrap up with a happy hour Guinness followed by a hearty Irish stew or salmon, broccoli, and colcannon—mashed potatoes with cabbage and other green things blended together. I loved the food—clearly I was so Irish.

So we were well fed as we drove hundreds of miles in a big circle around southern Ireland and visited places like the Blarney Castle and the Waterford crystal factory, whose slogan could be, "We make breakable stuff most people can't afford."

Before we'd left the USA, I'd made a reservation at Ireland's National Library's Genealogical Service, where the rest of the world can trace its Irish heritage. A librarian was waiting at the appointed time to finally connect all the dots from our ancestors.

"Mr. Doocys, it looks as if your family first settled in . . . oh . . ." She stopped in midsentence, as if she'd seen my mug shot the night before on *Ireland's Most Wanted*.

She started again. "Mr. Doocys, it appears your family's records . . . were destroyed in the fire."

Not the answer we'd expected. Ireland had lost our records? I imagined it involved a leprechaun . . .

"It was in 1922, the Four Courts fire, centuries of Irish history lost!"

I got the feeling she'd broken that same news to other families, because she paused only a beat and then she threw us a lifeline. "Of course the other possibility is that your name is misspelled." My dad spelled it out for her: D-o-o-c-y. "Oh, I know how you spell it, but sometimes the handwriting in the record books was hard to read, so the person writing up the file would make his best guess as to what it said. Sadly, many a name has changed through history because of bad penmanship."

So either Ireland has no record of us or it's a country of bad spellers.

"If you see an Irish name and it starts with the letter D, like Dewsy, Dancy, Dooley, or Deacy, there's a relatively good chance you're related," she said. We left wondering who the hell we really were.

For the rest of the trip, every time we went into a restaurant or shop, my father would make his way to the pay phone to examine the local phone book, looking for family members who spelled their names just like us. He found a couple that were close, but they always had an extra letter or two. Then, on a factory tour on the fifth day, I heard, "Stephen, come here!" Dad had found four families that spelled their names exactly like ours.

DOOCY

The trip just paid for itself.

We'd come all this way looking for relatives, and he needed a trophy, and this was it. Looking over his shoulder to the right, then the left, he ripped the page out of the phone book and wadded it up in his pocket. There was widespread phone book vandalism during our visit to the Emerald Isle.

On the flight home, I leaned over to my dad and said, "That was fun, wasn't it?"

He paused for a moment, then said, "I felt like I was thirty all over again."

At thirty he had been a traveling salesman, and I was ten. Every Saturday he'd call up the stairs, "Stephen, let's go," and I'd join him on a day-long sales call all across our part of Kansas. For lunch we'd stop at the closest cafe and order whatever the waitress said she'd have herself. Then, by midafternoon, after his sales calls, we'd wind up at Reilly's gas station, shooting the breeze with friends and total strangers while nursing Dr Peppers that always tasted best when they had half a bag of peanuts poured into the bottle, bobbing at the top of the neck. Mom would be waiting with supper as we'd pull up at dark, having spent the entire day talking and laughing about nothing in particular. I was my dad's sidekick, just like I was that week in Ireland.

The Doocys are from Ireland, right?

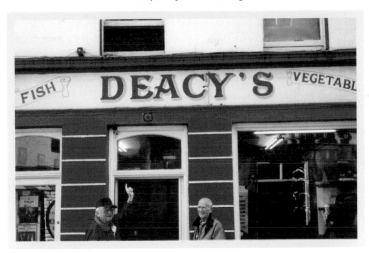

It starts with a D. We could be related!

I'll drink to that!

SWEET TEA FRIED CHICKEN

We love this recipe because it's an updated version of Shake 'n Bake, which is very old-school, but my mom used it when it was new-school, once upon a time. My dad loved this sweet tea recipe, because it's a combination of chicken and iced tea, which he drank all day. To save a couple hours of tea-steeping time, we use 5-minute cold-brew iced tea, for the sugary sweet tea marinade. It makes every piece of chicken taste great . . . although I'm not sure about the neck and gizzard (which he loved).

½ cup sugar
2 family-size Lipton cold brew tea bags
4 boneless, skinless chicken breasts
3 cups dried bread crumbs
2 teaspoons table salt
1 teaspoon freshly ground black pepper
½ teaspoon garlic powder
2 cups buttermilk
Vegetable oil, for shallow-frying

1. First, let's make the sweet tea! If you have a favorite way, by all means make it your way, but here's my fast method: Place the sugar in a 2-quart (8-cup) pitcher and pour in 2 cups of cold water. Mix until the sugar is completely dissolved, then fill the pitcher almost to the top with more cold water and give it a stir. Add the tea bags and let it cold-brew for 5 minutes, dunking the tea bags in the water a couple times with a spoon. Remove the tea bags, and if any sugar has settled to the bottom, use a long spoon to mix until it's dissolved.

2. Arrange the chicken in a large, deep bowl and add sweet tea to cover it (you'll have extra tea). Cover the bowl with plastic wrap and refrigerate for 1 hour.

3. Meanwhile, in a zip-top bag, combine the bread crumbs, salt, pepper, and garlic powder. Seal the bag and shake to mix. Pour the buttermilk into a shallow bowl.

4. Pour ¾ inch of vegetable oil into a large, deep skillet. Heat over medium-high heat. You'll know it's hot enough when you stick the end of a wooden spoon in the oil and little bubbles percolate to the surface. If it's bubbling all over, it's too hot; remove the pan from the heat and lower the temp a bit. Working with one piece at a time, remove the chicken from the marinade and coat it completely in the buttermilk. From there, place it in the bread crumb bag and give it a good shaking, then park it in the skillet. Don't crowd the pieces. Fry until deep golden brown on both sides, up to 10 minutes per side. The thicker the chicken, the longer it will need to cook. Check that the interior temperature of a thick piece has reached 165°F.

5. Set the chicken on paper towels to drain, then serve. Goes great with a side of mashed potatoes . . . and an ice-cold sweet tea.

PORK CHOPS IN MUSHROOM GRAVY

MAKES 6 SERVINGS

When we first moved to rural Kansas, I raised pigs as a 4-H project. Hands down my favorite pig was Arnold, named after Arnold Ziffle, the pig on the sitcom *Green Acres*. We'd never lived in the country and had no idea how to be farmers, so we raised Arnold the pig like a collie.

The pigpen fence was quite ineffective, and Arnold routinely did the limbo under the rails and would wander down the street to root under the bleachers at the ball diamond for popcorn strays, or farther down the road to the general store, for people to pet him. He spent more time outside the pen than in it. He was free-range pork before that became a thing.

Arnold lived a long life. He died of old age, or boredom, because some pigs are just too cute to become bacon—when they're not digging up the church flower bed.

My mom made this recipe a lot, when she wasn't trying to get Arnold home for his sponge bath.

3 tablespoons butter
3 tablespoons olive oil
1 onion, medium-diced
2 garlic cloves, minced
One 10-ounce container button
    mushrooms, stems trimmed, quartered
6 boneless pork chops, no more than 1 inch
    thick
1½ teaspoons table salt
1½ teaspoons freshly ground black pepper
½ teaspoon garlic powder
One 10.5-ounce can condensed golden
    mushroom soup
Mashed potatoes, for serving (optional)

1. In a large skillet, melt 1 tablespoon of the butter over medium-high heat. When almost melted, add 1 tablespoon of the olive oil and swirl to combine. Add the onion and garlic and sauté until they start to soften, 3 or 4 minutes. Throw in the mushrooms and sauté until they start to brown, 5 to 8 minutes. Remove to a plate and set aside.

2. Season the pork on both sides with the salt, pepper, and garlic powder.

3. Add the remaining 2 tablespoons butter and 2 tablespoons olive oil to the pan over medium-high heat and swirl to combine. Add the pork in a single layer and cook undisturbed until golden brown on the bottom, about 10 minutes. Flip and cook the other side, 5 to 7 minutes. Make a test cut into the meat to be sure it's cooked through.

4. Add the can of soup and ½ can of water to the pan with the pork chops, stir until well mixed, and return the onion-mushroom mixture to the pan. Return the heat to medium-high and bring to a boil. After 1 minute of boiling, reduce the heat to a simmer and cook about 2 minutes, until the mixture starts to reduce.

5. Serve the pork chops immediately with mashed potatoes, if desired, and spoon a bit of the mushroom soup mixture over the potatoes and pork. It's as good as gravy.

CHEESY SCHOOLHOUSE CHICKEN SPAGHETTI

MAKES 8 SERVINGS

If you grew up in the '50s, '60s, or '70s, you probably had hot lunch at school. I did, and I'm not embarrassed to say I liked it. You know why? Variety. While my mom was a great cook, she never made us pizza, enchiladas, or fish sticks with tartar sauce, but the lunch lady did. I even liked the mystery meat—because whatever it was, it was always doused with a savory gravy to conceal its donor animal's original identity.

In sixth grade I went to a one-room schoolhouse in Industry, Kansas, where the entire school body—of eleven students—was under the state-mandated supervision of our lone teacher, Hazel Lloyd. Each weekday she'd instruct us all at our various grade levels until late morning, when she would disappear into an adjacent room for about half an hour. Then the door would fly open and she would announce that lunch was served. After a good hot lunch, we'd go outside and run around until it was time to return to the classroom, where I would pretend I understood how to divide fractions.

This is a delicious version of Mrs. Lloyd's best recipe, creamy chicken and noodles. When I made it for Kathy the first time, because she is a cheese snob, she insisted I make it with Cheddar—even though the recipe calls for Velveeta. It was okay, but when I made it with Velveeta, she admitted it was much better.

Also, we've borrowed an ingredient from Dana Perino's Queen of Cable Queso recipe from our first cookbook. Dana also used Velveeta, plus Ro-Tel diced tomatoes, and we've started including those tomatoes in this recipe. They're a very nice addition if you like things a little spicy.

If you're craving a creamy comfort food, this is it. It reminds me of a simple, happy time when I wondered why other schools had all those unnecessary extra rooms, when everything I needed to learn could be done in a one-room schoolhouse.

Now, if you want to make it exactly as Mrs. Lloyd made it, put on a hair net before you get to cooking. Just don't forget to take it off before recess.

Cooking spray
1 pound spaghetti
1 tablespoon butter
1 tablespoon olive oil
1 yellow onion, roughly chopped
1 garlic clove, thinly sliced
One 4-ounce can mushroom pieces and
   stems, drained
One 10.5-ounce can condensed cream of
   mushroom soup
One 10-ounce can Ro-Tel diced tomatoes
   and green chilies
⅓ cup milk
One 16-ounce package Velveeta, cut into
   1-inch cubes
Shredded meat from 1 rotisserie chicken
½ cup shredded Cheddar cheese

1. Preheat the oven to 350°F. Coat a 3-quart casserole or 9 × 13-inch baking dish with cooking spray.

2. Cook the spaghetti according to the package directions. When it's done, remove it from the heat, but leave in the water for now.

3. Meanwhile, in a large skillet, melt the butter in the olive oil over medium-high heat. Add the onion and garlic and sauté until softened and almost golden, 3 to 4 minutes. Add the mushrooms, mushroom soup, Ro-Tel tomatoes, milk, and Velveeta and stir until the Velveeta is melted and smoothly mixed in, 5 to 8 minutes. Add the chicken and mix it in, then drain the spaghetti and stir it in as well.

4. Transfer the spaghetti-chicken mixture to the prepared casserole or baking dish. Scatter the Cheddar on top and bake for 15 minutes to melt the cheese.

LEMON PASTA AND SWEET PEAS

MAKES 6 SERVINGS

Our friend Madeleine learned to cook early. Her grandmother made dinner at night, but during the day her job was to screw lids by hand onto pickle jars in Greenwich Village, which was torture. She hated pickles. Her next job was to stuff pimientos into olives, so she wouldn't allow anybody in the family to ever buy olives, or eat them. Madeleine had no idea how delicious olives can be—*in a martini!*

After Madeleine's sisters and brother were big enough to finally all be enrolled in school, their mother, Nora, went back to work. So to make sure things still got done around the house, Nora assigned Madeleine and her sisters each a week-long task. Each week one girl would clean the bathrooms, another girl tidied the living room and den, and another would have to cook and then clean the kitchen, the hardest of the chores. Her brother was in charge of mowing and raking and all things outdoors. They didn't get an allowance for their labors; instead, they were allowed to live and eat there.

When Madeleine had her week in the kitchen, she remembers that the family had a set menu rotation. Sunday: roast beef. Monday: leftover roast beef sandwiches. Tuesday: pork chops. Wednesday: something chicken. Friday: pizza. Thursday night was pasta night. Madeleine would boil a one-pound package of spaghetti, make a sauce with tomato sauce and Spatini, and served it to the nine people around the table. Big family. Happy family. Zero leftovers.

She has happy memories of Thursday's noodle night growing up, but she's outgrown Spatini sauce, and today this lemon pasta recipe is her go-to. Madeleine says it's great . . . and not just because it's olive-free.

Table salt
1 pound spaghetti or other strand pasta, such as bucatini or perciatelli
One 12-ounce bag frozen sweet peas
½ cup fresh lemon juice (2 to 3 lemons)
3 tablespoons olive oil
2 large garlic cloves, minced
¾ cup grated Parmesan or Pecorino Romano cheese
½ teaspoon freshly ground black pepper

1. Bring a large pot of salted water to a boil. Add the pasta and cook about 1 minute less than the package directions say for al dente. Add the peas and cook about 2 minutes.

2. Reserving 1 cup of the pasta water, drain the pasta and peas and return to the pot, off the heat. Add the lemon juice, olive oil, and garlic and stir well to combine the flavors. Add the cheese, ½ teaspoon of salt, and the pepper and give it all a stir. It may be a bit dry, so add some of the reserved pasta water, which helps melt the cheese.

3. When all the noodles are coated with cheese sauce, serve pronto.

PETER'S CHICKEN PARM MEATBALLS

When we moved to New Jersey from Virginia, Peter, in second grade, selected chicken Parmesan as his go-to dish whenever we'd visit one of the state's great Italian eateries. Chicken Parm was everything a seven-year-old loved: lots of oozing cheese, buttery noodles, and rich red sauce all splayed out on a really big chicken finger. A dinnertime hat trick.

But now he's in his thirties, and as a network correspondent out on the road, he has to watch what he eats. This recipe allows Peter to enjoy his beloved chicken Parm and still fit into his pants.

Peter loves the way the cheese is hidden on the inside of the meatballs. Last time I made this for him he ate almost an entire batch, leaving three meatballs for his sister Sally, who was on the late bus.

By the time she got home, Peter had eaten the rest of the batch. He apologized and took her out for a slice of pizza. These meatballs are that good.

1½ cups panko bread crumbs
¼ cup grated Parmesan cheese, plus more
    for topping
1½ teaspoons table salt
1 pound ground chicken
1 large egg
½ teaspoon freshly ground black pepper
1 teaspoon garlic powder
½ teaspoon Italian seasoning
20 small pearl-size mozzarella balls, or
    ¾-inch cubes cut from an 8-ounce block
    of mozzarella
Olive oil, for shallow-frying
Jarred marinara sauce (we use Rao's)
Cooked pasta, for serving

1. Preheat the oven to 400°F.

2. In a medium bowl, combine 1 cup of the panko with the Parmesan and ½ teaspoon of the salt. Give a stir and set aside.

3. In a large bowl, combine the chicken, the remaining ½ cup panko, the egg, pepper, garlic powder, and Italian seasoning. Gently mix to combine.

4. To make a meatball, scoop up 2 tablespoons of the chicken mixture. Ball it up a bit and insert one of the little mozzarella balls or cubes into the center. Use your fingers to wrap the chicken mixture around the cheese, concealing it completely. Roll the meatball in the panko mixture to coat. Set the meatball on wax paper and continue to make the rest of the meatballs.

5. Pour ¼ to ½ inch of olive oil into a large skillet. Heat over medium-high heat until the oil starts to shimmer. Add the meatballs and cook until slightly browned all over, 2 to 3 minutes per side.

6. Use a slotted spoon to remove them to a sheet pan or baking dish. Bake until the chicken is cooked through and the cheese is melty in the center (cut one in half to make sure), 10 to 12 minutes.

7. Spread marinara sauce over the meatballs and crown each with a shake of Parmesan. Return to the oven to bake a few minutes to warm the marinara.

8. Serve with your favorite pasta, warmed and mixed with more marinara sauce to taste.

Yes, I autographed that plate.

This chicken is world famous.

BUTTERMILK FRIED CHICKEN
AND WAFFLES

MAKES 6 SERVINGS

When we moved to Kansas from Iowa when I was about five years old, I remember people were always telling my parents we had to drive an hour west to the Brookville Hotel to try their world-famous fried chicken. After years of hearing about that life-changing chicken we finally went, and it was amazing. The first time I took Kathy home to Kansas to meet her future in-laws, my parents wanted to show off a little, so we drove over to Brookville, and it did not disappoint. She loved the simplicity of the recipes, and on the way out she grabbed recipe cards for some of the dishes, which we still make today.

Kathy vividly remembers that trip because on the way home there was a tornado warning, My dad looked out the window and saw that the twister was right above us, so he pulled under an overpass and let it blow by. My dad then pulled out and we drove home, barely speaking of it. All Kathy could think of was the tornado in *The Wizard of Oz,* and she wanted to say, "Steve, we're not in Kansas anymore . . ." But we were in Kansas.

Back to the Brookville Hotel. The best part was the chicken, and the worst part was the hour-long trip to Brookville, Kansas, so it caused quite a commotion when it was announced that they were closing their doors and relocating to a new space about a thousand feet from the President's Best Western Inn that my parents had operated for decades. It was named that after President Eisenhower, who was from Abilene. Most people know that, as a Supreme Allied Commander during World War II, Eisenhower helped save the world, but if given a choice of visiting the Eisenhower Museum or the Brookville Hotel, most people would pick the chicken joint.

But I'm biased; my sister Lisa works there. I've been known to surprise her during her lunch shift. One of the last times I was there I autographed one of their signature serving plates at the request of the owners, and at last report it's still hanging on the wall of the main dining room.

This recipe reminds me of the crowd-pleasing chicken and happy family dinners at the Brookville Hotel. As you will see, we've added a Cheddar jalapeño waffle, because after our many travels through the South, we have become chicken and cheesy waffle people.

So if you're ever traveling on I-70 through Abilene, pull over at the Brookville Hotel and have a chicken dinner. Ask for my sister Lisa, who will probably tell you if you write your name on a plate with a Sharpie, you just bought that dish.

(continued)

CHICKEN

6 thin-sliced chicken breasts (4 to 6 ounces each)
1 cup buttermilk
3 cups panko bread crumbs
1 teaspoon table salt
½ teaspoon freshly ground black pepper
¼ teaspoon garlic powder
Vegetable oil, for shallow-frying

WAFFLES

1½ cups Krusteaz Light & Crispy Belgian waffle mix
1 large egg
2½ tablespoons vegetable oil
1 jalapeño, seeded and finely minced
½ cup shredded Cheddar cheese

SYRUP

½ cup maple syrup
1½ tablespoons Thai sweet chili sauce or 1½ teaspoons Frank's RedHot sauce

1. To marinate the chicken: About an hour before you want to start cooking, pour the buttermilk into a medium bowl. Place the chicken in the buttermilk and coat it well. Put plastic wrap over the bowl and refrigerate for anywhere from 1 hour to overnight if you're working ahead.

2. When you're ready to start cooking, in a zip-top bag, combine the panko, salt, pepper, and garlic powder and shake to mix.

3. Pour ¾ inch of vegetable oil into a large, deep skillet and heat over medium-high heat. The oil is ready when it shimmers as it kicks off the heat. One piece at a time, remove the chicken from the buttermilk, place it in the bag of panko, and give it a good shaking, then park it in the hot oil. Fry until deep golden brown on both sides, 6 to 10 minutes per side (the thicker the chicken, the longer it needs). Just test cut a piece to make sure it's cooked all the way through and to an internal temp of 165°F. As the chicken is done, set the pieces on paper towels to drain and cover with foil to keep warm as you make your waffles.

4. To make the waffles: In a medium bowl, blend the waffle mix, 2/3 cup water, the egg, oil, and jalapeño and stir until just combined. Add the Cheddar and stir until nice and smooth.

5. Preheat the waffle iron to medium heat.

6. Pour ⅓ cup of the batter onto the waffle iron, close the lid, and wait until the steaming stops, just a few minutes. I always let it grill an extra minute to make the cheese crispier. Carefully remove the waffle with a fork and cover it with foil to keep warm as you make the rest.

7. To make the syrup: When the last waffle is cooking, in a small microwave-safe bowl, mix the maple syrup with the chili sauce or Frank's and microwave it for 10 seconds to warm it up. Give it another stir.

8. To serve, place a piece of chicken on each plate and decoratively top it with a waffle. Spoon the syrup over the waffle (but it's also great on the chicken).

KANSAS CHICKEN-FRIED STEAK

MAKES 4 SERVINGS

Chicken-fried steak is such a happy memory of growing up in Kansas. Wherever I am, if it's on the menu, I'll order it. Most of the time it's just okay, but every once in a while it's amazing. Of course the best is always back home in Kansas.

On January 25, 2014, I was recognized by the Native Sons and Daughters of Kansas as their Distinguished Kansan of the year. Kathy and I flew to Topeka, and it was a great night as my family came from across Kansas to be there for that special occasion.

The next morning, before we had to fly back to New York, the Doocys all gathered at the Hanover Pancake House, not far from the capitol building in Topeka, where I started out as a correspondent. There the brunch menu featured chicken-fried steak, and my dad and I both ordered it. Afterward we both agreed it was divine. I took a picture of it with my phone,

(continued)

My dad could not have been prouder.

After lunch, it was time to fly back home. I was so proud that my dad had been able to see me honored as Kansan of the Year, which really was a reflection on him and my mom. I gave him a hug, took a selfie, got in the car, and left. It was the last time I would ever see my father alive.

You might think that I'd never have chicken-fried steak again, but that's actually another reason for me to have it, because it reminds me of my father and what a wise and wonderful man he was.

To me, this recipe just tastes like home.

2½ cups milk
1 large egg
1 cup plus 3 tablespoons all-purpose flour
1 teaspoon table salt, plus more to taste
½ teaspoon freshly ground black pepper, plus more to taste
½ teaspoon garlic powder
4 cube steaks or round steaks (4 to 6 ounces each), tenderized (see Note)
Vegetable oil, for shallow-frying
Mashed potatoes, for serving (optional)

NOTE: *Butchers have a machine that will tenderize cube or round steak, so if you can, buy your steaks pretenderized. But you can also do it yourself! Place the untenderized steak between two pieces of plastic wrap, wax paper, or parchment and use a meat tenderizing mallet or rolling pin to pound it to about ½ inch thick. Boom, it's tenderized!*

1. Let's build a chicken-fried steak assembly line: In a shallow bowl or pie pan, combine 1 cup of the milk and the egg and whisk until well blended. In another bowl or pan, evenly mix 1 cup of the flour, the salt, pepper, and garlic powder.

2. Place 1 steak in the flour mixture, completely coating it on both sides, then gently coat it on both sides with the milk-egg mixture. Next, it's back in the flour, making sure every speck is covered. Set the steak on a sheet pan or aluminum foil and repeat the process with the other steaks.

3. Pour ½ inch of oil into a large, deep skillet and heat over medium-high heat. Place all the steaks in the skillet, but don't crowd them—if they don't fit, cook them in batches. Fry until golden brown on one side, about 5 minutes, then gently flip and cook the other side until browned and cooked through, 4 to 5 minutes.

4. Set the steaks on paper towels to absorb any extra grease and cover with foil to keep them warm while you make the gravy.

5. Here's my mother's famous gravy recipe! Remove all but a few tablespoons of the oil from the skillet. Over medium heat, add the remaining 3 tablespoons flour and stir or whisk until smooth, scraping up any pan drippings. Once this roux is an even color and consistency, slowly mix in up to 1½ cups milk. You must go slowly so you can watch as the gravy thickens and stop adding milk when you get a texture you like. Taste and add salt and pepper until it is gravy perfection.

6. Serve the chicken-fried steaks on plates and top with the gravy. To add to the divinity, serve with mashed potatoes if you like.

CILANTRO PESTO CHICKEN

MAKES 4 SERVINGS

The Doocy family has a history deep in the world of chicken. My father and his siblings all worked through high school at Welp's Hatchery in Bancroft, Iowa, the world's largest family-owned chicken hatchery. My aunt Helen worked at Welp's for fifty-six years and Grandma Doocy worked there about fifty years. They knew everything about chicken.

I remember when I was a wee lad, around the age of five, we'd go over to Grandma Doocy's house for Sunday lunch. As I was the eldest grandchild, Grandma would ask me to help with meal prep. That meant going out back, opening the chicken coop door, and grabbing a live chicken. The chickens didn't like it and neither did I, because more than one started pecking my five-year-old arm and it freaked me out. So I eventually got wise and would go out as directed and try to look like I was chasing one, but I would never get close.

Grandma didn't have time to watch me pantomime Capture the Chicken, so she'd just wait for one to run past her, swoop down her left hand, grab a leg, walk to the stump in the middle of the pen, grab her nearby hatchet, and with one fell swoop, send that chicken to the big coop in the sky. Then she'd go back into the house to start the rest of the dinner and I'd pluck the feathers. Whoever said those were the good old days didn't have my history with poultry.

The chicken was so fresh, because the distance from farm to table was about twenty-five feet.

We serve a lot of chicken at our house today, and this is one of our current favorites.

(continued)

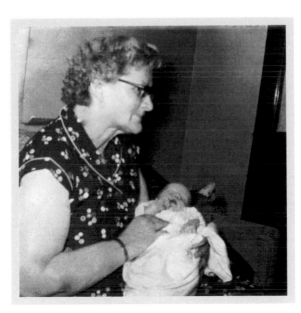

Grandma with future chicken chaser Stevie.

¼ cup pine nuts or slivered almonds
2 cups chopped cilantro (both leaves and
stems)
2 medium garlic cloves or 1 giant garlic
clove, chopped
1 tablespoon fresh lime juice
5 tablespoons olive oil, plus a splash if
needed
½ teaspoon kosher salt, plus more to taste
Freshly ground black pepper
2 tablespoons butter
4 thin-sliced chicken breast cutlets (4 to
6 ounces each)

1. In a dry small skillet, toast the nuts over medium heat, moving them around the pan for 2 to 3 minutes, until they start to turn a little golden. Remove them to a plate so that they don't burn.

2. In a food processor, pulse the nuts, cilantro, garlic, and lime juice until pulverized, scraping down the sides as needed to get all the big pieces. The mixture will be on the dry side. With the machine running, pour 3 tablespoons of the olive oil through the feed tube. If it needs another

splash of olive oil for a pesto-like consistency, add a little at a time until it's nice and smooth, occasionally stopping and scraping down the sides so every bit is perfect. Taste and season with the salt and a couple shakes of pepper, then give it a whirl until completely mixed. Transfer to a small serving dish, cover with plastic, and place in the fridge.

3. Now let's fry the chicken! In a large skillet, melt the butter in the remaining 2 tablespoons olive oil over medium-high heat. Swirl the pan to combine the butter and oil. Working in batches so as not to crowd the pan, add the chicken and season with a shake of salt and pepper. Cook undisturbed until the chicken has a little golden crispiness on the edges, about 5 minutes. Flip and cook until golden, no longer pink inside, about another 5 minutes.

4. Serve each piece of chicken topped with a nice dollop (2 to 3 tablespoons) of pesto. Leftover pesto is terrific on pasta, as a sandwich spread, or on salmon. Keep it in a closed container in the fridge for up to 3 days.

MARY'S MEATLESS MONDAY ZOODLE PIE

MAKES 6 SERVINGS

Kathy remembers the day our daughter Mary decided to eat healthier. They were watching Dr. Oz when he said that the average can of soda had about forty grams of sugar. Mary was drinking a soda right then, and that was the last soda, she vowed—except when she has the flu and her mother insists ginger ale doesn't count with Dr. Oz.

When our Mary was an undergraduate at Boston College she tried to eat smart, but it was hard. Also, because she was on the varsity crew team, every morning she was up at 4 a.m. paddling the often-icy Charles River, so she was more concerned with not falling asleep in philosophy class than the carb count on a Tater Tot.

When she graduated law school and moved to a job on Capitol Hill, she finally had a reliable daily routine and became a paragon of healthier choices. Today Mary cooks all the time, and a very common ingredient in her recipes is the zoodle, a spiraled noodle-like thing sliced from a zucchini. When I first heard of zoodle noodles, I thought they were the dumbest thing I'd ever heard of . . . until I tried them. They're great!

Mary told us she wanted a spiralizer to make her own spiraled zucchini noodles, so we bought her one, but Amazon delivered it to our house and not hers. When she came home to visit, she didn't have room in her bag to take it home, so I decided we were going to start spiralizing. I was shocked at how easy it was, and it's downright fun turning zucchini into noodles. This recipe is our way of using a lot of them, set in a delicious pie crust. As an homage to Mary, we'll make it on Meatless Mondays, but you can have it on Tasty Tuesdays, Wonderful Wednesdays, Thirsty Thursdays . . . you get the idea.

And while Mary owns a spiralizer, it's located 247 miles from her kitchen—in our house; so when she needs zoodles, she just buys them prezoodled at the grocery store. It's a speedy option, and one you might want to try to see if you're a zoodle fan!

(continued)

NOTE: *You can make this without the crust if you're counting carbs, but come on, it's pie crust!*

- 1 refrigerated pie crust, at room temperature
- 2 tablespoons olive oil
- 3 garlic cloves, minced
- 1 medium yellow onion, medium-diced
- 3 large zucchini, spiralized
- 2 large eggs
- ½ cup fat-free half-and-half
- ⅔ cup all-purpose flour
- ½ teaspoon table salt
- ¼ teaspoon red pepper flakes
- ½ cup grape tomatoes, seeded and quartered
- 1 cup shredded Cheddar cheese
- ½ cup grated Parmesan cheese

1. Preheat the oven to 350°F.

2. Fit the pie crust into an ungreased 9-inch pie pan and press it into the bottom and sides. Do a little trimming and fluting on the parts overhanging the rim. Set aside.

3. In a large skillet, heat the olive oil over medium-high heat. Add the garlic and onion and sauté until the onion starts to soften, 4 to 5 minutes. Top that with the spiralized zucchini and sauté the zoodles until they soften, about 10 minutes, stirring occasionally. Set aside.

4. In a large bowl, whisk the eggs and half-and-half. Add the flour, salt, and pepper flakes and whisk until entirely smooth.

5. Let's turn to the skillet with the zucchini. You'll see that at the bottom of the pan, some of the zucchini liquid has leaked out. Remove as much liquid as you can by tipping the pan to one side and spooning it out.

6. Transfer the drained zucchini and onion mixture to the egg mixture. Add the tomatoes and Cheddar and stir until the zoodles are coated. Pour the whole mixture into the prepared pie shell and top with the Parmesan.

7. Bake until firmed up and golden brown, 40 to 45 minutes. Let rest for 15 to 20 minutes so it's easier to cut, then serve. This makes great next-day leftovers and is delicious with a healthy side salad.

ROOMMATE'S REUBEN CASSEROLE

MAKES 9 TO 12 SERVINGS

When Kathy was single and looking for a place to live in New York, a friend of a friend told her about an opening in a safe apartment building shared by six flight attendants. One was a larger-than-life American Airlines flight attendant from Los Angeles, Mary Finnigan. A straight-talking, God-fearing, hilarious woman, Mary is to this day one of Kathy's best friends.

During that time, the biggest news story was that an orbiting American space station named Skylab was wobbling in space and at any moment could plunge to Earth. The planet was on edge. Nonetheless, life went on. Back then Mary had a boyfriend who had an annoying habit. It could be any hour of any day, the doorbell would ring, and it was Mary's boyfriend. Her roommates finally nicknamed him Skylab, because you never knew when he was going to drop in.

Skylab was smitten with Mary, and to show the world that they were a couple, he gave her his *Super Bowl ring!* He had worked for the Kansas City Chiefs once upon a time when they won the NFL's Super Bowl, and everybody in the organization got one. He gave it to Mary, who was not much of a football fan, but she knew it was a priceless piece of sports memorabilia so she hid it in a secure location.

Many years later, Mary got a call one night to say Skylab had passed away. They'd broken up long ago, but still it was a sad passing, and it raised the question, what would Mary do with that ring? Sell it, save it . . . it was hers now, right? She honestly didn't know. Nobody ever called and asked for it back, so

(continued)

Mary the roommate with Mary our lawyer.

when Mary eventually found the man of her dreams, a guy named Jack, she gave Jack the Super Bowl ring on a landmark birthday.

Whenever Jack wears it in public, people stare hard at him, because at five foot six he doesn't exactly have a classic football build. He can tell they're thinking, *How'd* he *get that ring*, and he'll simply say, "I was the kicker."

Of course, the person will think, *kickers can be any size, as long as their foot works*.

By the way, Mary says Jack always looks taller . . . when he stands on his wallet.

As for this recipe, Mary loves it because it reminds her of family gatherings and neighborhood buffets where people compliment her cooking rather than her husband's finger jewelry. Mary tells me it can be assembled in the morning and refrigerated until ready to bake, which is a good option, because just like Skylab, you never know when somebody hungry is going to drop in.

Cooking spray
6 to 8 slices rye bread
3 large eggs
1 cup milk or half-and-half
¼ cup mustard (we use French's)
1 pound sliced pastrami or corned beef
One 14.4-ounce can sauerkraut, drained
Thousand Island dressing (we use Ken's)
1 cup ½-inch-sliced dill pickles (we use kosher dills)
2 teaspoons caraway seeds
1 pound Swiss cheese, grated (thin slices of Swiss will also work)

1. Preheat the oven to 350°F. Lightly coat a 9 × 13-inch baking dish with cooking spray.
2. Tear 4 slices of the rye bread into random ¾-inch pieces and lay them in the dish in a single layer. If it's thin-sliced bread, you may need to use 1 or 2 more slices to cover the bottom. You be the judge. Place 2 more rye slices in a food processor and pulse into bread crumbs. Set aside.
3. Crack the eggs into a medium bowl. Add the milk and mustard and whisk until it's nice and smooth. Set aside.

4. We'll build this in layers, like lasagna. Distribute half the pastrami over the bread in the pan, then scatter the sauerkraut on top. Drizzle up to ½ cup of the Thousand Island dressing over the sauerkraut in a zig-zag fashion. Place the pickles evenly on top. Scatter 1 teaspoon of the caraway seeds evenly over the pickles and top with half of the grated Swiss.
5. For the next round of layers, spread the remaining meat over the cheese, evenly sprinkle the remaining 1 teaspoon caraway seeds on top, then evenly scatter on the rest of the grated Swiss cheese.
6. Gently pour the egg-milk mixture evenly over the casserole. I use a rubber spatula to make sure that the top is flat and everything is coated. Spread the reserved bread crumbs evenly on top.
7. Bake until the center is no longer jiggly, 40 to 45 minutes. Just be forewarned, when it's baking, it smells *exactly* like a Reuben sandwich, and it drives me crazy!
8. Let it rest 5 minutes, then use a sharp knife to cut it into squares. Serve with a side of Thousand Island dressing.

CHICKEN CURRY IN A HURRY

MAKES 6 SERVINGS

I am the first Doocy to graduate from college. To celebrate, my mom paid for my ticket that I'd charged on a TWA credit card. She didn't have enough money to pay it all at once, so every month for four years, she'd send me a check for the minimum monthly payment, and every month I was reminded of her kindness.

In London the only overnight accommodations I could afford was a youth hostel, which was super cheap but semi-terrifying, a dank dorm room with a dozen single cots. After I'd checked in, I found an unclaimed bed and lay down on it. The middle sagged about a foot, but I was so jet-lagged that I immediately fell asleep in my clothes (because my mom said there were pickpockets everywhere). I woke up a few hours later with a terrible stiff neck and checked to see if somebody had stolen the money belt I was wearing. They had not, so I went back to sleep until the next day, when I went sightseeing. I was still wearing the clothes I'd put on three days earlier in Kansas. It was okay, it wasn't as if I'd run into QE2 on the street.

You know I'm wearing a money belt, don't you . . .

London looks cool and almost everything has a history. At Buckingham Palace, I noticed a crowd had gathered at the gate, so I stopped to check it out. Within ten seconds there was a whistle, the people parted, and the gate opened for a Rolls-Royce. Clearly visible on the other side of a bulletproof window was Queen Elizabeth II. As she passed, she looked directly at me and gave that Windsor wave. I imagined she felt sorry for the young man with the stiff neck who was standing funny from sleeping with a money belt that cut off the circulation to his lower half.

Foodwise, I was prepared for classic British cuisine—Yorkshire pudding, kidney pie, things like that. What I didn't know about was London's large selection of very affordable Indian restaurants, where I had my first curry dish and fell in love. When our kids studied in England, I encouraged them to hurry to the curry joints. They did, and they love them, too. Happy memories of trips to the land of the kidney pie.

Of course if I told my children that the only reason I could go to England was because my mom had paid my TWA bill, they'd all ask the same thing: "Dad, what's a TWA?"

¼ cup plus 1 tablespoon olive oil
1 garlic clove, minced
1 large yellow onion, medium-diced
5 boneless, skinless chicken thighs, cut into
 ¾-inch chunks
⅓ cup all-purpose flour
1 tablespoon curry powder
1 teaspoon ground ginger
One 14.5-ounce can diced tomatoes
1 cup low-sodium chicken stock
One 5.3-ounce single-serve plain Greek
 yogurt
Cooked rice, for serving
Unsweetened coconut flakes, for serving
 (optional)

1. In a large skillet, heat 1 tablespoon of the olive oil over medium-high heat. Add the garlic and onion and sauté until the onion softens and turns a little golden on the edges, 3 to 4 minutes. Remove the garlic and onion to a plate.

2. In a large bowl, combine the chicken and flour. Toss to coat.

3. Add the remaining ¼ cup olive oil to the pan, still over medium-high heat. Add the chicken, season with the curry and ginger, and sauté until the chicken is browned and cooked through, about 10 minutes.

4. Stir in the tomatoes, chicken stock, and garlic-onion mixture and bring to a boil for a minute. Reduce the heat to medium and simmer for 15 minutes, stirring occasionally.

5. When you're ready to serve, remove the pan from the heat and stir in the yogurt until completely blended. Serve over cooked rice and sprinkle each serving with coconut flakes if you like.

FAVORITE FISH IN A FLASH

When Kathy and I were secure enough in our finances that we could join a club, we joined Price Club. Now of course it's Costco, and one of the main reasons we joined was the amazing slabs of salmon they had splayed across the blue Styrofoam. Salmon became our favorite fish.

Then the question became, how do we make it so that everybody loves it and it doesn't make a *big* mess in the kitchen? Salmon splatters take time away from you doing other important things, like teaching your golden retriever to speak Dutch because your show-off neighbor's schnauzer already speaks Italian. This recipe is that answer, and we cook it on the grill.

Eighteen minutes—that's how long this recipe took me to make last time. Once you prep and preheat, I bet you can cook it faster than DoorDash could dash it to your door. Trust me.

Cooking spray
Four 2-inch-wide salmon fillets, skin removed
Salt and freshly ground black pepper
1 bunch asparagus, ends trimmed
Olive oil, for dressing
One 1½-pound bag microwaveable fingerling or new potatoes, such as Steamables (or other brand of your choice)
2 tablespoons butter
2 tablespoons plus 1 teaspoon chopped fresh dill
⅓ cup mayonnaise
1½ tablespoons Dijon mustard
⅛ teaspoon garlic powder

1. Fire up the grill to medium-high heat. Away from the grill, coat a grill pan (not the grill grate itself) with cooking spray.

2. Sprinkle the salmon with salt and pepper. Place the fillets skin side down on the grill pan, close the grill lid, and grill until the edges start to crisp, about 5 minutes. Carefully flip and grill until cooked through, about another 5 minutes.

3. Right after you put the fish on the grill pan, place the asparagus on a plate, drizzle a little olive oil over it, and give it a shake of salt and pepper. Place the asparagus directly on the grill, perpendicular to the direction of the grill, or else the pieces will fall through! Cook until they have some nice grill marks, 6 to 10 minutes, rotating them a couple times. Place on a serving plate and cover with foil.

4. As soon as the salmon and asparagus are on the grill, prepare the microwaveable potatoes according to the package directions, which means they'll cook for about 10 minutes. Place the potatoes in a serving bowl and toss them with the butter. Garnish with 2 tablespoons of the dill.

5. To make the salmon sauce: In a small bowl, combine the mayonnaise, mustard, garlic powder, a pinch of pepper, and the remaining 1 teaspoon dill. Mix until smooth.

6. Serve the salmon topped with the sauce and with the potatoes and asparagus on the side. And if you can do it all in less than half an hour . . . welcome to the club!

MOM'S MEXICAN LASAGNA

MAKES 6 SERVINGS

After we got married, Kathy wanted to expand her meal-making menu from the lasagna she made on our first date to something, anything, else. She was baking a lot of whole chickens that gave us plenty of leftovers, so she looked for ideas using cooked chicken and found some in a cookbook given to her by her friend Mary. Mary's husband, Jack, is a great cook and makes delicious smoked tri-tips, but he is also very frugal, and when his mother passed away, Jack actually bought her coffin at a discount store called Caskets Direct. Can't wait for that reunion in Heaven . . .

Anyway, in that book Kathy found great chicken casserole recipes that didn't require a lot of cooking experience. This recipe has evolved over many years based on what the kids would eat at the time. Originally Kathy made it as individual enchiladas, but rolling them took extra time, so she started making it more like a lasagna with layers rather than individual enchiladas. Same taste, just faster.

Also, once when Kathy was almost done doing the prep work on this, she realized she didn't have any red enchilada sauce. In searching the cupboard for a substitute sauce, she found one that was much better than she'd intended: a very large a jar of salsa verde that she'd gotten coincidentally at Costco, where they also sell affordably priced caskets—who knew?

When Kathy's friend Mary would later take her mother shopping at Costco, she'd jokingly ask which discount casket she liked. Mary would say, "I think the Lady of Guadalupe model is my favorite." Her mother did not think it was nearly as funny as Mary did, so they'd head to the back of the store to load up on Kirkland Signature paper towels.

Cooking spray
1 tablespoon butter
1 tablespoon olive oil
1 garlic clove, minced
1 small red onion, finely diced
½ teaspoon freshly ground black pepper
¼ teaspoon chili powder
1 cup chicken stock
4 cups shredded cooked chicken (about 2 pounds)
One 8-ounce package cream cheese
One 16-ounce jar salsa verde (we use Herdez brand)
1 dozen 5-inch corn tortillas

1½ cups shredded cheese (we use a Mexican blend)
Optional, for serving: sour cream, sliced avocado, rice

1. Preheat the oven to 350°F. Coat a 10 × 10-inch (or similar size) baking dish with cooking spray.
2. In a deep saucepan, melt the butter over medium-high heat. Add the oil, garlic, onion, pepper, and chili powder and sauté with a silicone spatula until the onion is soft and translucent, 3 to 5 minutes. Pour in the chicken stock and bring to a boil. Remove from the heat.

(continued)

3. Add the chicken and cream cheese to the saucepan and mash away with the spatula until the cream cheese is melted.

4. Time to assemble. Pour just enough salsa verde to thinly cover the bottom of the prepared baking dish. Place 4 tortillas in the baking dish to form a single layer (this works perfectly in a 10 × 10-inch dish, but cut them to fit as needed). Spread half of the creamy chicken mixture over the top. Top with ½ cup of the shredded cheese.

5. For the second layer, lay 4 tortillas over the cheese, followed by the rest of the chicken mixture, ½ cup of cheese, and 4 more tortillas.

6. Pour the rest of the salsa verde jar over the top to keep the tortillas from drying out.

7. Bake for 30 to 35 minutes. Pull out the pan and top with the remaining ½ cup cheese. Bake until the cheese starts melting, about 5 minutes. Let the casserole rest for about 5 minutes to set and cool a little, as that cheese will be *hot!*

8. If you like, serve with sour cream and/or sliced avocado, and a side of rice is always appreciated.

SHEET PAN FAJITAS IN A FLASH

MAKES 10 FAJITAS

I remember the first time I tried Mexican food. It was 1965, and Lupe, our neighbor lady in Russell, Kansas, showed my mom how to fry tortillas. The first time my mom made them herself, she didn't remember exactly how long to fry them, and they were pretty limp and a tad greasy. But she did get the meat and spice combination right, and I remember that first warm bite as one of those *aha!* moments when you realize you could eat this every day of your life.

Years later, my dad and I had just ordered tacos and tostadas at a place in Junction City, Kansas, and were snacking on the chips when we heard a sudden loud hissing noise. It sounded like a gas main had ruptured and we'd be blown to smithereens before we got our churros. The sound was getting louder, and I swiveled around and realized that the scary sound was being carried into the dining room by a waiter. On a 500-degree pewter plate sat a sizzling skirt steak cut in slices. We all wondered what the dish was, and how soon we could order it. *Fajitas!*

By now you've seen the fajitas presentation in a restaurant a million times, but there's something magical about fajitas because they trigger three of your senses before you even take a bite. You *hear* them first, then you *see* the smoke, and then you *smell* the aroma. It's not just an entree—it's an experience.

But if you're pressed for time, you can easily make fajitas at home! We use chicken here, but you can use steak or shrimp if you like, and this is all done on a sheet pan so you can prep it, heat it, and then eat it—pronto. Just know there will be no loud sizzle; for that you'll have to go to a restaurant.

Cooking spray
2 red, yellow, or orange bell peppers, thinly sliced
1 red onion, thinly sliced
One 1-ounce packet fajita seasoning mix (we use Old El Paso)
1½ pounds boneless, skinless chicken breasts, cut into ½-inch-thick strips no longer than 1 or 2 inches
1 cup grape tomatoes, halved
1 avocado, medium-diced
Salt
10 fajita-size flour tortillas
Juice of 1 lime
1 cup shredded Mexican blend cheese
Sour cream, for garnish

Salsa verde, for garnish
2 tablespoons chopped cilantro, for garnish

1. Adjust an oven rack to the highest position and another to the center position. Preheat the oven to 400°F. Coat a sheet pan with cooking spray.

2. Place the peppers and onion in a large zip-top bag and add one-third of the fajita seasoning. Seal the bag, shake, and spread the vegetables evenly over one side of the sheet pan. (We traditionally kept the vegetables separate from the chicken in case one of the kids was going through a picky phase.)

(continued)

3. Place the chicken and remaining fajita seasoning in the bag, seal and shake, and spread the chicken on the other half of the sheet pan. Give everything on the pan a good shot of cooking spray.

4. Place the sheet pan on the top oven rack and roast for 15 minutes. Move the chicken and vegetables around with a spatula and roast until the chicken is completely cooked (cut and check to make sure), about 15 minutes more.

5. Meanwhile, in a medium bowl, combine the tomatoes and avocado and season with salt to taste. Set aside.

6. Loosely wrap the tortillas in foil and place them on the middle oven rack to warm up for 5 to 7 minutes (don't let them dry out). Set them aside, still wrapped in foil to keep warm.

7. Remove the chicken to a serving plate and drizzle with the lime juice.

8. Turn on the broiler and return the sheet pan to the top rack. Let the veggies scorch a bit, fajita-style, watching closely so they don't burn too much. Place in a separate serving dish.

9. Time to make the fajitas! The way you stack your fajita tortillas is a personal choice, but we put the cheese on the warm tortillas first (so it melts), then the chicken, vegetables, tomato-avocado mixture, sour cream, salsa verde, and finally a sprinkling of cilantro.

BRETT'S BBQ CUPCAKE CHICKEN

Condé Nast Traveler did an article on the top fifteen BBQ cities in America, and the number one best city for 'cue in the USA is . . . Kansas City, Missouri! In that town, if you're talking about KC Masterpiece you're referring to their bestselling sauce, not the Caravaggio hanging in the Nelson-Atkins Museum of Art.

When I was working at the ABC affiliate in Kansas City, I would make it a point to visit Arthur Bryant's or Gates Bar-B-Q at least once a week. Gates was my hands-down favorite, and when Kathy and I were planning our wedding rehearsal dinner, we both knew it had to be at Gates. My dad picked up the tab for the entire party, but that was okay because the most expensive item was six dollars.

"I do—love the burnt ends," I joked during a toast at Gates, practicing *part* of what I would say at our wedding twenty-two hours later.

Right now in our refrigerator you will find two bottles of Gates Original sauce, which we routinely ask Amazon to drive to our house and save a thousand-mile trip back to Missouri.

In the spirit of amazing smoked meats, this easy smoker recipe is from our Florida friend Brett Holmes, a competition barbecue guy. The prep is a snap, but it takes some time to refrigerate the chicken, and then there's a stretch in the smoker, which explains why you're spending time outside standing next to the smoker with your favorite cold beverage. It's perfect for family gatherings, football games, tailgating, or if you're lucky . . . wedding receptions.

12 boneless, skin-on chicken thighs
¼ cup BBQ rub (Brett's favorite is Butt Rub brand)
1½ sticks (6 ounces) butter
2 cups BBQ sauce (our favorite is Gates of Kansas City)
Optional, for serving: Coleslaw, beans, or potato salad

NOTE: *You can use a regular muffin tin for this dish, but it gets super smoked and is a pain to clean, so we use a disposable foil muffin tin from the aluminum foil section at the grocery store. It's worth the dollar.*

1. First, a little prep work before it's time to start smoking. Generously rub the chicken thighs with your favorite rub, coating them thoroughly. Place the thighs on a plate, cover with plastic wrap, and refrigerate for up to 3 hours.

2. When you're ready, set your smoker to 250°F. (We use apple- or cherrywood chips in the smoker for a sweeter taste—we don't like a real heavy smoke.) Let the thighs come to room temperature as the smoker heats up.

3. Working one at a time, roll a thigh into a ball and place it skin side down in one cup of a disposable aluminum muffin tin (see Note). It will be a tight squeeze, so press it in as far as you can. Repeat with the rest of the chicken thighs. Place a pat of butter on top of each and set the tin in the smoker, uncovered.

4. After 90 minutes, carefully remove the muffin tin and use tongs to carefully turn each of the

(continued)

thighs so the skin is facing up. Return to the smoker for 45 to 60 minutes, until the thighs reach 165°F on a meat thermometer.

5. The thighs are now ready to eat, but we like to dip them in our favorite BBQ sauce, then set them skin side up on a foil-wrapped sheet pan and smoke them for 20 to 30 minutes more to caramelize the sauce.

6. Remove from the smoker, place on a serving platter, and let rest 5 minutes. Brett loves to serve this up with a side of coleslaw, beans, or potato salad—they all taste great!

Peter imports Gates sauce twice a year.

PASTA BOLOGNESE WITH BACON

MAKES 6 TO 8 SERVINGS

The first time I took Kathy out to dinner it was to an Italian place in Northwest Washington. We went there because I knew she'd love the Bolognese. This recipe is inspired by that fateful night.

Kathy looked amazing when I picked her up. She was wearing for the first time a very expensive new cobalt blue suede suit she'd saved up to buy. She looked so stunning that she overwhelmed my caveman motor skills, because over the course of a two-hour meal I spilled a glass of red wine on her lap, and during dessert I spilled an entire cup of very strong coffee. "On the bright side, it's decaf!" I joked as she tried to stop my heart with an icy stare. Remember, this was the first date!

Driving her home, I apologized for everything, repeatedly. She just sat there. Her beautiful outfit smelled like she'd ridden out a 7.2 earthquake in a Starbucks basement.

When I got her to her door, I waited for her reaction. *Say something.* She was giving me the same look I gave my college roommate when I realized that for years, whenever he needed batteries, he took them out of the smoke detector.

"Do you want to come in for a drink?"

Wait, what? *Yes!*

That was more than thirty years ago—and it all worked out.

Today we still make a version of the Bolognese I ordered that fateful night, when ironically red sauce was the one thing she didn't get on her outfit. Over the years we've tweaked this recipe to fry the vegetables in bacon grease, which makes it taste as if it's been cooking all day. And it's all done in less than an hour!

NOTE: *This dish is doubly divine served with a side of Aldo's Amazing Cheesy Toast (page 89).*

Cooking spray
4 slices bacon, cut into ¾-inch pieces
1 yellow onion, roughly chopped
2 garlic cloves, minced
½ cup finely chopped carrots
2 celery stalks, cut into ¼-inch slices
1½ pounds meatloaf mix (ground beef, veal, and pork)
1 teaspoon Italian seasoning
1 teaspoon table salt
1 teaspoon freshly ground black pepper
¼ teaspoon freshly grated nutmeg
One 28-ounce can crushed tomatoes
One 6-ounce can tomato paste
¾ cup red wine (Cabernet is our favorite)
1 pound pasta (rigatoni is perfect)
⅓ cup half-and-half
Optional garnish: Whipped ricotta cheese, fresh basil

1. Coat a large saucepan with a little cooking spray. Add the bacon and fry it over medium-high heat, separating the pieces so they don't stick together. Use a slotted spoon to transfer the bacon to paper towels to absorb any excess oil.

2. Reduce the heat to medium. Add the onion and garlic to the pan and sauté for 1 or 2 minutes to soften the onion, scraping up the browned bacon bits in the pan. Add the carrots and celery and sauté until softened, 3 or 4 minutes. Use the slotted spoon to remove the vegetables to a plate.

3. Add the meat to the pan and cook over medium-high heat, mixing in the Italian seasoning, salt, pepper, and nutmeg and breaking up the meat as it browns. When the meat is cooked through, with all the pink gone, reduce the heat to medium and add the tomatoes, tomato paste, wine, and cooked bacon and vegetables. Bring to a simmer, stirring occasionally, until the wine reduces a bit and the sauce thickens, about 15 minutes.

4. Twenty minutes before it's time to eat, cook the pasta according to the package directions. Leave it in the water until serving.

5. Just before you're ready to serve, remove the Bolognese from the heat and stir in the half-and-half. Give it a minute to warm up.

6. Drain the pasta and serve it with the Bolognese. We love to top it with a healthy scoop of whipped ricotta, and if you have some fresh basil leaves, shred them and toss on top.

Can we cook this, Dad?

There's a bear in camp!

Dad, I'm burning food, like you!

CLASSIC CAMPFIRE FISH

MAKES 4 SERVINGS

As a lad growing up in Kansas, I was a Cub Scout and then a Boy Scout, and when Peter listened to my boyhood stories of adventures like throwing axes, shooting BB guns, and sleeping under the stars until I had strep throat, he knew that when he was old enough he'd want to become a young man in uniform, like his father.

He loved the Pinewood Derby and winning ribbons for pumpkin carving, but Peter's Scouting highlight had to be when we drove west to Camp No-Be-Bo-Sco in the Kittatinny Mountains of New Jersey. I didn't know at the time that this camp is where they filmed the first *Friday the 13th* movie, which meant if Jason showed up at our tent at midnight in a hockey mask, it wouldn't be the first time for that venue.

The weekend was calm until it was discovered that despite being told not to bring doughnuts, a couple dads had broken the rule . . . and attracted some of the neighbors. "Dad, there's a bear in the camp!" Peter yelled into our tent jolting me from a really good nap. By the time I got my shoes on, Peter was fearlessly running toward a 200-pound black bear as if it were a labradoodle or an animated character at Chuck E. Cheese, because kids think animals are cute and they could be friends. Eventually the adorable bear retreated to the woods after finishing the contraband box of glazed Dunkin' Donuts and all of our marshmallows, canceling that night's s'mores-a-thon.

The next day during the fishing derby, Peter went to find nightcrawlers to use as bait. As he was threading one on a hook I realized it wasn't a worm, it was a very small (and apparently nonpoisonous) redbelly snake. That was the last time we went fishing for anything other than compliments.

Of course Scouting memories like those come at a substantial cost, which meant the boys had weekly fundraisers selling all sorts of stuff we didn't need. Being good parents, we did what every family in our neighborhood did—whatever Peter was selling, we bought his entire quota so he wouldn't have to knock on the doors of neighbors who watch only CNN.

This fish recipe wrapped in tinfoil is something my Scout leader taught us how to make when I was a Scout. We cooked it directly on the coals, and of course it was super charred, but delicious in a "I burned this all by myself" way. And sitting that close to the campfire always made our eyes water. I wish I'd packed my hockey mask.

(continued)

4 tablespoons (½ stick) butter, at room
   temperature
1 tablespoon finely chopped fresh dill
Table salt
Cooking spray
1 large russet potato, peeled and cut
   crosswise into ¼-inch-thick slices
   (we use a mandoline)
Freshly ground black pepper
½ pound asparagus, ends trimmed
1 red bell pepper, cut into ¼-inch-wide
   rings
4 salmon fillets (about 6 ounces each), skin
   removed

1. At least 1 hour before you start the meal, make the herbed butter: In a medium bowl combine the butter and dill, give it a shake of salt, and really mash it up with a fork to mix it evenly. Roll out a 1-foot square of plastic wrap and spatula the butter mixture onto the center. Cover the butter loosely with plastic wrap and use your hands to roll out a butter log that's about 1 inch thick. Close up the ends and refrigerate for at least 1 hour.

2. Preheat the grill to medium-high (400° to 425°F), with one side getting indirect heat.

3. Tear off four 30-inch lengths of foil. Make a single fold in the middle of one piece to double it up. Coat about an 8-inch area in the center of the foil with cooking spray. First, place about 6 potatoes slices in the middle, forming a rectangular single layer, leaving at least 1½ inches of empty foil on the top and bottom. Give them a shake of salt and pepper. Place 3 or 4 asparagus spears on the potatoes, then 2 or 3 rings of bell pepper. Next goes a salmon fillet, with the skin side facing down. Salt and pepper the works and give a final spray of cooking spray. Now let's close it up. Fold up the long sides of the foil, join them by crimping the top, roll down the seam to create a compact packet, and crimp the two ends. Repeat to fill and seal the other packets.

4. Grill the packets over indirect heat for 25 to 30 minutes, carefully rotating them once or twice.

5. Remove the packets from the grill and open them carefully as they are steaming hot. Check to make sure the salmon and potatoes are done. If not, close the foil and grill another 5 to 10 minutes. When done, get the herbed butter out of the fridge, slice off about a tablespoon, and place it on the very top of the salmon. Close the top of the foil again and let the packets sit for 2 minutes for the butter to melt and butter-ize the entire entree.

6. To serve, open the packets and carefully drain the excess liquid out of one end. Spatula the works onto plates or eat them out of the foil . . . just like a Boy Scout. But don't expect a merit badge—you have to sell things like popcorn and lightbulbs to earn those.

ZOODLES 'N' SHRIMP SCAMPI

MAKES 4 SERVINGS

For twenty-five years we have lived in New Jersey, which is, according to our license plates, the Garden State. Clearly backyard gardens are a state requirement, so we've dutifully grown bumper crops of tomatoes, basil, and zucchini. I'd spot a good-looking tomato in the morning and think all day about how I'd plan to use it at suppertime, only to go out at the end of the day to pick it and find a mouthful missing. Frustrated at living on the set of *Wild Kingdom*, I erected a welded-wire fence around the garden. Think Checkpoint Charlie with irrigation. That worked great at keeping animals out, but it also made it really hard for me to harvest the crops. Then Peter found a solar-powered animal repeller online. Perfectly harmless, it's a motion detector that lights up when critters come near, discouraging them from eating our vegetables and encouraging them to shop elsewhere. Sorry, neighbors!

This is a delicious way to use up fresh zucchini; they go right in the spiralizer so they're quick to whip up. As for the rabbits that live in our backyard, sorry, the zucchini are ours, but if you text me, I'll spiralized some carrots and leave them outside by the back door.

You're welcome.

2 tablespoons olive oil
2 garlic cloves, minced
¼ cup chopped shallots
1 pound large frozen shrimp (31/40), peeled, deveined, and tails removed
½ cup white wine or chicken stock
Juice of 1 lemon
½ teaspoon table salt
½ teaspoon freshly ground black pepper
3 medium zucchini, spiralized, or 5 to 6 cups store-bought zucchini zoodles
4 tablespoons (½ stick) butter or healthy spread

1. In a large skillet, heat the olive oil over medium-high heat. Add the garlic and shallots and sauté until they are softened and starting to turn golden on the edges, 2 to 3 minutes. Remove them to a plate.

2. Add the shrimp in a single layer and cook undisturbed for 3 to 5 minutes, until they just turn deep pink. Flip, cook the other side until pink, and spatula them onto the plate with the garlic and shallots.

3. Add the wine, garlic, lemon juice, salt, and pepper to the skillet and bring to a boil for about 1 minute, stirring constantly. Add the zucchini noodles, tossing them a few times to coat with the juice, and sauté until soft but not mushy (think al dente), about 5 minutes.

4. Slide the noodles to one side of the skillet and return the shrimp and shallots to the pan so they heat up for 1 or 2 minutes on the skillet bottom. Remove from the heat.

5. Stir in the butter until it melts, then serve pronto.

Steve's parents, Jim and JoAnne, 1955.

AIR-FRIED CHICKEN AND ARUGULA SALAD

MAKES 4 SERVINGS

When I was about twenty-five, my dad told me he'd read an article somewhere and insisted that I start the day by drinking two tablespoons of apple cider vinegar. Supposedly it lowered cholesterol and blood sugar levels and got rid of your belly. He promised it worked, saying, "Look at me!" But at six feet tall, he'd never weighed more than about one hundred fifty pounds. He said it was the vinegar, but I thought it was the Pall Malls.

My mom endorsed it as well, so I tried the vinegar thing for a couple months and stopped. Didn't like it. Now I read that famous celebrities swear by it. Guess my parents were right.

When I was about thirty, Mom and Dad sent me jars of a green barley powder. "Lots of super nutrients," Dad told me, and announced he was the new regional salesman for the stuff. I tried it for a couple months and stopped; it tasted awful. Now I see how many famous celebrities swear by powdery green health drinks. Were my parents right again?

Five years later, a big box arrived at our house, a birthday present from my parents. It was a convection oven. This was years before homes had convection ovens, and this version sat on the countertop and had a big plastic dome, big enough for a whole chicken. "Cuts cooking time in half," Dad told me. We roasted a whole chicken that night, and it took half the time. Correct again.

(continued)

Thirty years later.

Kathy made an oven-stuffer roaster chicken once a week in that gizmo, which we called the whirly-bird. It was such a time-saver . . . until the dome cracked and it stopped working. Then we discovered that the company had stopped making it. The party was over for quick chicken.

Fast-forward to last year, when on TV Paula Deen gave me an air fryer that reminds me a lot of the whirly-bird, but it's much more durable and really amazing. Some weeks I can go without ever turning on our big oven, and the air fryer is a snap to clean up. This recipe is super easy to make—you'll be amazed at the taste, and it reminds me that I was lucky to have had caring parents who had some pretty good ideas . . . I just didn't realize it at the time.

Mark Twain famously said, "When I was a boy of fourteen, my father was so ignorant I could hardly stand to have the old man around. But when I got to be twenty-one, I was astonished at how much the old man had learned in seven years."

Maybe I should have listened more . . . but that green powder drink thing really was awful.

2 tablespoons balsamic vinegar
6 tablespoons olive oil
1½ teaspoons mustard (Dijon is great)
1 garlic clove, minced
Salt and freshly ground black pepper
1 large tomato, cut into ½-inch cubes
3 scallions, green parts only, chopped
½ cup mozzarella pearls (optional)
2 large eggs
1 cup dried bread crumbs
¼ cup grated Parmesan cheese
4 thin-sliced chicken breast cutlets (about
    4 ounces each)
Cooking spray
3 cups baby arugula

1. In a medium bowl, whisk together the vinegar, olive oil, mustard, garlic, and salt and pepper to taste. Add the tomato, scallions, and mozzarella pearls (if using) and stir to combine. Refrigerate and let the flavors combine.
2. Let's make a little assembly line for the chicken. In one shallow bowl, whisk the eggs. In another shallow bowl, combine the bread crumbs, Parmesan, and a sprinkling of salt and pepper. Stir to combine.
3. Drag a chicken cutlet through the egg, coating every bit of the chicken, then give it a good coating of the bread crumb mixture. Repeat to bread the rest of the chicken cutlets and set aside.
4. Preheat the air fryer to 400°F (it only takes 3 minutes to preheat).
5. Because of the size of the fryer basket, you'll need to cook in two batches, but it goes fast. Spray 2 of the cutlets all over with cooking spray and place them in the air fryer. Cook them for about 10 minutes. Flip and spray with more cooking spray and cook for 10 minutes more, or until completely cooked through. Remove to a plate, cover with foil, and air-fry the other batch.
6. While the chicken is cooking, remove the tomato mixture from the fridge and add the arugula. Give it a good toss to evenly coat the salad. To serve, place a piece of chicken on a plate and top with a nice mound of salad.

BLT PASTA

When you see those people on TV, you ever wonder how much they make?

In 1979, when I was the weekend weatherman and statehouse correspondent at the NBC affiliate KTSB-TV in Topeka, I started at four dollars an hour, and earned enough per month to cover my rent and expenses, with fifty dollars left over to buy food. Cash-strapped and always hungry, I lived on a lot of ramen noodles and pot pies, often priced ten for a dollar. I loved the chicken pot pies, and the beef were okay, but I'd only eat the tuna on Fridays during Lent.

The real money-stretcher all-star was a one-pound box of macaroni. I could get three or four complete meals out of a single package. Of course today we call it pasta, but back then it was spaghetti, noodles, or macaroni. At that price point, I called it a miracle.

Thankfully I had a go-to recipe that was so special I could eat it four times a week: bacon carbonara. In high school, my friend Gary Shorman's family had hosted a foreign exchange student from Italy by the name of Antonio. We all had many questions for him, mainly about how to pronounce various curse words in Italian. Our teachers never had any idea what we were saying; they were just impressed we were expanding our international vocabulary.

One night the Shormans invited me over for a special meal—Antonio was going to make a real Italian dinner. He was the only authentic Italian I had ever met in Kansas, and I was ready to learn. Antonio boiled the noodles like my mom did, but then he pulled out a big skillet and fried a pound of bacon—bacon at suppertime? What a game changer! Then he separated some eggs, the yolks from the whites, which I had never seen done before, and dumped the yolks in a bowl with a healthy portion of Kraft grated Parmesan and gave it a stir. He was quickly narrating the whole thing in Italian (I presume in appropriate language, as Mrs. Shorman was standing right next to him).

In a span of thirty seconds, Antonio turned off the skillet, dumped in the noodles, and stirred in the egg and Parm mixture, which cooked completely from the heat of the noodles and pan. He served it up immediately, and it was perfect.

Just know that in the last few years, I've updated and expanded the ingredients to include shallots and arugula, which I had never heard of growing up.

(continued)

TV weatherman, four dollars an hour.

Before iPhones, people made movies with actual cameras.

Table salt
1 pound strand pasta (spaghetti, fettuccine, and bucatini are all great), broken in half)
½ pound bacon, cut into 1-inch pieces
1 pint cherry or grape tomatoes, halved
1 garlic clove, thinly sliced
1 shallot, thinly sliced
¼ teaspoon red pepper flakes
Freshly ground black pepper
3 large egg yolks
1 cup grated Parmesan cheese
3 cups baby arugula

1. Bring a large pot of salted water to a boil and cook the pasta according to the package directions. Scoop out 1 cup of the pasta water and set aside. Leave the noodles in the water until ready to use.

2. While the pasta is cooking, in a very large skillet, brown the bacon over medium-high heat. Remove the bacon to a plate, leaving the grease in the pan. Add the tomatoes, garlic, shallot, pepper flakes, and a sprinkling of salt and black pepper. Sauté for about 5 minutes, until everything has been bacon-flavorized.

3. Add ½ cup of the reserved pasta water to the tomato mixture and bring to a boil. Stir in the pasta and toss to coat it with the tomato mixture for a couple minutes, until heated through.

4. In a small bowl, whisk the egg yolks. Remove the skillet from the heat and stir in the egg yolks. The eggs cook very quickly in the hot noodles and residual pan heat, and if it's too hot they can turn into scrambled eggs; you don't want that. But if you're worried that the eggs are not cooked enough, put the pan back on the stove for a couple minutes over medium heat, add a tablespoon or two of the extra pasta water, and keep stirring to avoid scrambling, until done to your liking. Stir in the cheese, then the arugula and bacon and season with salt and pepper to taste. Serve it up in bowls.

8

HOLIDAYS

RECIPES FOR ONCE OR TWICE A YEAR

THE FAMILY CLASSICS IN THIS HOLIDAY COL-
lection are so special they are sometimes
only made once or twice a year. Some
are more elaborate than the rest of the
cookbook recipes, but that's because at important
gatherings we often congregate in the kitchen for
hours, so while we're there chewing the fat, we
might as well put all those hands to good use and
make something fantastic that tastes like home.

Today when I ask my kids what recipe reminds
them of growing up at our house, they'll say hands
down it was what I'd make for thirty years of Sunday mornings, and it took very little time at all: the
classic egg in a nest, which was simply an egg fried
in a hole cut in a piece of bread.

"Dad, why do they call it egg in a nest? It's egg
in toast," said Mary, our future litigator.

She was right, and her question inspired me to
go on an almost generation-long odyssey to devise
a dish that looked more like its name.

Sunday mornings, for years, I'd attempt a twist,
but nothing was ever just right. When we agreed to
write our first cookbook, Kathy and I really wanted
to include egg in a nest, because the kids loved it,
so I made it a goal to invent a new look for this
breakfast classic, because every version still looked
like egg in toast. Dozens of eggs, nothing perfect.

Finally, on the day before the cookbook was
due, it was 7:30 a.m. Sunday morning and I was
sitting in church, and as they were passing the
collection plate I thought about how after mass I
should try making one last version. But I had no
brainstorm, so I looked up at the face of Jesus, and
I thought to myself, *You got any ideas?*

Nothing.

The agony of defeat! We simply would not
have a recipe for egg in a nest in the cookbook
that was due in twenty-eight hours. I took one last
look up at Jesus's face, glanced up at his crown of
thorns, and realized for the first time after years in

Eggs-perimenting.

that church that the crown of thorns around his head looked like *a nest*.

It was right there the whole time. What did we cook with that I could use to make something that looked like a nest? Instantly it dawned on me—*hash browns*. I practically ran to the store next door, and by the time the kids and Kathy got up an hour later, I'd made them twice. They were terrific, and they appear as the first breakfast recipe in our first book, *The Happy Cookbook*.

Divine intervention or just coincidence? You be the judge.

I have always been a spiritual person and a regular churchgoer. It's where I've sat and thought about the big questions in life. I remember when Grandpa Doocy died, and I was five, I had no clue why everybody was crying and carrying on, then at the funeral I asked my mom why Grandpa was sleeping in that box at the front of the church. She told me, "He's gone to heaven . . ."

I followed up by asking where exactly was this place, and would we ever see him again? I still remember her saying, "We'll see him again in heaven, it's where everybody goes when they die, Stephen—if they're good . . ."

Wait. "Are *you* going die, Mom?" I asked, terrified that she'd leave Dad and me in the big church, with Grandpa in the box.

And to this day I remember it as if she said it yesterday, "Don't worry about me, I'm never going to die." Because she was my mom, my ultimate authority, I heard her say it and never gave it a second thought until Christmas morning, 1997, when my sister called to say Mom had passed away unexpectedly at sixty-two.

Losing a parent is as bad as it gets for a child. I was in my thirties and had trouble falling asleep for over a year, until one night about 2:30 a.m., the phone rang next to our bed and I answered it. It was my mom. We had a nice conversation that lasted a couple minutes; she was fine, she told me. She was watching me do the morning show; apparently they have cable up there. And then I woke up.

A few months later at bedtime, I was staring into space through the skylight in our bedroom and as I looked at the face of a full moon, I made a direct appeal, and it was simple. God up there in heaven, give me a sign. Let me know there is a second act, there's got to be something else. Mom, if you're up there, somewhere—show me.

I tossed and turned for a couple hours but there was no sign. The alarm clock went off at 3:27 a.m. and I was awoken by Z-100, New York's Top 40 radio station. Almost immediately I remembered that I'd asked for a sign and was disappointed that I didn't get one. I was about to turn off the clock radio when Janet Jackson started her hit song, "Together Again," about how one day she would be reunited in heaven with a lost loved one. I listened to the whole song with goose bumps the size of saucers. *That was some impressive signage*, I thought, and I felt a wave of something good wash over me. That song made my day. Of course there are people who would say that it was just the luck of the draw that I asked for a sign and then heard a song about someday seeing somebody in heaven. Coincidence.

Years later, our nine-year-old golden retriever Charlie died of cancer. The kids all came home from college and jobs to be at his side when the vet put him to sleep. When my mom had died, they were very little kids, but when Charlie died, they were young adults and had spent most of their lives with him. He wasn't a dog to them; he was like their brother.

The next day, back on TV, I was announcing a

segment called "This Day in History," and the last story had me reading this exact copy: "And it was this week in 1997 that Janet Jackson had the number one song in America with 'Together Again.'" And then the audio guy turned up the music and Janet sang that same song I'd heard years ago when I asked for a sign from above.

Coincidence, again?

Father Jerome Fasano baptized two of our children at St. Catherine of Sienna Catholic Church in our Virginia neighborhood outside Washington, DC. I attended with great regularity, and Father Fasano became a very good friend and loved Kathy's lasagna. Once the Father invited me to attend a meeting in the rectory to hear the eyewitness account of Ivan Dragicevic, one of six young people who in the 1980s claimed to have seen the Virgin Mary in Medjugorje, Bosnia. Of course I said I'd go, because I love to hear personal recollections of historical events, plus there was always cake at evening occasions at the rectory.

When I arrived, there were about twenty people in a circle made of folding chairs, and in the back of the living room was Father Fasano with the actual visionary and his translator. I got the last chair by the door and sat down. As soon as I did, Father Fasano said that before we heard the speaker's story, we would pray the Rosary, which I knew, kind of. At that time I'd probably heard the Rosary once in my life; I remembered it was the Our Father and Hail Mary over and over, and then some other prayers, which we read out of a book. While I was waiting for somebody to hand out the cheat sheets, the room started praying out loud in unison. Somebody handed me a rosary and I immediately put my finger on the first bead; everybody else was holding the crucifix, so I backed up one.

As long as everybody prayed out loud, in uni-

son, I'd be fine. And I was—until everybody stopped and then the first person in the first chair across the room from me started praying aloud—alone. This just got better—he'll pray for us. But then he stopped and the person next to him started. When that person wrapped up, the third person took over. That's when it dawned on me—soon I would be expected to lead the most religious people in my parish in a prayer I did not know. So quietly I counted the number of people left to speak and then calculated the remaining number of beads. The news was not good; I was to be leading the group in a series of prayers based on the Joyful, Sorrowful, or Glorious Mysteries, each one recited on a different day of the week. Those prayers were a mystery to me. Holy cow, my goose was cooked. With three people left before it was my turn, I was about to be revealed as a lifelong Catholic who always sat in the back row, and for good reason—*he did not know how to pray properly!*

The person to my right was just starting; I would be next and excommunicated by the time the cake was cut. I could already feel a combination of flop sweat and embarrassment when I said to myself, *God up there in heaven, please help me.*

The person next to me stopped talking. It was showtime. I cleared my throat for my public confession, hesitated awkwardly for a moment, and started to speak . . .

But just then the doorbell rang. A reprieve? I jumped up to open the door and standing there was a guy I'd sat next to many times in the back pew of our church, Supreme Court Justice of the United States of America Antonin Scalia, perhaps the most famous Catholic in the country!

"Good evening, Justice Scalia," I said. "We are wrapping up the Rosary; please take my chair. We're on that bead—and *it's your turn.*"

Charlie, their brother.

It's your turn? Where did that come from?

Scalia didn't hesitate; he sat in my chair and recited the correct Mystery to the appreciative room. He's a Supreme Court justice *and* he knows the Sorrowful Mystery? That's our Nino . . .

Antonin Scalia was my guardian angel. How many people can say that?

Okay, it could be another in an amazing series of coincidences . . .

But as we celebrate our holidays, remember, they're not just about a great menu to wow your friends and family members but also a chance to reflect on what you find spiritual.

In my life I've had big questions and asked them to the universe, and I've gotten some pretty direct answers.

As a priest once told me at a spiritual retreat, "Coincidence is God's way of remaining anonymous."

So maybe it is just a coincidence, but then again a lot of us are praying that somebody is actually listening.

Next time you have a house full of people and you pray that your soufflé doesn't fall, and it doesn't, you're either a good cook—or maybe you're getting a hand from above.

ARTICHOKE PIE

When I asked Brian Kilmeade, my TV couch-mate on *Fox & Friends*, what foods made him happy, he told me about artichoke pie. "It reminds me of our family's holidays, because there was always one on the dinner table."

I assumed it was his mother's recipe and, as it turned out, it *was* his mother's recipe. But it was also his aunt's recipe, and a recipe made by every card-carrying Kilmeade in the family.

"It was a recipe that didn't belong to any one person," Brian told me during a commercial one day. "It belonged to everybody, because every time there was a family gathering, somebody had to make it. It was done on a rotation basis, so everybody learned how to do it."

Brian thinks the recipe was probably from his Italian grandmother on his mother's side of the family, Louise D'Andrea. Brian's mother Marie's younger sister, Cathy (D'Andrea) McGoey, was the designated scribe who wrote it down and guided me through the instructions, which you'll find on the next page.

"We used to put a crust on the top, but then one time we tried toasted panko," Cathy told me, and because the change was happily received, "we've been making it that way ever since."

Aside from the panko, there's one other choice you have to make, and that's whether or not to include a meat like salami or pepperoni. Cathy says the family is split—half the family likes it with, the other half of the family without, like every other family in America. At least they're not polarized over panko . . .

This artichoke pie is so easy and delicious that it's become part of the Doocy holiday table. Give it a try and you'll see why.

Thanks, Kilmeades.

(continued)

Two 14-ounce cans artichoke hearts
1 tablespoon plus 2 teaspoons olive oil
1 large garlic clove, thinly sliced
½ cup panko bread crumbs
6 large eggs
½ teaspoon freshly ground black pepper
1½ cups shredded mozzarella cheese
    (about 6 ounces)
½ cup grated Pecorino Romano cheese
½ cup diced hard salami or sliced pepperoni
    (optional)
1 frozen deep-dish pie crust

1. Preheat the oven to 350°F.

2. Drain the artichokes, then squeeze out any extra liquid. Cut them into ¾-inch chunks.

3. In a skillet, heat 1 tablespoon of the olive oil over medium-high heat. Add the garlic, give it a stir to flavorize the oil, then add the artichokes.

Sauté until the garlic starts to turn a little golden on the edges, a minute or two. Transfer the garlic and artichokes to a plate to cool down.

4. In a small bowl, combine the panko and remaining 2 teaspoons olive oil. Mix with a fork to distribute the oil evenly. Set aside.

5. Crack the eggs into a large bowl, then add the pepper and whisk until smooth. Add both cheeses and give a nice stir. Add the slightly cooled artichokes and stir well. Mix in the salami or pepperoni (if using).

6. Transfer the mixture to the pie crust, level it out, and sprinkle with the panko. Bake until golden brown, about 50 minutes. Let it sit for at least 5 minutes to compose itself, then cut it pie-style and serve warm.

FRANK THE BANK'S CREPE-STYLE MANICOTTI

My neighbor Frank, aka Frank the Bank (he works for a major mortgage company), remembers having this dish at every major holiday meal of his life. Thanksgiving, Christmas, Easter—this crepe-style manicotti was always there. For years Frank was parked at the kids' table at Grandma Jenny's house, where once you walked in the door, you would talk and eat until the time you walked out. If people left hungry, Grandma hadn't done her job.

Jenny would start every holiday off with the antipasti course: a kaleidoscopic array of meats and cheeses. Next, still in the appetizer-y phase, she'd present platters of these wonderful manicottis, but instead of tube noodles, they were made with light, delicate crepes that were a taste of cheesy heaven. They are unforgettable! Just know that making these crepes is easier and faster than you think, and it's so worth it—that's why this is a family classic. The crepes would be followed by the main dishes of lemon chicken, a veal or pork roast, plus another kind of pasta, building to a culinary crescendo with a dessert table that would stretch across the dining room.

"Lotta food—it was a long day," Frank told me.

This recipe wasn't passed down to Frank from Grandma Jenny. He got it from his father, who once was an accountant for Volkswagen USA. When VW announced its plan to relocate operations from northern New Jersey to Detroit, Frank's dad quit.

But now that he was out of work, how would he feed his family? Luckily an aunt asked if he'd like to help her run an Italian deli she owned in Hasbrouck Heights, New Jersey, famously called Famiglia, which means "family" in Italian. Frank's dad jumped at the chance to join a family business. What would you rather do, sit at a desk at Volkswagen HQ studying Jetta and Passat cost-per-unit sales or run an Italian deli, surrounded by fresh mozzarella, sausages, and the most tempting foods in the world? "A fresh batch of ravioli . . . I'm gonna have to taste test it!" What a great job! When Frank's aunt retired, his father took over and ran the place for decades.

Today Frank the Bank, who loves to cook and has won various cooking contests, makes this recipe for his entire family, who now gather at his home every holiday, I know this because he lives across the street from our house. Frank loves it because it reminds him of growing up in New Jersey and being part of a big, proud, noisy Italian family. I mention noisy because when Frank hosts family dinners, I can always hear a lot of laughter.

(continued)

CREPES

6 large eggs
½ teaspoon table salt
2 cups all-purpose flour

FILLING

2 large eggs
1½ pounds (24 ounces) ricotta cheese
½ cup finely grated Parmesan cheese, plus more for garnish
2 tablespoons chopped Italian parsley
½ teaspoon table salt
½ teaspoon freshly ground black pepper

FOR FINISHING

Olive oil cooking spray or 2 tablespoons olive oil
Your favorite jarred marinara (we use Rao's brand; Frank makes his own)

1. To make the crepes: In a large bowl, whisk the eggs. Add 3 cups of water and the salt and whisk again. While whisking constantly, add the flour. The batter will not be thick. Place in the fridge to chill while you make the filling.

2. To make the filling: In another large bowl, combine the eggs, ricotta, Parmesan, parsley, salt, and pepper and mix until well blended. Place the filling into a gallon-size zip-top bag, seal it, and squeeze it toward the bottom of the bag. Place in the fridge to chill.

3. To cook the crepes, warm a nonstick skillet or crepe pan over medium heat. You can lightly coat the pan with olive oil cooking spray, but I do what Frank does: pour a couple tablespoons of olive oil in a little bowl, then dunk a paper towel in the oil and carefully and lightly rub it over the bottom and just up the sides of the pan.

4. Using a soup ladle, measure out enough batter to cover the bottom of the skillet or crepe pan and pour the batter into the pan, moving it around to make sure it's in a thin round layer. After about a minute, move the pan side to side to make sure the crepe is not stuck to the pan. Cook the crepe for about 3 minutes, watching for the top to start to dry out. When the whole top appears dry, carefully run a spatula all the way around the edges, then flip. Cook the other side a few minutes, until golden-brown dots appear, then set it aside on wax paper. Repeat to make the rest of the crepes, placing wax paper between them so they don't stick.

5. Adjust an oven rack to the center position and preheat the oven to 425°F.

6. Frank uses one of those 12 × 20-inch disposable aluminum foil steam table pans you can get at the grocery. You can use any very large baking dish or ovenproof pan. Spread at least ½ cup of the marinara thinly on the bottom (this will keep the manicotti from sticking). Lay a crepe out on a flat surface. Cut 1 inch off a corner of the bag of cheese filling. Using the bag as you would a piping bag, squeeze out a log of the cheese from one side of the crepe to the other, then roll up the crepe and place it seam side down in the pan. Repeat until you've filled them all, then top each crepe with an equal amount of the marinara sauce and sprinkle with Parmesan.

7. Cut foil to cover the pan and spray it with cooking spray so it won't stick to the crepes. Cover and bake until the cheese is melty and the crepes start to turn a golden brown, 20 to 25 minutes.

8. Let rest a few minutes, then serve. *Delizioso!*

THANKSGIVING CORN SPOONBREAD

MAKES 9 SERVINGS

Going through some family photographs, I found a great one of Kathy making an early Thanksgiving dinner. She has such a big smile as she bakes a batch of Pillsbury crescent rolls, with the empty turkey pan behind her, the bird already parked on a platter. Behind that, the imported fruit and herb tile that I installed myself to save money. Of course I didn't know how to do it when I started, but I got a book from Home Depot, and I've been doing kitchen backsplashes ever since. My grout lines are great.

We loved that kitchen and made a lot of great memories there. A few years later, when we were moving to New Jersey, we needed help cleaning the house—fast—so we hired a cleaning lady who we were told was expensive but fast, and when she left the house it was gleaming. Next day, the home inspector called and said that he couldn't approve the sale because the inside of the oven was ruined. Apparently our expensive cleaning lady had used scouring pads and abrasive oven cleaner that wrecked the self-cleaning function. Who knew? When the new owners moved in, they had a brand-new oven that we could never afford. You're welcome!

Looking at those early Thanksgiving photos, we had the same menu as today, with a few exceptions. In the beginning she'd just microwave a box of corn, dump it in a bowl, add a pat of butter, and dinner was served. Then, after a visit to the legendary chicken joint the Brookville Hotel in Kansas, she asked the waitress for the secret to their cream-style corn. "Hold on," the waitress said, and returned to the table with the secret recipe professionally printed on a postcard. Their secret ingredient was whipping cream.

After making this new favorite for twenty-five consecutive Thanksgivings, Kathy was on the hunt for a new corn dish, and we found it during one of our summer vacations to the Lowcountry of South Carolina, when we tried spoonbread. Which didn't make any sense, because it wasn't served with a spoon and it certainly wasn't bread. It's more of a soufflé of corn. You could call it corn soufflé, but spoonbread just sounds like somebody's grandma made it with love.

A perfect complement to your turkey and green bean casserole, it takes only five minutes to prep, and cleanup is easy. And it's not going to destroy your oven . . . use the cleaning lady for that.

Cooking spray

2 large eggs

1 cup ricotta cheese

½ cup fat-free half-and-half or milk

One 8.5-ounce box corn muffin mix
(Jiffy brand works great)

1 tablespoon sugar

1 teaspoon table salt

½ teaspoon freshly ground black pepper

One 14.75-ounce can cream-style sweet
corn

One 15.25-ounce can whole corn, drained

½ cup grated Cheddar cheese

2 jalapeño peppers, halved, seeded, and
minced (optional)

1. Adjust an oven rack to its highest position and preheat the oven to 400°F. Coat an 8 × 8-inch baking dish with cooking spray.

2. In a large bowl, whisk the eggs. Add the ricotta and half-and-half and mix until smooth-ish. Add the corn muffin mix, sugar, salt, and pepper and stir until just combined. Fold in the cream-style and regular corn and stir in the Cheddar and jalapeños (if using) for a little color.

3. Pour the mixture into the prepared pan. Bake until the spoonbread is golden on top and the center is no longer jiggly, 35 to 45 minutes.

4. Let it rest a few minutes, cut it into 9 squares, and serve.

One of Kathy's early Thanksgivings.

MIMI'S SOUTHERN CORN BREAD DRESSING

MAKES 8 SERVINGS

You'll love this dressing from Ainsley Earhardt's grandmother Mimi who made this super-easy and delightful dressing for important family meals.

"It is one of my favorites for many reasons," Ainsley says. "First of all, it's delicious, especially with gravy drizzled on top. Second, it reminds me of home, holidays, celebrations, and of course my sweet grandmother."

Ainsley called her Mimi, but her name was Ann Giles, and she had a lasting impact on Ainsley's life. "The most loving Christian lady," Ainsley calls her.

Ann was also a clever cook, and this recipe uses a pan of home-baked corn bread, prepared with onion and celery to kick it up a notch. Mimi would use turkey drippings and stock from the turkey, which is our first choice, but if you're in a hurry (and who isn't) you can use melted butter instead of the drippings and store-bought turkey stock. Either way, it's simple, and a nice change of pace from typical dressings served at big family events.

Thanks to Ainsley's aunt, Lynn Giles Young, for kindly sharing this family recipe.

CORN BREAD
Cooking spray
One 8.5-ounce box corn muffin mix
   (Jiffy brand works great)
1 large egg
⅓ cup milk
1 medium yellow onion, finely chopped
3 celery stalks, finely chopped

DRESSING
5 large eggs
One 8-ounce package Pepperidge Farm
   Herb Seasoned Classic Stuffing
⅔ cup (1⅓ sticks) butter, melted, or turkey
   drippings
1 cup turkey or chicken stock, homemade
   or store-bought
Turkey gravy, for serving

1. Preheat the oven to 400°F. Coat an 8 × 8-inch baking dish with cooking spray.

2. To make the cornbread: In a medium bowl, mix the corn muffin mix, egg, milk, onion, and celery until just combined, then pour into the prepared baking dish.

3. Bake until it has a nice golden top, 20 to 25 minutes. Set aside to cool.

4. Reduce the oven temperature to 350°F. Spray an 8 × 13-inch baking dish with cooking spray.

5. To make the dressing: In a large bowl, whisk the eggs and add the seasoned stuffing. Crumble the homemade corn bread into the bowl. Pour in the melted butter and turkey or chicken stock. Mix until all the dry items are moistened, then evenly spoon the dressing into the prepared baking dish.

6. Bake until browned on top, about 30 minutes. Cut into pieces. Serve with turkey gravy for drizzling.

JIM'S DANDY MAPLE BACON ACORN SQUASH

MAKES 4 SERVINGS

My dad loved acorn squashes.

If my mom was baking something that would require the oven to be on for about an hour, she'd always make my father an acorn squash. So easy—a little brown sugar, butter, and maple syrup—she never measured, and I never saw her watch the clock, because she had other methods to tell when food was done. One of her secrets was placing a strip of bacon across the top of each half-squash, and when the bacon was crispy the squash was perfect, having soaked in sugar and butter for about an hour.

When I was living on my own as a bachelor, this was the one thing I knew I could make exactly as it was from my childhood. Clearly, vividly, perfectly. If only life were this simple.

When my mom made acorn squash, it took an hour to bake and sometimes it still wasn't done. Thanks to microwaves, it's done in half that time, and just as tasty.

2 acorn squashes
2 teaspoons pure maple syrup
2 teaspoons light brown sugar
4 tablespoons (½ stick) butter
(2 tablespoons melted and
2 tablespoons unmelted)
¼ cup chopped cooked bacon (for speed we
use Oscar Mayer Real Bacon Bits)

1. Preheat the oven to 400°F.

2. Slice the squashes in half through the stem and scrape out the seeds. Place cut side down on a microwave-safe plate and microwave for 3 to 4 minutes, depending on the size of the squash.

3. Meanwhile, in a small bowl, mix the maple syrup, brown sugar, and melted butter to form a delicious sweet confection.

4. Place the squashes in a 9 x 9-inch baking dish, cut side up. Brush the cavities with the sugar-syrup-butter mixture and then place a pat of butter in each one.

5. Bake until the edges start to turn a little brown, about 15 minutes.

6. Dip a brush into the melted butter mixture in the cavity of the squash and use it to brush the cavity and cut sides. Toss the bacon crumbles on top. Let the squash halves cool down a few minutes before serving.

BACON-BRAIDED
SMOKED TURKEY BREAST

MAKES 6 TO 8 SERVINGS

Make this turkey for your holiday meal and your guests will not only rave over how smoky and delicious it is, but this could be the first bird you've ever cooked where everybody wants to take a picture of it instead of assembled family members.

The reason is simple: "People love bacon," John McLemore told me, and he's right.

You've seen John on *Fox & Friends* many times, working magic with his world-famous Masterbuilt smokers. He came up with this recipe by combining a smoked turkey with his famous Fatty. What's a Fatty? A Fatty is a lattice weave, as on a pie crust, only made of bacon. Can this man please be awarded the Nobel Prize for Pork?

It's this kind of clever thinking that's made his company an industry leader. In the 1970s his father, Dawson, started making fish fryers in their backyard and selling them out of the back of his truck. A man of deep faith, he made a deal with the Almighty. It was simple—if God could help him, he'd name the company after Him. The fish fryers started to take off, and Dawson kept his word and named the company after the Lord. God is the Master, and Dawson was the builder. Master + builder = Masterbuilt.

To this day their priorities are faith first, family second, then the rest.

One of the early challenges was that most people had no idea how to use their cooking machines. So not only did they sell them the equipment, they told them what to cook on it with recipes. The early Masterbuilt recipes were classic American dishes the family grew up eating from their mom and dad's kitchen, but they adapted them to use with whatever they were selling, whether it was a fryer, smoker, or grill.

In this recipe, because it is just the turkey breast, it's faster than smoking a whole bird, but it's still hours in the smoker, so plan accordingly. Just know you need two pieces of special equipment: a smoker (we have a Masterbuilt) and a meat or marinade injection syringe, easily found online or in cooking supply stores.

As for this bacon-braided smoked turkey, why does it make John happy?

"It's fun to make, and when you serve it, people go . . . *Wow!* If you want something elegant, with great table presence, especially at Thanksgiving, this is it."

(continued)

One 6- to 7-pound bone-in turkey breast
One 16-ounce bottle apple cider vinegar
One 12-ounce bottle honey
¼ teaspoon cayenne pepper
16 slices bacon (about 1 pound)
2 tablespoons freshly ground black pepper

1. Preheat a smoker to 275°F. We use applewood chips.

2. Let's start with some turkey prep. A bone-in turkey breast will come with the back and ribs. With kitchen shears, cut the back off the turkey breast and remove the ribs, trying to do it in such a way that when the breast sits right side up on the cutting board, the bottom will be flat. Remove the skin.

3. John is very clever in how he uses the vinegar and honey bottles as mixing jars. It saves on cleanup, and it's easy to eyeball measurements. Pour 1 cup of the apple cider vinegar (half the bottle) into the smoker water bowl to give it a nice flavor. Pour ½ cup of the honey into the half-empty vinegar bottle. Add the cayenne, cover the bottle, and really give it a shake. Fill the marinade injection syringe with this mixture and inject the turkey breast all over to flavor the meat from the inside. Use about 1 ounce (2 tablespoons) of marinade per pound.

4. Now for the creative part! Let's make the bacon weave. On a piece of wax or parchment paper, lay 8 bacon slices side by side horizontally. On the left side of the strips, starting at the bottom, fold that first slice to the *right* a few inches, along with the third, fifth, and seventh slices.

5. Place a slice of bacon on the left side running vertically (perpendicular to the other slices). It will cover the pieces you did not fold. Unfold the 4 strips to cover the perpendicular strip.

6. Fold the second, fourth, sixth, and eighth horizontal strips to the *left*, over the first vertical strip. Place a slice of bacon flush with that first vertical slice. Unfold the 4 folded bacon slices.

7. Now you have the pattern for the entire weave! Repeat the process with the remaining 6 bacon slices. (If you need more help, look online; there are plenty of bacon-weave videos that make it easy to understand.)

8. Flip the turkey breast, so it's upside down in the middle of the bacon weave. Cinch up the sides of the bacon weave so it's evenly spaced over the breast, then flip over the whole turkey and flatten the bacon on the sides. Place the bacon-braided breast on the middle rack of the smoker and set the smoker for 3 hours.

9. While the turkey is smoking, let's make the glaze. Add the black pepper to the remaining honey in the bottle, cover, and shake like crazy. Set it aside at room temperature.

10. After 2 hours of smoking, remove the turkey and drizzle half of the honey bottle glaze over the top of it. Return to the smoker for 1 hour more, until the internal temp of the turkey is 165°F.

11. Present your bacon-braided smoked turkey to friends and family for a quick photo session.

12. To cut for serving, make a single incision down the breast plate and pull the whole half-breast off. Place it on a cutting board and cut it into ¾-inch-thick slices, holding the bacon in place on top. Drizzle more of the honey on top and serve.

MARCUS LUTTRELL'S MAMA'S PRIME RIB

MAKES 8 TO 10 SERVINGS

From deep in the heart of Texas, this is a Luttrell family favorite meal. It must have special powers, because Marcus's mother, Holly, always made it on major holidays, and the Luttrell twins, Marcus and Morgan, both grew up big and strong and eventually both became Navy SEALs.

To this day, Marcus will request it "every time Mama whips up a big meal."

Marcus's wife, Melanie, shared this recipe with us; she's been collecting recipes from patriotic families all over America, including some of the families of the SEALs who died in Operation Red Wings, which the movie *Lone Survivor* was based upon. One day Melanie would like to be able to share all those recipes, and she told me if she ever published a patriotic cookbook she'd write that service starts at the dinner table. She says she'd call the book *Served*, which seems just about perfect.

How good is this prime rib recipe? One time a professional photographer was at the Luttrell home taking pictures while a prime rib was in the oven, and he said he was a vegetarian but the smell was driving him crazy. Eventually he asked for a tiny taste.

"Wow, that's good! Would you have enough to send me home with a plate?" And they did.

Holly says, "I turned a vegetarian into a carnivore with this prime rib . . ."

This will take a couple hours roasting in the oven, so while it's cooking, raise a glass to the Luttrell family of patriots who shared this hearty and delicious recipe with all of us, and another toast to all of those who have *Served!*

One 5-pound bone-in prime rib
6 garlic cloves, cut lengthwise down the
    middle, making 12 pieces
¼ cup vegetable oil
Six 1-ounce packets beefy onion soup mix
    (Lipton works great)
2 tablespoons sea salt
¼ cup cracked black pepper
2 tablespoons seasoned salt (Lawry's is
    terrific)
Jarred horseradish sauce (optional)

1. Let the roast sit out for about 30 minutes to come closer to room temperature.

2. Adjust an oven rack to the lowest position and preheat the oven to 350°F. Line a large roasting pan with foil and set a roasting rack inside.

3. The secret to the flavor is inserting the garlic deep into the roast. Make twelve 2-inch-deep cuts between the ribs and push a slice of garlic deep into each cut. The thinner the garlic slices, the easier they are to insert.

4. Rub the roast with the oil, then the soup mix, entirely covering the meat. Liberally season the roast with the sea salt, pepper, and seasoned salt.

5. Place a meat thermometer in the thickest part of the roast and set the roast fat side up on the prepared roasting rack. The roasting time is about 2 hours, but you'll need to monitor the internal temperature throughout the roasting; you'd hate to overcook such a beautiful piece of beef! The USDA's recommended safe cooking temperature for beef is 145°F. Keep in mind that the temperature of the meat will rise 5° to 10°F after it comes out of the oven.

6. Remove the roast from the oven, wrap it in foil, and let it rest for 20 to 30 minutes. Slice it up and serve it to smiles all around. Some of the Doocys like a touch of horseradish on the side, and maybe someone will at your house, too, so that's also a nice option. The day after we made this for one Christmas dinner, Marcus wrote me to say, "The prime rib is great for breakfast if y'all have some left . . ." Too late, no leftovers on this one!

GLORIOUS LEFTOVERS GALETTE

The day after Thanksgiving is the biggest shopping day of the year, and it's also the biggest leftover day of the year. Unless you're like our friends who on the big day had just taken the turkey out of the oven and had gone into the TV room to watch the football game as the bird rested for the prescribed 20 to 30 minutes. When they returned to the kitchen, they immediately noticed that about 10 pounds of the 16-pound turkey were missing. They turned to their dog, who was under the bird and offered them nothing but a guilty look.

But if your dog didn't eat the turkey, what are you going to do with all those leftovers? Don't just warm everything up again and palm it off as new; whip up this easy-to-make recipe, inspired by our daughter Mary's friend Martha, who is the best cook Mary's ever met. Martha grew up in Wisconsin and Illinois and hosts once-a-week baking parties, where she got Mary hooked on galettes.

This is an easy way to give you a different taste of Thanksgiving in every bite. When I taste the stuffing, it reminds me of Kathy's; the sweet potatoes remind me of the Market Basket store in New Jersey where Peter worked as a stock boy in high school, and the turkey takes me back to every one of my mom's Butterballs.

The listed amount of leftovers is just a suggestion; whatever you've got will be just fine if it's close. And remember, this is also a joyous recipe, because it marks *the end of the leftovers*! Tomorrow we get new food . . .

2 refrigerated pie crusts, at room
    temperature
1 to 2 cups diced or shredded leftover
    turkey
2 cups leftover mashed potatoes
1 cup leftover sweet potato casserole
1 cup leftover stuffing
1 cup turkey gravy

1. Adjust an oven rack in the center and preheat the oven to 400°F.

2. A single store-bought pie crust is just too small for this extravaganza, so we're going to make it bigger. Lay out a stretch of parchment paper that will fit inside a sheet pan. Unroll one pie crust in the center of the paper, then unroll the second pie crust and place it right on top of the first, so that it's a double thickness. Gently crimp the edges with your fingers to fuse the crusts together. Use a rolling pin to roll out the dough, making it as round as you can and as large as you can. Don't go too thin, and keep the round no wider than the parchment paper. Place the paper with the rolled-out crust on the sheet pan.

3. Arrange the turkey all over the crust, leaving a couple inches empty around the edges, because at the end you'll be folding the edges up and over the leftovers.

4. Let's spoon the spuds over the turkey and smooth them out. We like to create colorful potato zones for variety. Starting in the center,

(continued)

make a small pile of mashed potatoes and then take a spoon and level them out so they create a 3- to 4-inch round of spuds that's about ½ inch deep. Place the sweet potato casserole in dollops in a ring around the mashed potatoes, still leaving an inch or two empty at the edges. Smooth out the sweet potatoes.

5. Crumble the stuffing over the potatoes and then drizzle the gravy evenly over all those savory leftovers. There is no wrong way to do this— just be artistic! Like snowflakes, no two leftover galettes are ever the same.

6. Time to fold the crust! Start on one side and slowly go all the way around the crust, folding the dough edges up and in toward the leftovers while pleating them closed. It's not supposed to look perfect; it's supposed to be rustic.

7. Bake for 45 to 50 minutes to heat through and brown the crust. If you spot the gravy bubbling up from the middle, that's a good sign it's heated up and ready to devour.

8. Let the galette rest for 10 minutes. Use a pizza cutter to cut it into 6 pie-style wedges and serve. You'll never look at Thanksgiving leftovers the same way again!

Fox & Friends Thanksgiving 2019.

SHOW-OFF PUMPKIN PIE WITH CINNAMON ROLL CRUST

MAKES ONE 10-INCH PIE

In the last year, we've had all the kids' bedrooms repainted. At one point I had all their diplomas off their walls out in the hall, and it dawned on me that people rarely go into their rooms. It seemed a shame that the diplomas they'd worked so hard to receive were so hidden away. So I decided I would put them together in one place. But where? We settled on one wall of the dining room. You'd never see them from the front door or the hall; you'd have to be seated at the table. But when I sat down and looked up at that wall of achievement, as any proud father, the first thing I thought was, *Do you know what those diplomas cost me?* It's the most expensive wall art in Doocy family history.

We had some neighbors over for dinner a few weeks ago, and halfway through, one of them took a look at all those diplomas and said, "Whoa . . . are you showing off?" I hadn't thought about it like that until right then. I guess we were—but it was really about pride.

It's okay to show off every once in a while, and we consider this recipe a good way to show off in the kitchen for a big meal. With its clever cinnamon roll swirled crust, this is a showstopper of a pie. You can't buy it in the store, it's pretty easy to make, and everybody will want a piece.

By the way, this past Thanksgiving, as we gathered around the table, Peter, our TV reporter and professional observer, mentioned something that we'd never thought about: Mary's Boston College diploma is in Latin and unreadable—to us at least. Did she actually graduate? Not sure; what I do know is I'd love another piece of this pie, right after I Instagram a photo of it.

2 large eggs
One 12-ounce can evaporated milk
One 15-ounce can unsweetened pumpkin
    puree
1½ teaspoons pumpkin pie spice, plus more
    for garnish
1 cup plus 2 tablespoons granulated sugar
¼ cup packed dark brown sugar
1 teaspoon ground cinnamon
2 refrigerated pie crusts, at room
    temperature
2 tablespoons butter, melted
Cooking spray
1 cup cold heavy cream
½ teaspoon pure vanilla extract

1. Preheat the oven to 375°F.

2. In a large bowl, whisk the eggs and evaporated milk well. Add the pumpkin puree, pumpkin pie spice, and 1 cup of the granulated sugar and whisk until smooth. Set aside.

3. In a small bowl, combine the brown sugar and cinnamon.

4. Roll out the pie crusts flat and paint the tops with the melted butter. Sprinkle both crusts with the brown sugar–cinnamon mixture. Starting at one end of each crust, roll the crusts into two tight logs. With a sharp knife, cut off the ends of each crust log, then cut each crust into ½-inch

(continued)

pieces. Try to keep the log as round as possible during the cutting.

5. If you have a 10-inch glass pie plate, use that, so more of the crust is visible—remember, this is a show-off pie! Pull off a sheet of parchment paper that's about 15 inches long. Place it slippery side down on a work surface, then flip your pie plate upside down in the center of the paper. Use a pencil to trace a circle on the paper that's about 1 inch wider than the pie plate, to give you an idea how big to roll out the crust. Set the pie plate and paper aside.

6. Pull off another piece of parchment paper, about 15 inches long. Set it slippery side up. Starting in the center of that paper, lay the pie crust rings in one flat layer to form a round. Set the pencil-marked parchment paper over the pie crust rings, pencil side up, and arrange it so the pie crust rings are within the pencil circle.

7. Use the palms of your hands to gently push down on the rings to flatten them a bit, then use a rolling pin to carefully roll out the crust, extending it to just inside the pencil marks. If one side is a little lopsided, roll the pin in that direction a few times with a little extra pressure until you meet the line. Try not to make the crust too thin in any spot. Carefully peel the top piece of parchment off the crust. Look how pretty that is!

8. Coat the pie plate with cooking spray (including the top lip), then invert the plate over the crust and carefully flip it into the plate. Carefully peel the parchment off the crust and adjust the crust. I don't crimp or cut it on the top like a regular crust; I like to see the round tops of the flattened cinnamon rolls right up to the outer edge of the pie plate rim. Use your fingers to close any holes or spots where the crust has pulled apart. Pour the filling into the crust and cover the crust edges with foil strips to keep them from browning too quickly.

9. Bake for 40 minutes. Remove the foil and bake until the center is no longer jiggly, another 15 to 25 minutes.

10. Let the pie cool at room temperature, then refrigerate it for at least 2 hours.

11. For the whipped cream, refrigerate a medium bowl and the mixer beaters for at least 15 minutes. Right before serving the pie, in a small bowl, combine the heavy cream, remaining 2 tablespoons granulated sugar, and the vanilla. Whisk well. Pour the mixture into the chilled bowl and, using the chilled beaters, start mixing on medium speed, then on high speed until stiff peaks appear when you pull the beaters out.

12. You can spread the whipped cream over the entire pie or dollop it onto single wedges. Dust lightly with pumpkin pie spice if desired and serve. Store any leftovers in the fridge—like there are going to be leftovers—ha!

CHRISTIE'S CHRISTMAS COOKIES

MAKES ABOUT 5 DOZEN COOKIES

There are some things that are so good we only make them once or twice a year, to keep them special. These snickerdoodles are one of those recipes.

The original test kitchen for this recipe was actually a public school cafeteria kitchen in Michigan, where our friend Christie de Nicola's Grandma Jack was one of the lunch ladies. Lunch ladies have very high food standards, and these cookies were such a hit that they passed the recipe around to one another and would occasionally even treat the schoolkids to this little taste of heaven.

Christie's family has been making this recipe for more than fifty years. She still has the original 3 × 5 index card in the handwriting of a wonderful grandmother who loved kids so much that she served them lunch every day, for decades—with a smile.

Christie makes these once a year, because they are the quintessential Christmas cookie.

2¾ cups all-purpose flour
2 teaspoons cream of tartar
1 teaspoon baking soda
1 teaspoon table salt
1½ cups plus 6 tablespoons sugar
2 teaspoons ground cinnamon
1 cup Crisco
2 large eggs
1 teaspoon pure vanilla extract

1. Preheat the oven to 375°F.

2. Over a medium bowl, sift together the flour, cream of tartar, baking soda, and salt. (Why sift the flour? It makes it lighter and easier to mix when making cookie dough. If you don't have a sifter, simply whisk the ingredients in the bowl.) Set aside.

3. In a small bowl, combine 6 tablespoons of the sugar and the cinnamon. Give a stir to mix it up well. Set aside.

4. In a bowl, with an electric mixer, combine the Crisco and remaining 1½ cups of sugar. Start the mixer on low speed. When you have those two ingredients going, add the eggs one at a time, then the vanilla. Slowly add the flour mixture and continue mixing until you have a smooth cookie dough.

5. Take a walnut-size dab of dough (1 big tablespoon) and roll it lightly into a ball (don't press or pack the dough). Roll the ball in the cinnamon-sugar to coat and set it on an ungreased baking sheet. Repeat to make the rest of the balls, spacing them at least 1½ inches apart, as they spread *waaaay* out when baked.

6. Bake until the edges are a little golden, about 10 minutes. Remove the baking sheet to a counter and let the cookies sit for 5 minutes; the bottom will keep crisping. Use a spatula to remove them to a cooling rack or sheet of foil, until the kids raid the kitchen and eat half the batch.

LEFTOVER PUMPKIN PIE GROWN-UP SMOOTHIE

MAKES 2 SERVINGS

You had a twenty-pound Thanksgiving turkey, and you had to move quickly, because leftovers are only safe in the fridge for three, maybe four days. Luckily you had many menu choices: turkey pot pies, turkey quesadillas, turkey enchiladas, turkey Cobb salad, turkey soup, turkey tetrazzini, turkey chili, and open-faced turkey sandwiches.

But then there's the leftover pumpkin pie. There are only two ways to eat it: plain or with a topping. It gets boring on Day Two.

My daughter Mary, the smoothie maker, and I came up with this recipe one morning when we didn't have fruit for a smoothie, but we had pie! It's become a holiday highlight after brunch or dinner.

This is so easy and so tasty—and if you're of legal age you can add a hint of hooch with a splash of bourbon. Obviously, don't let kids drink bourbon or whiskey; first of all, it's illegal, and second, they're kids and will find the taste revolting. As a six-year-old, I sipped my dad's Coors and gagged . . . until college, when I made a miraculous recovery.

Most kids have never had any alcohol and aren't interested anyway, right? A friend of mine, who had installed a bar in his man cave, had just poured himself a Cabernet and then turned to his fourteen-year-old and asked, "What'll it be, son?"

A very shy young man, his son paused and meekly said, "Really, Dad?"

His grinning father answered, "Sure."

"In that case, Pops, gimme a Jack 'n' Coke, twist of lime."

His father was stunned. Does that sound like any kid's *first drink*? What happened to starting out simple with a beer or White Claw? And who before the age of twenty ever ordered *Jack 'n' Coke, twist of lime* other than Kid Rock?

As for this recipe, the bourbon is for the adults only. Feel free to card people at the table—it's a great conversation starter.

2 scoops vanilla ice cream (dairy-free ice cream also works)
¼ cup milk (soy or almond milk also works)
1 slice leftover pumpkin pie
1 cup ice cubes
1, 2, or 3 teaspoons bourbon (optional, for an adult version)
Whipped cream (optional)
Pinch of pumpkin pie spice (optional)

1. In a blender, add the ingredients in this order: ice cream at the bottom, then milk, pie, and ice cubes. If you'd like an adult version with a taste of bourbon, add it now. If you wouldn't, skip it.

2. Secure the lid and pulse until the ice cubes are pulverized. The mixture will be smooth and maybe a little grainy from the pie crust; that's perfect. If too thick to pour, add a little more milk and blend some more, or add a few more ice cubes if needed.

3. Divide into two glasses or mugs, and then give the tops a shot of whipped cream and a dusting of pumpkin pie spice on the top if you'd like. Straws are good but spoons are better. Now those are good leftovers!

PAVLOVA

Two of my Fox News bosses, Rupert and Lachlan Murdoch, congratulated me on the success of *The Happy Cookbook* one day during a commercial break on *Fox & Friends*. I told them that almost everybody could identify with the book's premise, which was that there are some foods that make them feel happy. When I asked Lachlan what his was when he was growing up in Australia, he paused for less than a second and said, "I *loved* pavlova!"

I immediately nodded in approval, despite having no idea what that was.

Lachlan described it as a meringue with whipped cream, and I knew *exactly* what it was—our friend Madeleine Van Duren made it all the time. Her aunt ran a restaurant in Ireland and this was her specialty. When Madeleine started cooking, her aunt gave her the recipe, but in European measurements. Clever; that's one way to always be the best cook in the family . . . bequeath a recipe that nobody can make!

Over time she figured out how to make it taste exactly as it did at the family restaurant in Ireland—and it's wonderful, whatever it's called.

Lachlan also tells me that it's traditional in Australia to add some canned passion fruit syrup on top as the very last thing. Again I nodded with approval, despite having no idea what canned passion fruit syrup was. But I found it, used it, and it's a tasty treat!

3 egg whites
¼ teaspoon cream of tartar
¾ cup granulated sugar
1 cup heavy cream
3 tablespoons powdered sugar
½ teaspoon pure vanilla extract
Fresh fruit for serving, such as strawberries, raspberries, or blackberries
Canned passion fruit syrup for topping, if you can find it (optional)

1. Preheat the oven to 225°F.

2. Cut a 15-inch length of parchment paper to fit a sheet pan. With a pencil, in the middle of the paper, draw about an 8-inch circle (the size of our salad plates). It doesn't have to be exact. Flip it over onto the sheet pan so the pencil markings are on the bottom. (You can also draw a heart for Valentine's Day, or a wreath around Christmastime—just make sure it's about the same size.)

3. To make the pavlova meringue: In your mixer bowl, use the wire whip attachment to beat the egg whites and cream of tartar on medium speed until foamy. Slowly add the granulated sugar, then turn the mixer to high and beat until stiff peaks form. Do not underbeat or it will ooze all over the place.

4. Spoon the meringue in a round onto the parchment paper, fitting it within the circle you drew earlier. Think of it as the first layer on a two-layer cake, with rounded sides and a flat top. Use a spoon to give the outside edge a slightly raised "curb," which will hold the whipped cream in place later. (Clean the mixing bowl and set it in the fridge to chill for later.)

5. Bake for 1 hour 30 minutes. Turn off the oven but leave the meringue inside for another hour; the top will appear dry and even cracked. Remove from the oven and let it cool on the sheet pan.

6. When you're ready to serve, make the whipped cream in the cold mixing bowl. Beat the heavy cream, powdered sugar, and vanilla on high speed until stiff peaks form.

7. Decorate the top of the pavlova with the whipped cream. We like to place it on top of the meringue as if it were a second layer, straight up the sides from the pavlova and flat on the top, to essentially make it twice as tall as it was. We top the whipped cream with fresh berries; Lachlan Murdoch tops his with canned passion fruit syrup.

CLASSIC RICE PUDDING WITH A SURPRISE

Suzanne Scott, the CEO of Fox News and Fox Business, has a wonderful Christmas Eve family tradition that started generations ago at her Aunt Astrid's home. She would lead the family in Christmas caroling and then have a legendary dinner for their entire Gunderson family, many of whom had immigrated to New Jersey directly from Norway.

After the holiday dinner, and before the gifts were exchanged, Astrid would serve everyone authentic cookies called *krumkake* and a dessert they waited a year to have, a small dish of rice pudding, or as the Norwegians call it, *riskrem*. It was always a high point, not because it's delicious and simple, but because at the bottom of one single dish was a nut that Astrid would hide before her guests arrived.

"I've got it!" somebody would holler, and Astrid would proudly present that one person with a gift that went with finding the nut. The gift varied year to year; it might be a fancy piece of chocolate, a little soap, or maybe a board game, nothing too extravagant. Yet to the family member who got it, it was like winning a Rolex.

It's a happy memory from her childhood, and Suzanne keeps this tradition alive by hosting an annual Christmas Eve dinner at her home. She leads the family in Christmas carols (Suzanne still has her aunt's original sheet music), and after dinner she serves the rice pudding and somebody gets a prize. Of course it's a competitive family that keeps track of who got the nut the previous year, and if that person finds the nut *a second year in a row*, Santa has explaining to do.

A wonderful holiday tradition—if you're looking for one for your family, this is a great one.

1 cup Arborio or white basmati rice
Salt
2 cups whole milk
2 cups half-and-half
½ cup sugar
½ teaspoon pure vanilla extract
½ teaspoon ground cinnamon
½ teaspoon ground nutmeg
Whipped cream, for topping
One almond, or the nut of your choice
  (optional)

1. In a medium saucepan, combine the rice, 2 cups of water, and a pinch of salt. Bring to a boil over medium-high heat, give it a good stir, cover, and reduce the temperature to low. Simmer until all the water is absorbed and the rice is tender, about 20 minutes.

2. Uncover and stir in the milk, half-and-half, and sugar. Increase the heat to medium-high and cook, stirring often, until the mixture boils. Stir, put the lid back on, and reduce the heat to low. Cook until the rice is super creamy, stirring occasionally, about 25 minutes.

3. Remove from the heat and stir in the vanilla, cinnamon, and nutmeg. Let the rice pudding rest for about 10 minutes to thicken.

4. You can serve the rice pudding warm, or cover it, refrigerate, and serve chilled (we like it best that way). It's great with a little whipped cream on top, and the stakes are heightened when one serving hides a single nut.

9

TASTY TREATS AND DESSERTS

OUR KIDS ARE GROWN. THEY'VE PICKED up and left town, and we're thinking about downsizing.

Don't get me wrong, I love this house; it's where all my kids grew up and ran down the stairs every Christmas (good chance you saw that video on TV!). When we moved to New Jersey, into a house we could barely afford, I told Kathy that because I had moved a dozen times by the age of twenty, I never really knew where home base was, and it was important that we not move from this house if we could help it. That way when the kids thought of home, they'd think of one place.

And I love the decades we've lived here. It's where I miscalculated and built a treehouse that was *waaaaay* too tall, and Kathy declared it unsafe for her children. At 3:30 one morning, on the way to work, I backed up in the garage and the garage door collapsed on the roof of my Ford Explorer, which is what happens when you don't open the garage door before trying to exit.

And it's the house where the carbon monoxide detector went off one afternoon after I turned on the furnace for the first time that season, and I had to call the fire department—as Kathy tidied up and did the dishes—and let in a dozen men in firefighting gear, who arrived in three minutes with lights and sirens. Because it was a volunteer fire department, most of the guys were our neighbors, and as they went scouting for the source of the CO, they walked through every room and opened every door and closet.

"The good news is there's no carbon monoxide," our friend Todd the fireman told us. "The bad news is your basement is a disaster . . ."

Todd was right—it was a disaster. We're not

Thirty years later and they're still running down the stairs on Christmas.

hoarders, but right now in our basement we have almost every toy the children ever had growing up, still scattered on the carpet as if they'd left them there twenty minutes ago. But it was actually almost twenty years ago.

I have a confession. I think we kept all their toys because not a single toy from my Wonder Years survived my childhood. I had one: After his army service in Germany, my dad bought a stuffed toy tiger, which lived on my bed with me every day of my life until one of my younger sisters thought it would be hilarious to pull his head off. I was of course heartbroken, but I was a good friend to the tiger, and right through college it sat on my bed at home, awaiting my return, decapitated like something out of a Tim Burton movie. No idea what happened to my tiger.

We couldn't bring ourselves to part with a single toy. However, I'm getting to the point that if the kids don't want to take this stuff to their places and they don't have their own children to play with them, maybe we should donate them. Although I have no idea what charity would want a Fisher Price cash register chewed on by three-year-old Peter Doocy.

So we're at a crossroads, and for the last year, every time the kids come to visit, I'll suggest we go down and "streamline" the basement.

To Peter the basement is his official National Archives, curated by parents who would never throw anything out—or so he thought. But if I could get the girls on board, I was renting a dumpster. Sally knew my intentions and shocked me, saying, "I will always remember and love these things, but, Dad, you can't keep them forever." She helped me fill up Hefty bag after Hefty bag.

One kid left to convince: Mary, who was studying a doll she'd slept with for two years.

"Let's donate Kirsten; some lucky little girl somewhere will love her as much as I did," she said. But as I started to put Kirsten in a Hefty bag, she balked. "Wait . . . I think I want to save *that one*."

"Okay, how about this?"

She was momentarily in a trance, remembering where she was when that item was the most important thing in the world to her. "That's another one I'd like to keep." So I put that on top of her Boston College collection. She looked around, gave me the sad face, and said, "Dad, I would like to save everything. Is that okay?"

No, I wanted to clean the basement, because I knew we had carpet under there somewhere. But at the same time, I'd been saving everything for them—for their kids, their memories—and this was validation that I'd done the right thing.

Mary looked at the bags of toys Sally had marked for the garbage. "Sally doesn't know this, but she's going to want some of these things someday," she said, and with that Mary picked up the bag and dumped it on the floor. "Look," she said, "it's Sally's whole childhood. You can't throw that away, Dad."

She was right, I couldn't throw her childhood away, and I didn't. It's all still down in the basement of the house we'll never move out of. Kathy has nostalgically placed the kids' iconic toys—things like Curious George, teddy bears, and childhood blankies—in Plexiglass shadow boxes that today live just a few feet from where the kids fell asleep with them for a generation. When I see them, I'm instantly transported somewhere in time when the kids were little and Kathy and I wondered what the future would hold for them. So far, so good.

Our cookbook's intent is simple: to provide you with recipes that remind you of happy times and help you to create new memories. It's like a

We'll always have Curious George.

time capsule that you access by turning on the stove. We hope you enjoy making the recipes and hearing the behind-the-scenes stories of life at our house, which we bet is a lot like life at your house.

Next time the kids are all home, I'll ask them if they can help me carry something up from the basement, and then I'll ask them if there's anything down there they want to get rid of, and they'll say yes but really mean no. It took me thirty years and three kids to realize it.

We all want to hang on to the past, but not if it keeps you from a ranch house with the master bedroom on the first floor.

Peter's salty hat.

CRACKER CRUST PEANUT BUTTER PIE

We'd just moved from Virginia to New Jersey, and on the first day of Mary's pre-K, in a new school in a new state, Kathy felt like an outsider. After the kids bravely marched into the classroom, some happy for the adventure, others already missing their parents, most of the moms stood in the parking lot and chatted. Kathy could tell they all knew one another. The lone exception was the blond woman in the minivan with the Michigan plates. Kathy had Virginia plates, and that was her conversational icebreaker as she introduced herself to Christie de Nicola, who is now Kathy's most long-term friend in New Jersey.

Because all the kids are close in age, Kathy and Christie spent a lot of time together with them trick-or-treating, sledding on snow days, howling as they played Capture the Flag, and going to the neighborhood swimming hole. Our kids grew up together and had a lot of fun.

Christie's husband, Tony, was Peter's confirmation sponsor at our church, and whenever Tony's business takes him to Washington, he always makes it a point to call Peter and meet at the very fancy Hay-Adams hotel bar, Off the Record, for a drink or dinner. They have a good laugh, talk a little politics, *off the record*, and then Tony will pretend that the cell service is terrible there and he has to take a phone call outside, leaving Peter to pay the bill.

Kidding . . .

In 1987, at Christie's wedding shower, her mother presented her with a gift that she treasures to this day: a simple recipe box filled with heirloom family recipes. All the foods of her childhood in one box, so she could re-create all the happy foods of her early life during their marriage, and she has. This peanut butter pie is one of those recipes. Christie remembers its origin was her mother's ladies' church group in Michigan.

We love this recipe for its completely different kind of pie crust; and because Ritz crackers are extra-buttery, it pairs perfectly with the peanut butter. Christie's family demands it with great regularity, and she happily makes it for birthdays, family celebrations, and important milestones.

Tony usually requests this as his birthday dessert, when he's not in DC leaving Peter with a significant bar tab.

(continued)

50 Ritz Original crackers (about 4 of the short cracker stacks)

1 stick (4 ounces) butter, melted

4 ounces cream cheese (half an 8-ounce package), at room temperature

½ cup chunky peanut butter

1 cup powdered sugar

½ cup milk

One 8-ounce container Cool Whip, thawed for 4 hours in the refrigerator

¼ cup salted peanuts (optional)

Chocolate syrup, for serving (optional)

1. Crush the Ritz crackers. We put them in a zip-top bag, leaving the top slightly unzipped, and pulverize them with a rolling pin. Very therapeutic. But don't go crazy: If you turn them to dust, they don't make an efficient crust. Dump the crumbs into a 9-inch glass pie plate (it freezes better than metal), reserving a couple tablespoons of crumbs for garnish, and add the melted butter. Mix thoroughly and press the crumbs into the bottom and sides of the pie plate to form a crust.

I like to use the bottom of a 1-cup measure to make the surface nice and level. Set aside.

2. In a large bowl, with an electric mixer, combine the cream cheese, peanut butter, and powdered sugar and beat on medium speed until smooth, scraping down the sides occasionally. Slowly pour in the milk and mix on low until you have a perfectly smooth slurry (apart from the peanut butter chunks). With a rubber spatula, fold in the entire container of Cool Whip, which makes it fluffier than the mixer would. Pour the mixture into the crumb crust, smooth it out, and garnish the top with the reserved cracker crumbs.

3. Freeze for at least 4 hours—although longer makes it better.

4. Take the pie out of the freezer 10 to 15 minutes before serving to soften a bit. The Doocys like to amp it up a little and top with salted peanuts and a squirt of chocolate syrup.

5. Wrap the leftovers (if there are any) in plastic wrap and return to the freezer.

APPLE DUTCH BABY

Years ago a neighbor invited Kathy to a living room party to demonstrate and sell clever kitchen products. Kathy bought measuring cups, a steamer basket, a salad spinner, and an item that I immediately fell in love with, a deep-dish stoneware baker. The instruction book included a recipe for a puffy pancake, so I made it one Sunday morning, and a star was born. The wow factor was that it always rose up into a crazy shaped puffy thing, and the kids *loved it*!

I probably made the recipe fifty times before somebody dropped the stoneware dish and it shattered. I went online to look for a replacement but couldn't find the same thing. So many frowny faces on Sunday mornings when the kids realized there would be no crazy puffy pancake thing.

I was telling a friend about the magical properties of the dish, and he told me he thought it wasn't the dish, that it was probably the fact that it was super preheated before you poured in the batter. His family made a similar recipe called a Dutch Baby, and they used a cast-iron skillet.

"Why do they call it a Dutch Baby?" I asked.

"No idea."

Forget the name. Here's why you should try it—it's unbelievably tasty and super easy to make, and its randomly crazy puffy shape is a crowd-pleaser. And a cast-iron skillet will never break if you drop it on the floor . . . especially if it lands on your toe!

½ cup milk
2 large eggs
1 teaspoon pure vanilla extract
½ cup all-purpose flour
4 tablespoons (½ stick) butter
2 Granny Smith apples, peeled, cored, and thinly sliced

1 teaspoon ground cinnamon
2 tablespoons light brown sugar
2 tablespoons chopped walnuts, pecans, or almonds
Powdered sugar, whipped cream, or ice cream, for serving (optional)

1. Preheat the oven to 450°F.

2. Once the oven is at temperature, preheat an 8- or 9-inch round pie pan or similar size cast-iron skillet in the oven. To make a puffy Dutch baby, it has to be very hot.

3. Batter up! In a medium bowl, whisk the milk, eggs, and vanilla. Add the flour and whisk until silky. Set aside.

4. In a medium saucepan, melt 2 tablespoons of the butter over medium-high heat. Add the apples and toss to coat. Cook until softened, 10 to 12 minutes, occasionally moving them around the pan. Stir in the cinnamon and brown sugar and cook until they have the texture of apples in an apple pie, 5 to 10 minutes. Toss in the nuts and cook for a couple quick minutes. Remove the pan from the heat.

5. Now back to the really hot dish in the oven. Remove the pan and add the remaining 2 tablespoons butter. When the butter has melted (it will be *fast*), carefully (the pan is hot) swirl the butter to coat the bottom, then pour in the batter. Bake until the edges are raised up and curled and it's turning golden brown, 15 to 20 minutes.

6. Remove the pan from the oven and spread the apple mixture over the Dutch baby. Remember that the pan or skillet is *very hot!*

7. To serve, cut into 6 wedges, shake some powdered sugar on top, or do what the Doocy kids do and top it with whipped cream or vanilla ice cream.

TRES LECHES SUPERSTAR CAKE

MAKES 15 SERVINGS

When I was promoting *The Happy Cookbook*, *Fox & Friends* held a nationwide contest to hear Americans' stories about the foods that make people happy and why. This was one of the winning recipes, because it's delicious—and what a story behind it.

Cristina Montero was born in Costa Rica, and when she was very young, she was adopted by parents in the United States. When she was seven, after a long naturalization process, Cristina was granted US citizenship. To celebrate that landmark, her second-grade class in Florida threw her a party and gave her an American flag that had flown over the US Capitol on the very day she was naturalized.

Now every March 13th she makes this cake to remind her where she comes from. It's a Costa Rican recipe, but she tops it with berries that make it look like a delicious Old Glory.

"This recipe is symbolic of the gift that this nation grants to each and every one of its citizens," Cristina told us, "the unparalleled blessing to live in the world's most extraordinary nation, with the right to life, liberty, and, above all, the pursuit of *happiness*."

We flew Cristina and her mother, Linda, to New York, where she made us her cake and told us her story.

Kathy and I loved the story so much that we've started making our own version of Cristina's tres leches cake, which means "three milks." It's quick to put together, but it takes hours in the fridge for the milk flavors to blend into something scrumptious, so plan ahead.

Cristina's cake features the stars and stripes to remind her of "the countless blessings that have been bestowed upon me by this great country."

With our version, we make a cake, but rather than the whole flag, we feature a single star, a *super*star . . . like Cristina.

Cooking spray
One 15.25-ounce box Duncan Hines Classic
   Yellow cake mix (see Note)
⅓ cup vegetable oil
4 large eggs
One 12-ounce can evaporated milk
One 14-ounce can sweetened condensed
   milk
1 cup heavy cream
1 teaspoon pure vanilla extract
8 ounces strawberries, hulled and thinly
   sliced
1 teaspoon sugar

One 8-ounce container Cool Whip, thawed
   for 4 hours in the refrigerator
2 cups blueberries

NOTE: *You can use another similar major brand of yellow cake mix, but follow the package instructions for preparation, because times and the required added ingredients (like eggs and oil) may vary.*

1. Preheat the oven to 350°F. Coat a 9 × 13-inch baking pan with cooking spray.

(continued)

2. In a large bowl, with an electric mixer, combine the cake mix, vegetable oil, eggs, and ¾ cup of water and beat on medium speed until the mixture is smooth, about 2 minutes, scraping down the sides of the bowl once or twice.

3. Pour the batter into the prepared pan and bake until the top has nicely browned and a toothpick inserted in the center comes out clean as a whistle, 28 to 35 minutes. Let the cake cool for 15 to 20 minutes.

4. Meanwhile, in a medium bowl, combine the three milks (aka *tres leches*)—the evaporated milk, sweetened condensed milk, and heavy cream—and the vanilla. Whisk until combined and set aside.

5. Use a fork to gently puncture the top of the cake all over, taking care not to rip up the surface. The holes will help the creamy milk mixture to distribute through the cake. Slowly and evenly pour the milk mixture over the cake. You will be shocked at how thirsty the cake is. It all fits in there; trust the trickle-down theory.

6. Cover with plastic wrap and refrigerate for at least 4 hours to allow the milks to make magic inside that cake.

7. In another medium bowl, combine the strawberries and sugar, cover, and refrigerate.

8. When it's time to serve, spoon the entire container of Cool Whip over the cake and make a nice even layer to cover the top. For years Kathy has turned this cake into a fruit flag, with stars and stripes, but this past year we've started making a large star from blueberries in the middle and adding a border of sliced strawberries around the edge. This is so pretty . . . so carve it up and enjoy! Serve any leftover fruit alongside pieces of cake that are bereft of a berry topping.

LEMONY BLUEBERRY BARS

MAKES 9 SERVINGS

A guy at work gave me a travel tip. Chatham, Massachusetts, he said, was a terrific family weekend. Two weeks later, after a nine-hour drive, mainly up I-95, we were in the motel lobby when the manager gave a welcome we were not expecting.

"Spell the name again? I don't see anything . . . and I'm sold out."

These were pre-Expedia days, and the only printed piece of paper we had regarding the trip was a nine-page MapQuest printout giving us directions to a hotel with no rooms. One of the kids was at my side when this happened, and when I said we'd have to turn around and drive home, they burst out loudly into tears. I think the manager must have been a father himself, because after about ten painful seconds of wailing, he announced, "I have one room, but it's being painted. If you don't mind the primer, you can stay in it." I took it.

We opened the door, and it wasn't a regular hotel or motel room with two queen beds; for some reason it was a room with four single beds, all pushed together.

"Where's Sally going to sleep?" Kathy said. I'd already asked the front desk guy for a crib for one-year-old Sally, but they were all being used, and we certainly didn't want her rolling off the bed in the middle of the night. I paused for a moment, weighed our options, and remembered something I'd seen in a movie. I walked over to the chest of drawers under the TV, pulled out the bottom drawer, lined it with a cozy blanket, and announced, "She'll fit in there."

And she did, for three nights. She slept like a baby, because she was a baby.

We loved that first vacation and have gone back many times. But on that first trip, Kathy ordered some lemon bars for the room, and the kids loved them. When we got home, Kathy started making her own version, occasionally topping them with fruit to make them even more delicious.

I know this is a cookbook, not a travel guide, but if you have never been to Cape Cod, visit sometime—it's great. They have sixteen legendary lighthouses, the seashore is pristine, and the shops and restaurants are top-notch. But when leaving, don't forget to check out that bottom dresser drawer. You don't want to leave a kid behind.

(continued)

NOTE: *Here's another fast and easy recipe that does require a couple hours of fridge time at the end, so plan ahead!*

One 16.5-ounce tube Pillsbury refrigerated
   sugar cookie dough
Cooking spray
Two 8-ounce blocks cream cheese, at room
   temperature
2 large eggs
½ cup sugar
¼ cup fresh lemon juice
1 pint blueberries
Whipped cream, for serving (optional)

1. Preheat the oven to 350°F. Coat an 8 × 8-inch baking dish with cooking spray.

2. First, let's make the *easiest lemon bar baked crust in history.* Open the tube of refrigerated sugar cookie dough, but instead of slicing it into cookies, crumble the dough into the prepared baking dish and use your fingers to press the crumbles into a single even crust layer.

3. In a large bowl, with an electric mixer, beat the cream cheese briefly on low speed until it's pretty pliable, then add the eggs, sugar, and lemon juice and beat until smooth, using a spatula to scrape down the sides a couple times during mixing.

4. Pour the cream cheese mixture evenly over the crust. Sprinkle as many blueberries as you like on top, but don't stir them in.

5. Bake until firm in the center, 45 to 55 minutes. Let it rest 20 minutes to cool down, then refrigerate for a couple hours, until thoroughly chilled.

6. To serve, cut into 9 squares. A little whipped cream on top never hurt anybody . . .

PECAN CHOCOLATE PIE

MAKES ONE 9-INCH PIE

Kathy is a mother beloved by her children because she's kind and compassionate. But what will one year win her the United Nations Mother of the Year award is the fact that if there is leftover pie in the house, she's serving it to the kids for breakfast.

We checked, and it's not against the law in our town—yet.

"Wait, you only eat pie at night—why?" Sally once asked a neighbor kid, who was at our house hitching a ride to school—as the kid finished his second piece of pie with whipped cream. It was 7:20 a.m.

This is one of our favorite pies; it was actually my father's favorite. We've adapted my mom's recipe by adding dark chocolate to the bottom, which gives it a marvelous extra taste.

A snap to make, this pie brings back the happy memories of my father sitting in his La-Z-Boy watching *Murder She Wrote* and having a piece of this pie. And two generations later, our children are enjoying this family tradition—at breakfast!

One 9-inch refrigerated pie crust, at room temperature
One 4-ounce bar semisweet chocolate, finely chopped (we use Baker's brand)
3 large eggs
1 stick (4 ounces) butter, melted
½ cup dark corn syrup
½ cup pure maple syrup, plus more for brushing
¾ cup packed dark brown sugar
1 tablespoon all-purpose flour
2½ cups roughly chopped pecans
Whipped cream or ice cream, for serving

1. Preheat the oven to 350°F.
2. Roll out the pie dough and place it in an ungreased 9-inch pie plate (glass is best). Crimp the edges to the rim of the plate or the crust will shrink. Sprinkle the chocolate evenly into the crust. Set aside.
3. In a large bowl, combine the eggs, melted butter, corn syrup, and maple syrup and whisk well. Add the brown sugar and flour and whisk until smooth. Fold in the pecans and carefully pour the mixture over the chocolate pieces. Do not overfill the pie plate. Move the pie plate gently back and forth on the countertop to help the mixture settle evenly.
4. Place the pie plate on a baking sheet (to avoid drips) and bake for 30 minutes. Remove the pie, wrap foil over the crust so it doesn't get too brown, and bake until the center stops jiggling, 20 to 30 minutes more—this time varies, so don't be shocked if it takes longer.
5. Set the pie on a cooling rack and lightly brush the top with maple syrup. Cool completely, then keep in the fridge until it's time to eat.
6. Serve with whipped cream or ice cream. Store in the refrigerator.

SALTED CARAMEL AND CHOCOLATE PRETZEL CAKE

MAKES 24 SERVINGS

I baked my first cake in a high school class called bachelor living, which was essentially home ec for guys who would rather be driving their pickups than stuck in a classroom learning to boil water. It was more laughing than learning, but we picked up enough kitchen know-how to keep us from starving.

My friend Gary reminded me not long ago that the highlight of that semester was the day we were told by our teacher we could make any meal we wanted as long as we brought in the materials. I made a hamburger-something. So I started frying it up, glancing around the room and noticing that several of my classmates had teamed up at one of the stoves. There was a lot of whispering and giggling, and when the teacher walked over to them, they hushed up, slamming the oven door closed. She kept walking and they started giggling again.

What was so funny? Mostly sons of farmers and ranchers, many of us had freezers filled with prime cuts of beef and pork, but those mischievous boys over at the avocado green Kenmore range in the corner thought it would be hilarious to prepare *possum*.

I don't know where they got it—it could have been roadkill—but after they'd briefly hidden the possum in the oven, they pulled it out and started pan-frying it. The howls of laughter were short-lived. What they didn't know was unless you cage and feed a possum a clean diet of grain for two weeks before butchering, its system will be full of whatever the heck it ate rooting through garbage cans and ditches. We didn't have Google back then.

Never in my now sixty-odd years did I ever smell anything quite that . . . ripe. Neither had the teacher, who rushed over to investigate. "You said we could make anything we wanted!" the teacher was reminded. She turned off the stove, sacked up the possum, and took it to the trash, but the damage was done. Opening the windows didn't work, nor did flinging open an exterior fire escape door. So she adjourned the class and sent us to the library, where we all sat and cackled about the catastrophic Critter Casserole, which is still legendary, forty years later.

It was in that class that I learned how to bake a cake from a mix. My mom showed me how to amp it up; she'd often swap out the water Betty Crocker called for with a cup of instant coffee, mainly because it made the cake smell amazing, but with five kids, she was usually exhausted and certainly needed an afternoon pick-me-up.

(continued)

CAKE
Cooking spray
4 large eggs
1 cup black coffee (unflavored)
⅓ cup Crisco
One 15.25-ounce box Duncan Hines Devil's
 Food cake mix

FROSTING
1 stick (4 ounces) butter
¼ cup unsweetened cocoa powder
¼ cup plus 2 tablespoons half-and-half or
 milk
1 teaspoon pure vanilla extract
One 1-pound box powdered sugar (about
 3¾ cups)
¼ teaspoon table salt

GARNISH
24 salted mini pretzels
Sea salt (optional)
Store-bought salted caramel sauce

1. Preheat the oven to 350°F. Coat a 9 × 13-inch pan with cooking spray.

2. To make the cake: In a large bowl, with an electric mixer, combine the eggs and coffee. Next, in goes the Crisco; blend briefly on low speed. Add the cake mix and blend at least 1 minute on medium-high speed, then stop and use a rubber spatula to scrape the batter from the sides and bottom of the bowl. Mix on medium-high speed for 1 minute more, then pour into the prepared pan.

3. Bake until a toothpick inserted into the center of the cake comes out clean, 25 to 30 minutes. Set the cake aside to cool.

4. To make the frosting: In a small saucepan, melt the butter over medium heat. Add the cocoa and whisk to combine, then add the half-and-half and vanilla and whisk gently until it's smooth. Remove from the heat.

5. In a clean large bowl, with an electric mixer, combine the powdered sugar and salt. Mix briefly. Add the still-warm cocoa mixture and beat on medium speed for at least 2 minutes, until all the lumps are gone and the frosting is super smooth. Make sure you scrape down the sides of the bowl so all the powdered sugar is incorporated.

6. Spread the warm frosting by pouring it in a thin line down the cake. It may flow so freely across the top that you don't even need to use a spatula to spread it out.

7. To garnish: Press the pretzels one at a time into the frosting. We set a pretzel at the center of each piece of cake, spacing them so there are four rows of six, for 24 pieces. Sprinkle with sea salt if you like a little extra salty taste. Let the cake rest for at least 5 minutes for the frosting to set. When ready to serve, zig-zag as much caramel sauce as you like over the top.

BANANA-CARAMEL PIE

MAKES ONE 9-INCH PIE

To celebrate being the first Doocy in our family's history to get a four-year degree from a university, something big was in order, but of course I was living below the poverty level, so it had to be something big—on a shoestring.

In the days before Expedia.com, I looked at the Sunday papers for trips overseas. I actually had a number of European options to consider, thanks to my mastery of various languages. I had taken three years of college French and four years of Spanish. So I chose . . . England. It was the cheapest trip, and I was 50 percent fluent in their language.

Earlier in this book I told the story of how during that first trip to London I fell in love with curry. It was such an eye-opener—flavors I had never had in my life just all rolled up into one neat dish. There was also one dessert that these many years later I still remember. It's Banoffee pie, the name a mash-up of *bananas* and *toffee*. It was supposedly invented in England, but it reminded me of my Kansas-based mom's banana cream pie, with a toffee twist. The distinctive taste has become a Doocy kids' favorite, and we often make it for holidays. Just know it needs a few hours in the fridge to firm up—but it's so worth it.

(continued)

I went to London and learned how to make pie.

I've asked waiters in the UK how Banoffee pie was made, and I've heard lots of different versions. This is our hybrid, and it's super easy. Years ago I made dulce de leche by heating a can of sweetened condensed milk in the oven for an hour, but we're in a hurry and now use store-bought dulce de leche, which you'll find in the international foods aisle. Use a store-bought pie crust and the pie takes literally five minutes to assemble.

And the taste is, as we said in my French class, *merveilleuse!*

Or in my Spanish class, *maravillosa!*

And as I often heard in my English class, "Why are you late again, Mr. Doocy?"

3 large ripe bananas, thinly sliced
1 store-bought graham cracker crust
2 cups store-bought dulce de leche
One 8-ounce carton heavy cream
2 tablespoons sugar
½ teaspoon pure vanilla extract

OPTIONAL TOPPINGS
Melted chocolate
Chocolate shavings
Cocoa powder
Caramel sauce

1. Chilling the mixing bowl and wire beaters will make cream whip faster, so park both in the refrigerator about 20 minutes before you start this recipe.

2. Layer the banana slices on the bottom of the graham cracker crust. When you have four or five layers, pour the dulce de leche over the bananas, letting it seep to the bottom.

3. In a small bowl, whisk the heavy cream, sugar, and vanilla. Pour the mixture into the chilled bowl and whip first on medium and then on high until stiff peaks form. Slather the whipped cream over the bananas and dulce de leche.

4. Refrigerate the pie for at least 3 hours.

5. When it's time to serve, top with melted chocolate, chocolate shavings, a dusting of cocoa powder, or caramel sauce if you like!

GOOEY CHOCOLATE CHEWIES

MAKES 16 COOKIES

When Kathy was growing up in Los Angeles, every summer she and her brothers all got jobs. Their mother was fascinated by show business and would line up the kids with auditions for jobs as actors in TV commercials. If you're old enough to have watched TV in the 1960s and 1970s, there's a better than average chance you saw Kathy and her brothers show off a toy, eat a snack food, or happily ride in an amazing new automobile in a thirty-second spot.

To make the commercials, the family would fly to New York every summer. Then at the end of the summer they'd all fly home. But one summer they decided there were a bunch of places between LA and NYC that they'd never seen, so instead of looking down at middle America from 35,000 feet, they drove an Oldsmobile 88 Cutlass west from Gotham to discover America.

They really had no itinerary other than getting back before school started in a couple weeks, so they were in no huge hurry. Kathy clearly remembers driving into downtown Holland, Michigan. Just like the European Holland, this Holland was famous for its Tulip Festival. The festival had happened months earlier and the tulips were now dead. But Holland did feature a living relative of Kathy's family—a close enough family member that Kathy's mom got a free night in her spare bedroom.

As they were packing up the car to hit the road, the relative presented them with a Tupperware container filled with these chocolate-coconut bars. She called them chewies and gave them a handwritten copy of the recipe. Kathy has since made this with some regularity her entire life.

It's a happy taste from a summer of travel to the land of Michigan to visit what's-her-name.

Names are hard to remember and cookies are hard to forget.

Cooking spray
One 11-ounce box vanilla wafer cookies
¼ cup sugar
⅓ cup (⅔ stick) butter, melted
One 14-ounce can sweetened condensed milk
One 12-ounce package semisweet chocolate chips (we use Nestlé Toll House)
1 cup pecans, roughly chopped
1½ cups sweetened coconut flakes
Store-bought caramel sauce (we use salted caramel flavor; optional)

1. Preheat the oven to 350°F. Line an 8 × 8-inch baking dish tightly with foil, for ease in removing the bars later. Coat the foil on the bottom and sides with cooking spray.

2. Place 50 to 55 vanilla wafer cookies in a food processor (or just use three-fourths of the box, if you don't have kids to make a game of counting them). Pulse the cookies until finely processed.

3. Into a medium bowl, measure 2 cups of the crumbs. Add the sugar and melted butter and mix well until the butter seeps into all of the crumbs, giving them a deeper color. A rubber spatula works great.

(continued)

4. Dump the crumb mixture into the prepared pan, level it out, and then use the bottom of a flat measuring cup or spatula to firmly press the crumbs into the pan, forming a nice flat even crust.

5. Pour the sweetened condensed milk onto the crust, making sure it covers all the crumbs. Next, make an even layer of chocolate chips and top that with the pecans. Do a nice layer of coconut, at least ½ inch thick, then take the measuring cup or spatula that you used to level out the crust and press the layers down firmly. Finally, if you like, give the coconut a squirt of caramel sauce in a zig-zag fashion.

6. Bake until the chocolate chips are melty and the coconut is golden on top, up to 30 minutes.

7. Set aside to cool, then carefully lift the bars out by the foil liner and allow them to firm up on a flat surface. Cut them into four rows of four and serve.

SIX-MINUTE STRAWBERRY PIE

MAKES ONE 9-INCH PIE

After our wedding, the gifts started arriving, and Kathy was thrilled to open a couple of big Tiffany boxes with two dozen Elsa Peretti crystal water glasses carefully packed inside. They were made from the thinnest, lightest crystal I'd ever seen, and they must have cost a fortune.

We used them at our first dinner party, and a friend who'd volunteered to help was cleaning up in the kitchen. I asked him to make sure to put the Tiffany glasses on the top rack of the dishwasher.

"Tiffany? I thought they were plastic! I'm so sorry . . . they're in that thing," he said, pointing to the trash compactor.

We also got a beautiful pie plate as a wedding gift, but Kathy wasn't yet a pie maker, so it sat in a lonely cupboard for years until the kids came along. They loved creamy pies, so Kathy saw fresh strawberries at our local farm stand and started making this super-light strawberry pie once a week. The original recipe had about an hour's worth of hands-on time involved, and with some adaptations, Kathy got it down to less than ten minutes. I can make it in six minutes. How long will it take you? Ready, set, cook!

1 pound strawberries, hulled and halved lengthwise, with a few reserved for garnish
½ tablespoon sugar
One 8-ounce container Cool Whip, thawed for 4 hours in the refrigerator
2 cups strawberry yogurt (whole milk works great)
1 store-bought 9-inch graham cracker crust

1. Start the clock after you've prepped the strawberries. Place the strawberries in a food processor, sprinkle the sugar on top, and pulse a few times until the strawberries are nicely chopped. If you pulse too much and wind up with strawberry juice on the bottom, spoon it out.

2. Transfer the strawberries to a large bowl. Add the Cool Whip and strawberry yogurt. Use a rubber spatula to mix until nice and smooth.

3. Scoop the strawberry filling into the graham cracker crust. There is no limit to the height of this pie; just make sure it's symmetrical.

4. Set the pie in an open space in your fridge and chill for at least a couple hours. Kathy would make it at breakfast and it would be perfect by lunch.

5. Garnish with the reserved strawberries and enjoy this flavor-packed treat. It sure made our kids happy in a hurry! Store leftovers in the refrigerator.

RED, WHITE, AND BLUE-TIFUL SKILLET COBBLER

MAKES 8 SERVINGS

Pete at the hardware store has been asking me for the last couple of years, "When you gonna break down and buy a new grill?" He'd sold me the last one, fifteen summers earlier, and it still worked okay. During Superstorm Sandy, with no power in the house for ten days, our grill was the only way we could make a meal. I had bought it during the Bush administration, and it had worked all the way through the Obama years, and the first three Trump years. *Maybe* it was time for a change.

"Go look in our showroom and see if you like anything," he said, knowing that I had a weakness for the stainless steel. I took a quick glance around and then I spotted it. Seventy-five inches wide and stainless steel (of course), it was a gleaming Temple of High Temperatures. It was love at first sight. Classic story of boy meets grill.

For you grillers, here are the specs. It's a Weber Summit S-670, natural gas model. Six burners with snap-jet ignition, each roaring out 60,000 BTUs per hour, a smoker, a side burner, a sear station that makes the perfect steak every time, and something my dad had on his grill but I never did—a rotisserie motor. But unlike my father's, this new grill had a motor *and* an infrared rotisserie burner. Pinch me, heaven was missing a grill.

It was delivered the next day, and I pledged to Kathy that if I was going to take the cover off and make a meal on the grill, it was going to be a *whole* meal. With 634 square inches of cooking space, I had room to cook everything from appetizer to dessert. That meant I had to come up with a way to make our favorite summertime dessert, the classic cobbler. Kathy started making it years ago, when the blueberries go on super-sale in the middle of the summer. I remembered that Grandma Berndt made cobbler in a cast-iron skillet, so that's what I did that day, and what I do now.

With the cobbler's red, white, and blue colors so bright and beautiful, if you're flying a flag in the front yard, this looks like something you'd be making in the backyard—when you're cooking with gas.

Of course I'm giving you oven directions as well.

(continued)

8 ounces strawberries, hulled and sliced
(about 1½ cups sliced)
1 cup blueberries
½ cup plus 2 tablespoons sugar
½ teaspoon pure vanilla extract
1½ cups Original Bisquick mix
¾ cup milk
4 tablespoons (½ stick) butter, plus more as
needed to test the skillet if grilling
Vanilla ice cream or whipped cream, for
serving
2 tablespoons strawberry jam (optional)

1. If grilling, place a 10¼-inch (or similar size) cast-iron skillet over indirect medium heat. If using the oven, preheat it to 375°F and set the cast-iron skillet inside. Either way, it will take 10 to 20 minutes for the pan to get hot enough (we'll test it in step 4 below).

2. In a medium bowl, combine the strawberries and blueberries with 1 tablespoon of the sugar and the vanilla. Stir until all the berries are coated with sugar and set aside.

3. In a larger bowl, combine the Bisquick, milk, and ½ cup of the sugar and whisk until it's as smooth as you can get it. This will take a moment, as it tends to be lumpy.

4. Time to make the cobbler magic happen!

If using the grill: Test the temperature of the skillet by putting a little bit of butter in it. If the butter immediately smokes and turns brown, the skillet is *waaaay* too hot. Carefully paper towel the burned butter out of the pan, reduce the temperature, and wait a few minutes for the pan to cool down. Do the butter test again—you'll know it's right when it starts melting without the smoke. Keep it moving with a silicone spatula and add the rest of the butter, stirring the entire time, until melted. It won't take long.

If using the oven: Add the butter to the skillet and watch it melt. Oven temperatures are more predictable than the grill, so the butter shouldn't smoke.

5. Immediately pour the batter into the butter in the hot pan, but do not mix the batter with the butter. Place the berries evenly on top: Don't bunch them in the center; scatter them right up to the edge. Don't stir the berries into the batter. Sprinkle the remaining 1 tablespoon sugar over the berries and batter. Set the pan back on the grill and close the grill lid (or return to the oven).

6. Bake until the crust is golden and a toothpick inserted into the center comes out clean as a whistle, about 30 minutes.

7. The pan is *super* hot! Carefully set it aside to cool for at least 10 minutes.

8. Finally, cut into 8 wedges, serve pie-style, and top with vanilla ice cream or whipped cream. If desired, make a strawberry drizzle for the ice cream or whipped cream: In a microwave-safe bowl, lightly blend the strawberry jam and ½ tablespoon water with a fork and microwave for 20 seconds so it's pourable.

CRAZY-QUICK COCONUT CREAM PIE

MAKES ONE 9-INCH PIE

As we were approaching the less-traveled Hawaiian island of Molokai, the flight attendant noticed we were the only nonlocals on the plane and inquired why we chose this island for our honeymoon.

"Opened a map, closed our eyes, and pointed at this island!" I said, sounding like the ultimate jet-setting bachelor who was finally settling down with his perfect wife. "What an adventure!"

"You know you picked the island with the leper colony—right?" she said, walking back the drink cart. Wait . . . what?

Yes, many years ago this was the island where Hawaiians with leprosy were quarantined! Not gonna lie—it kind of freaked us out for a minute. But after the welcome mai tai, we completely forgot. The scariest part was our visit to a coconut farm, where a sign warned us of the potential for brain damage if a coconut clocked us in the noggin.

Nonetheless, we love coconut. Sally's favorite dessert in the world is a coconut cake from Café Panache in northern New Jersey. This is a super-quick pie version, with five minutes of prep and some time in the freezer. It reminds me of my mom's 1970s version, which she made with Dream Whip. Remember that stuff? This is delicious.

Falling coconuts? I'm not in Kansas anymore . . .

Two 3.4-ounce boxes Jell-O instant vanilla pudding
2 cups milk
1½ cups sweetened shredded coconut
One 8-ounce container Cool Whip, thawed for 4 hours in the refrigerator
1 store-bought graham cracker pie crust

1. In a large bowl, combine the contents of the pudding boxes and the milk and blend with a wire whisk or electric mixer for a couple minutes until creamy. Add 1 cup of the coconut and hand-mix to combine. Open the Cool Whip, scoop out 1 cup, and fold it in until evenly mixed (it will be a little lumpy from the coconut). Scoop the filling into the pie crust and even out the top, nice and smooth. Freeze it for at least 3 hours if possible; it's ready after 2 hours, but the longer the better.

2. When ready to serve, toast the remaining ½ cup coconut in a nonstick skillet over medium heat, moving it constantly around the pan until it's nice and golden brown, 2 to 3 minutes. Don't get distracted—keep stirring! Put the toasted coconut on a plate to cool.

3. Remove the pie from the freezer and spread as much of the remaining Cool Whip as you'd like on top of the pie. Sprinkle the toasted coconut on top and serve. Refrigerate any leftovers.

COOKIE CRUST ICEBOX PIE

MAKES ONE 9-INCH PIE

Growing up, New Jersey chef Kevin Kohler was proud of the fact that his mother would bring her famous homemade apple pie to any local event. People would cut a piece, marvel at the texture and consistency, and rave, "It's so flaky!" Kevin's mom would beam with pride. And when she baked it, it filled the house with that unmistakable warm apple pie smell.

Through the years, Kevin's mom apparently developed a secret technique to make the pie so consistently perfect, and Kevin was so inspired by his mother and a love of food that he became a professional chef. After working in some of the best New York City kitchens, today Kevin owns and operates Café Panache in Ramsey, New Jersey. It's our favorite restaurant in the New York area.

Always looking for a wonderful dessert for his menus, he asked his mother for the recipe for her apple pie. She promised she'd write it down . . . "one of these days." Years passed, and he continued to bug her to tell him how to make a pie that was so delicious he dreamed of it at night. Finally, she relented. "Kevin, honey . . ." She paused, then dropped a bomb. "It's a Mrs. Smith's pie. They're in the frozen foods at every grocery store."

Not in a million years would he ever have suspected that. Today, Kevin's family vividly remembers that just before Mom would pop one in the oven, she'd sprinkle sugar and cinnamon on top, which helped give it that slightly imperfect homemade look and just-baked smell. She'd been passing off a frozen factory-made pie as her own signature dessert for years, and everybody bought it. *Awesome!*

There's one dessert Kevin knows his mother did make from scratch, because he'd seen her make it with his own two eyes: no-bake refrigerator pies. We love them, too! Kathy has been making this one for close to thirty years. She knew I loved pie and the kids loved Oreos, so this covered all the bases. It's chocolatey and cooling and reminds us of those happy times. And it's ready in a flash—even if it has to spend some quality time in the fridge after that.

One 3.5-ounce box instant chocolate
    pudding
1½ cups whole milk
One store-bought 9-inch Oreo pie crust
One 8-ounce package cream cheese, at
    room temperature
1 cup powdered sugar, sifted to remove
    lumps
One 8-ounce container Oreo-flavor Cool
    Whip (or regular Cool Whip)

OPTIONAL GARNISH
2 Oreo cookies, crushed
Chocolate syrup
Caramel sauce

1. In a large bowl, with an electric mixer, combine the pudding mix and milk and beat on medium speed for a couple minutes, stopping halfway through to scrape the sides of the bowl with a spatula. Pour the mixture into the Oreo crust and refrigerate.

2. In a clean large bowl, with an electric mixer, beat the cream cheese on medium speed for 30 seconds, until creamy. Add the powdered sugar and beat until smooth and well combined, again scraping down the bowl. Gently fold in 1 cup of the Cool Whip by hand until evenly mixed.

3. Remove the pie from the fridge and top it with the cream cheese mixture. Give it some artistic swirls and garnish with a crushed Oreo or two if you'd like.

4. Return the pie to the fridge for at least 4 hours. When it's time to serve, let it sit at room temperature for about 10 minutes before cutting. A squirt of chocolate syrup or caramel sauce is always an amazing addition.

A family cruise on the May River, Bluffton, South Carolina.

HAPPY HAZELNUT CROISSANT

Kids who study abroad all seem to return to America with a greater appreciation of . . . Nutella, and our girl Mary was no different. After six months at the University College of London, she returned nutty for Nutella, which she reported was created in 1946 by an Italian pastry maker named Pietro Ferrero. Pietro called it Gianduja, which is an odd thing to name *perfection*, so about twenty years later, his company renamed it *Nutella*. The rest is history . . . actually, that is the history.

I remember reading in the *New York Times* a few years ago that after students at an Ivy League university requested that the school serve Nutella at every meal, the university complied and was shocked at how much of the stuff students slathered upon all manner of food items—including foods you wouldn't normally associate with Nutella. Reportedly, because they loved it so much, they'd *borrow* that big jar from the condiment table in the dining hall and keep it in their dorm rooms. Suddenly the university was spending thousands of dollars on Nutella each week. The university denied the story, but when you think about it, it's better that they're spending thousands a week on hazelnut spread than Grey Goose, am I right?

Back to Mary: Before she fell in love with Nutella in college, she loved croissants in high school, so this recipe is a beautiful marriage of both, along with a heavenly blend of strawberries and bananas that we crisp on a waffle iron.

Cooking spray
4 store-bought croissants
Nutella
6 large ripe strawberries, hulled and sliced
1 banana, sliced
Whipped cream, for serving (optional)
Ice cream, for serving (optional)

1. Coat the inside of a waffle iron with cooking spray and preheat it to medium heat.

2. Cut each croissant in half horizontally with a sharp knife. Spread a layer of Nutella on each of the cut surfaces, sticking more to the middle of the croissant and not going all the way to the edges. It will want to leak during the waffling. Put the croissant tops back on.

3. Place a croissant in the middle of the iron, lower the lid, and give it a little pressure to squash it a bit but not too much. We want to keep the Nutella in the croissant! Cook until a bit crispy, 2 to 3 minutes. Because waffle irons vary, your cooking time may be longer. Remove the croissant from the waffle iron and let it rest while you make the rest of the croissants. Let the last croissant rest a couple minutes before serving.

4. To serve, top with the strawberries and bananas. If desired, garnish with whipped cream (and use a fork) or serve with ice cream (and use a spoon).

SALLY'S BITE-SIZE S'MORES PIES

MAKES 6 MINI PIES

Peter was in the summer program at our local YMCA, and the highlight was a once-a-year campout when we packed up the SUV and drove exactly a quarter mile to Lake Fairfax Park in Virginia. Although we were only 1,320 feet from our house, as a protective parent I had to be ready for any situation, so we overpacked with enough wardrobe changes to clothe the entire *Friends* cast for two seasons.

The highlight was always the ritualistic burning of food on the bonfire, and we did plenty of that. Standing downwind from that smoky blaze first to half-cook hot dogs, then to ignite s'mores, we spent the rest of the night two feet from the flames, because it was cold, and really dark.

That was more than twenty-five years ago. We still have the leather vests we wore that weekend in a space bag in the bottom of my closet, and I can report that they still smell like a smoldering stump.

Mary and Sally both preferred the more refined campfires of Palmetto Bluff in South Carolina, a movie set–like town with stunning homes and facilities, where you'd get around on bikes and in golf carts and evenings were spent "porching" with the parents at the River House Lounge, sipping a sweet tea (or more often a highball) as the kids would stand entirely too close to the roaring fire. Once their marshmallows were fully engulfed in flames, the kids would run willy-nilly in the dark, waving them like sparklers.

Kids running with flaming pointy sticks. What could go wrong?

Actually, nothing ever did. It's a cherished passage of childhood. It's s'mores, people!

For this recipe we use tiny Keebler pie crusts that we found in the baking aisle. These treats take less than 15 minutes from start to finish, and making them is a good activity for the kids as you stand nearby with a highball, reminiscing about the days when you'd catch things on fire over a campfire.

No flame needed for this recipe.

One 4-ounce package mini graham cracker pie crusts
1 cup chocolate chips
¾ cup salted peanuts
One 16-ounce container Marshmallow Fluff

1. Set the 6 mini crusts on a sheet pan.

2. In a microwave-safe bowl, heat the chocolate chips for 30 seconds. Remove and give a stir. Microwave another 30 seconds; remove and stir. You're getting the idea. Keep adding 30 seconds and stirring until the chocolate chips melt into a beautifully smooth chocolate soup.

3. Scoop out a heaping tablespoon of the chocolate into each of the little crusts. Whatever you have left over, divide among the crusts. Top each with some salted peanuts—they add a lot of flavor.

4. Preheat the oven broiler.

5. Scoop most of the container of Marshmallow Fluff into a large zip-top bag, seal it, and squeeze

(continued)

as much as you can toward one of the bottom corners. Snip off a small bit of that corner and you've got a homemade piping bag! Using both hands, squeeze it gently to pipe the fluff onto the tops of the little pies in a circular pattern, covering the nuts and chocolate.

6. Broil until the golden highlights on the fluff turn almost brown . . . very s'mores-y. Don't step away because they will burn quickly!

7. Serve immediately.

Kids, sticks, chocolate, and fire. What could go wrong?

PUMPKIN SPICE CRÈME BRÛLÉE–STYLE

For much of my adult life, my favorite dessert has been crème brûlée. The key is the crunchy sugar top, which, once cracked, lets you into the chilled creamy absolute heaven below.

When I first worked in New York, on big celebratory nights, Kathy and I would go to the Royalton Hotel's Forty Four, on 44th Street in Midtown, and I'd order a New York strip—medium-rare, wedge salad, tall rum and Coke—and top the evening off with one of their classic crispy-topped crème brûlées. If we were hit by a meteor on our way home, I'd go out with a smile on my face.

For my birthday one year Kathy bought me the one tool I needed to make crème brûlée at home, a gas torch. I had learned how to use a torch in high school, back in the 1970s. Future jobs were uncertain then, but my dad made it clear that I'd never go hungry if I had a trade. So I learned how to use a torch, weld, and even do plumbing . . . and if I could do both arc and acetylene welding, I could certainly caramelize sugar.

I was great at torching the tops, just saying, but the process of making a correct crème brûlée was very labor- and time-intensive, with the water bath and whatnot, and since this cookbook's theme is "happy in a hurry," I wanted to share with you my secret shortcut method. It's pretty darn good and features a seasonal hint of pumpkin spice.

Also, you don't need to have a torch; you can simply use your oven broiler. Just make sure you don't burn yourself. Crème brûlée won't taste as good after a trip to Urgent Care.

One 3.4-ounce box Jell-O instant vanilla
   pudding
1½ cups half-and-half
1 teaspoon pumpkin pie spice, plus more
   for topping if desired
Turbinado sugar, for caramelizing
Whipped cream, for serving

1. In a medium bowl, combine the pudding mix, half-and-half, and pumpkin pie spice. Quickly blend with a wire whisk until smooth and the pumpkin pie spice is evenly distributed. Using a rubber spatula, immediately divide the mixture into 3 shallow ovenproof custard dishes or ramekins. Refrigerate for at least 1 hour to chill and firm. I'll make them early in the day and they're ready to go at suppertime.

2. Adjust an oven rack to the second level from the top and preheat the broiler.

3. Close to serving time, sprinkle a teaspoon of turbinado sugar over each dish, creating a thin layer. Place the dishes on a sheet pan and broil for about 5 minutes, keeping the door ajar and watching pretty constantly so that they don't burn. They are done when the sugar is melted and caramelized.

4. Let them cool a little. When ready to serve, top with whipped cream, plus a very light dusting of pumpkin pie spice if you like.

ACKNOWLEDGMENTS

Thank you to Perry Spencer, a self-taught engineer who when working at Raytheon Corporation in 1941 noticed that a chocolate candy bar in his pocket had melted while he was working with magnetrons. Wondering why, he did some experimenting then with popcorn and eggs, and the man with the chocolatey pocket would eventually be credited with inventing the microwave oven. There is probably no other person in modern times who has helped us put dinner on the table faster than Perry.

The theme for this cookbook is Happy in a Hurry, but for a moment let's slow down and give thanks to some very special people who helped make this cookbook possible. I'd like to start by thanking one of America's greatest food photographers, Andrew Purcell, and food stylist Carrie Purcell, for making these recipes look not only beautiful, but delicious. Thank you both so much.

So many of these recipes are from the kitchens of so many friends and family members: Christie de Nicola, Frank "The Bank" Sedita, Madeleine Van Duren, Todd Van Duren, Marcus and Melanie Luttrell, Mary Finnigan Vossler, Brett Holmes, Cathy D'Andrea McGoey, Lynn Giles Young, Amy Baier, Ali Sadri, Aldo Cascio, Tom DiSarno, John McLemore and Masterbuilt, Cristina Montero, and Lisa Doocy.

Fox News is not only America's number one cable channel, it's also number one when it comes to colleagues who cook and share their recipes and food stories. Special thanks to Suzanne Scott, Lachlan Murdoch, Sean Hannity, Brian Kilmeade, Ainsley Earhardt, Janice Dean, Jillian Mele, Bret Baier, Dana Perino, Stephanie Freeman, and Judge Jeanine Pirro.

Then there are friends who helped us remember stories and details. Thanks to Father Jerome Fasano, Kevin Kohler, Kathy and Charles Theofilos, Ira Fenton, Gary Shorman, and Gary Schreier.

Others who helped us this year in so many ways include Dr. Patrick Clancy, Dr. Carol Shields, Dr. Jerry Shields, Wills Eye Hospital, Sileshi Petro, and the professionals at the UPS Store, Wyckoff, New Jersey.

Our Washington-based literary lawyers, Bob Barnett and Daniel Martin—thank you for making this project so easy and keeping my name out of the Mueller Report.

Behind the scenes at Fox News and *Fox & Friends*, we have a wonderful team of executives, producers, bookers, writers, and creative geniuses—thank you sincerely for the incredibly hard work you do with great skill at my real job.

Brian, Ainsley, Janice, Jillian, what can I say . . . you're all the best.

And to my longtime colleague and predawn coffee mate, Gavin Hadden, thank you for your daily quest for greatness, because as you remind us all every day, "Freedom isn't free."

William Morrow, the publisher of this cookbook, assembled an amazing team that is responsible for so many of America's most popular cookbooks. Kathy and I are flattered that the best in the business pulled out all the stops to make this book possible. Especially our editor, Cassie Jones, who always picked up her office phone when it said simply "New Jersey" because she knew it was me, and always had the right answers to my questions. Always.

And thank you to the rest of the team, including Jeanne Reina, Jill Zimmerman, Rachel Meyers, Tavia Kowalchuk, and Anwesha Basu. Kathy and I wrote this book for a year, then emailed you three hundred pages of stories and ingredients and directions and snapshots in a shoebox, and you turned it into this beautiful book, suitable for coffee-table display. But don't put an actual cup of coffee on it; that's why they invented coasters.

And to all of our friends, families, brothers, sisters, and spouses who helped with family recipe retrieval, revival, and general storytelling, you're not only good at helping with cookbooks, you're great at always being there for Kathy and me.

Many thanks and God bless,
Steve & Kathy Doocy

UNIVERSAL CONVERSION CHART

OVEN TEMPERATURE EQUIVALENTS

250°F = 120°C

275°F = 135°C

300°F = 150°C

325°F = 160°C

350°F = 180°C

375°F = 190°C

400°F = 200°C

425°F = 220°C

450°F = 230°C

475°F = 240°C

500°F = 260°C

MEASUREMENT EQUIVALENTS

Measurements should always be level unless directed otherwise.

⅛ teaspoon = 0.5 mL

¼ teaspoon = 1 mL

½ teaspoon = 2 mL

1 teaspoon = 5 mL

1 tablespoon = 3 teaspoons = ½ fluid ounce = 15 mL

2 tablespoons = ⅛ cup = 1 fluid ounce = 30 mL

4 tablespoons = ¼ cup = 2 fluid ounces = 60 mL

5⅓ tablespoons = ⅓ cup = 3 fluid ounces = 80 mL

8 tablespoons = ½ cup = 4 fluid ounces = 120 mL

10⅔ tablespoons = ⅔ cup = 5 fluid ounces = 160 mL

12 tablespoons = ¾ cup = 6 fluid ounces = 180 mL

16 tablespoons = 1 cup = 8 fluid ounces = 240 mL

INDEX

Note: Page references in *italics* indicate photographs.

NOTES

NOTES

THE HAPPY IN A HURRY COOKBOOK. Copyright © 2020 by Steve Doocy and Kathy Doocy. All rights reserved. Printed in the United States of America. No part of this book may be used or reproduced in any manner whatsoever without written permission except in the case of brief quotations embodied in critical articles and reviews. For information, address HarperCollins Publishers, 195 Broadway, New York, NY 10007.

HarperCollins books may be purchased for educational, business, or sales promotional use. For information, please email the Special Markets Department at SPsales@harpercollins.com.

FIRST EDITION

All photos courtesy of the author except page 53, courtesy of the Ronald Reagan Presidential Library, and page 147, courtesy of Megan Robinson Photography.

Library of Congress Cataloging-in-Publication Data has been applied for.

ISBN 978-0-06-296839-5

20 21 22 23 24 LSC 10 9 8 7 6 5 4 3 2